The Library

COLBY JUNIOR COLLEGE

COLBY JUNIOR COLLEGE FOR WOMEN
PARATI · SERVIRE
MENS · ANIMUS
CORPUS
1837

W9-CIH-980

☆

THE NATION AND THE STATES
Rivals or Partners?

☆ ☆ ☆ ☆ *The* **NATION** *and*

the **STATES,** *Rivals or Partners?*

by WILLIAM ANDERSON ☆ ☆ ☆

☆ ☆ PUBLISHED BY THE UNIVERSITY

OF MINNESOTA PRESS · *Minneapolis* ☆ ☆

JK
325
.A73
1955

Copyright 1955 by the

UNIVERSITY OF MINNESOTA

All rights reserved. No part of this book
may be reproduced in any form without the
written permission of the publisher. Permission is hereby granted to reviewers to quote
brief passages in a review to be printed
in a magazine or newspaper.

PRINTED AT THE LUND PRESS, INC., MINNEAPOLIS

Library of Congress Catalog Card Number: 55-7201

PUBLISHED IN GREAT BRITAIN, INDIA, AND PAKISTAN BY
GEOFFREY CUMBERLEGE: OXFORD UNIVERSITY PRESS, LONDON, BOMBAY, AND KARACHI

35722

"The Constitution, in all its provisions, looks to an indestructible Union, composed of indestructible States."

— Chief Justice Chase
IN Texas v. White, 7 Wallace (United States Supreme Court Reports) p. 700 (1869)

About This Book

THIS volume is concerned with a fundamental problem of American government one that has been much debated and written about since the days of Hamilton and Jefferson and one that will probably continue to stimulate heated discussion in and out of print for many years to come. At present, public interest in this problem has reached one of its periodic peaks, as strikingly evidenced in the creation by Congress in 1953 of a commission to study and report on intergovernmental relations. This was the first time in one hundred and sixty-five years of experience under the Constitution that a commission had been established for such a purpose.

Since it was from my association with the Commission on Intergovernmental Relations that the impetus for the present book came, a brief comment about the commission seems in order.

The appointment of official national commissions of inquiry upon major questions of public policy is in itself nothing new. At least since the administration of President Theodore Roosevelt the national government has frequently set up special temporary commissions to investigate and report upon urgent public issues of particular gravity and complexity. In more recent years there has been the commission of the middle thirties that studied problems of social security and worked out the social security system; later came the two "Hoover commissions," one in the late forties and one in the fifties, created to study the national administration and to propose reorganizations and economies.

Such commissions have a number of advantages over legislative and executive bodies for purposes of inquiry. Given a reasonable appropriation for staff and expenses, a commission can not only draw on all existing sources of reliable information, both public and private, but can also carry out independent studies through its own staff. Being created and set apart by law for the one purpose of investigating the problems assigned to it, a commission can, almost by its very existence, focus public attention on those problems and gain such public support for its proposals as their soundness and wisdom deserve.

The membership of a commission can and usually does include persons of specialized knowledge and experience along with others of broad general experience in business, the professions, and government. Officials and lay citizens can be combined in one body. For example, the Commission on Intergovernmental Relations included at the time of its formation in 1953 twenty-five members in all, of whom five were United States senators, five representatives in Congress, three persons in high national government positions (one of these a former governor), one other former governor, four governors, a state "secretary of state," a mayor, a businessman, a former dean of a law school, two university administrators, and one university professor.

In such a body there will be members with exceedingly varied points of view and widely diversified experiences which can be brought to bear on the questions at issue. Having no responsibility as a group for current legislative and administrative problems, a commission can concentrate its attention on the particular task before it and presumably take a broad, calm, and objective view of the facts and problems involved.

This is, of course, the ideal situation. In practice such detachment is not fully possible. Members of Congress, national administrative officials, governors, and other public officers are unavoidably distracted from the work of the commission of inquiry by the constant and compelling demands of public office and of campaigning for re-election to office. It is the nonofficial members who must carry a large part of the burden. This may limit the amount of work a commission is able to do.

And, of course, the time available to it further limits the activities of any commission. So it is with the Commission on Intergovernmental Relations. Under present law it must report its findings and go out of existence by March 1, 1955. In so short a time the commission could not search deeply into all the many issues that are involved in intergovernmental relations. It may be compelled to limit its main report to some of the more immediate and urgent questions in the field of fiscal relations between governments—overlapping national and state taxes, for example, and grants-in-aid.

The members of the commission and other leaders of public opinion, both in and out of public office, are fully aware, however, that there are fundamental issues and principles to be considered, and that current proposals must be placed in their historical context if they are to be seen in their long-term significance. Early in its work the commission established a committee on the principles and historical development of American federal government. As a long-time student of intergovernmental relations and the author or editor of various works in the field, I was appointed to membership on this committee.

The committee was at first without any special staff to assist it and the members were all busy people who did not have the time to delve into the many intricacies—political, financial, constitutional, and historical—that make the federal republic of the United States what it is today. Therefore, I volunteered to prepare a summary of the history and present status of national-state relations in the United States. This was offered to the committee as a "working paper," for their information, but I retained the right to revise and to publish it as my own if I so desired.

As work on the paper progressed, it appeared that this might well grow into a small book of some potential value to the public in helping it to appraise not only any proposals that the Commission on Intergovernmental Relations might make but also the recommendations of other groups and agencies.

My working paper for the committee concerned largely the

constitutional issue. For the present volume I have added a brief survey of the federal system as it exists today, a discussion of certain fiscal and policy issues, and a suggested program of action.

Because the book had to be produced with considerable speed if it was to be published before the commission report, I do not pretend that it is a final work of scholarship. It is still in a sense a draft, a working paper, but, I venture to hope, not less useful because of that. If it helps some readers to see the basic elements in a complex set of intergovernmental relations, and makes for more informed public discussion, it will have accomplished my purpose.

In order to be most useful to lay readers, the book had to be brief enough to be read by busy people, clear enough to be understood without consulting other works, comprehensive in its coverage of the major problems, and as objective and balanced in its statement of the issues and arguments as a person of reasonably strong convictions could make it.

The last criterion was the most difficult to meet. Perfect objectivity and balance are not humanly attainable. I have acquired certain convictions about the subject that it would be futile to try to conceal. Indeed a book about public affairs in which the author does not positively state his reasoned convictions does not make its full potential contribution to public understanding. I will therefore state in advance the general position I have reached concerning national-state relations under the Constitution and supplement this from place to place throughout the book by more specific conclusions upon particular points. The personal pronoun will be a flag of warning to the reader that "here the author is giving his own views for whatever they may be worth."

(It must be clearly understood, of course, that this book is the work of an individual member of the commission and except by mere coincidence it in no way represents the views of other members or of the commission as a whole. The commission's report will speak for the commission.)

The following statement of my position (or of my bias, if anyone wishes so to name it) is not the product of a youthful enthusiasm but the end result of many years of study of governments. It is a statement that is not likely to satisfy the perfectionists of either the right or the left, but it is one that I believe conforms with the evidences of political history as I have found them.

I believe that the system of government of the United States under the Constitution is probably the greatest achievement of the entire human race up to now in the construction of a political system that will provide strong and active government for every national and local need and emergency, and at the same time ensure a maximum of attainable personal liberty and popular control over what the government does I can think of no foreign system that I would be willing to substitute for it.

I believe in all parts of the system—national, state, and local; legislative, executive, and judicial. I believe in the system not only as it came from the hands of the founders in the late eighteenth century, but also as it has been developed through trial and error, through thought and decision, from that day down to the present. I believe that the relations that have been worked out among national, state, and local governments are based upon sound principles of good government, suitable to the needs of this nation. I believe too that those relations are in accord with the Constitution.

I believe that the American people today, operating through their system of government, provide the most important, yes the one indispensable tower of strength among the free nations of the world as they face the forces of militant world communism. Not only for the sake of other nations, but for the sake of their own liberties, institutions, and national independence, the American people have a duty to keep the nation strong to meet every emergency. This requires, I believe, that the national government, and indeed the whole system of government, be kept strong and vigorous. In the face of the Communist menace, who can say that the government is too big, or that it is too strong? Who would dare weaken it in this hour of destiny?

Certainly there are changes that can be made at various points in the system, changes that seem necessary to some groups and that would mean no weakening of the national structure. Indeed some of them might bring added strength. The tests that I would apply to every proposal are these:

Will the proposed change almost certainly bring an actual increase in the strength and effectiveness of the governmental system as a whole in the meeting of foreign and domestic needs and emergencies?

Is it a change that will ensure higher standards of public service, or one that will bring the risk of lowered standards?

Is it a change that will increase the loyalty and support of the people, or one that may bring popular dissatisfaction and disgruntlement?

Is it one that will strengthen popular support of the American economic and political system, or one that may give arguments and weapons into the hands of the Communists and other subversive groups?

These are severe tests to apply, but I think not too severe. I for one am not willing to gamble on some proposed change in the mere hope that it *may* bring *some* improvement. I want to see substantial and pertinent evidence and to hear persuasive argument that there is an actual evil to be corrected; that the proposed remedy is one that will clearly tend to correct the evil; and that no undesirable consequences are likely to follow from the change. I will be more impressed by actual historical evidence and experience than by wish and theory. As a result of my own study and experience, also, I will be forced to consider the source or sources from which a proposed change is put forth, and whether it represents an informed majority opinion, or a scientific opinion as to public needs, or something less impressive and more limited.

I do not know as I write this what the Commission on Intergovernmental Relations is going to recommend in its report. Neither do I know how I shall vote as a member of the commission. I flatter myself that the conclusions I have reached up to now are in accordance with the considerable body of evidence that I have found in my own studies. On several points my views today are not what they were earlier, because later evidence convinced me that my former views were not well supported. I hope that I have retained enough flexibility and scientific objectivity to be willing to change again if the weight of new evidence is sufficient to override earlier opinions. My votes in the commission, coming for the most part after this book was written, may not therefore accord fully with the views expressed herein. I shall not be intransigent. If the commission proposes reforms that hold good promise of advancing the national public welfare, as I have every reason to believe that it will, I will not set up a perfectionistic standard; I will go along with what I consider to be an improvement even if it does not in every way meet with my highest expectations.

Whatever the proposals of the commission, obviously they will not settle for all time, and not wholly even for the present, the problems created by governmental interrelationships. New issues will rise with new conditions, domestic and foreign. Other groups will put forth suggestions in accord with their own special interests. Possibly the commission will have its greatest effect, not through its specific proposals, important as they may be, but in stimulating greater public awareness of the problems in intergovernmental relations and in encouraging more informed public discussion of needed changes. It is my hope that this volume too may in its own way thus stimulate and encourage. For the vitality of a democratic system depends upon the lively and informed participation by all citizens in the affairs of government.

W. A.

University of Minnesota
October 1, 1954

Acknowledgments

To MAKE acknowledgments to all those from whose knowledge I have gained something valuable toward the writing of this book would be impossible. My debts on this account go back to and even beyond the men who in 1787 framed the original and major portion of the Constitution of the United States. Two of those framers in particular, namely Alexander Hamilton and James Madison, the principal authors of *The Federalist*, have placed all Americans under a heavy debt for their brilliant interpretation of the original Constitution, as well as for their able and patriotic efforts in helping to get the Constitution written and adopted. But these men were only two in the first group of a long succession of statesmen, jurists, teachers, and scholars, who by their actions and decisions in crucial stages of the development of the Constitution, as well as by their expositions and interpretations of it, have helped to develop the American federal system into what it is today. We owe a debt of gratitude to the many citizens of this land, past and present, who have contributed constructively to the development of the Constitution and the governmental system as a whole.

My more immediate obligations are to the University of Minnesota for time and research funds to devote to problems of the United States federal system; to the Rockefeller Foundation for a generous grant of money for a study, not yet fully published, of the intergovernmental relations of Minnesota; to those who assisted me in the latter project; and to my colleagues and graduate students in political science at the University of Minnesota for many a helping hand along the way.

ACKNOWLEDGMENTS

Although they are in no way responsible for anything in this book, the members of the Commission on Intergovernmental Relations by their discussions, and the members of the subcommittees and research staff of the commission by their studies and explanations, have done much to enrich and clarify my thoughts on the whole subject of intergovernmental relations.

Finally, warm words of thanks go to Louise P. Olsen for an excellent and speedy job of typing, and to Jeanne Sinnen of the editorial staff of the University of Minnesota Press for numerous excellent suggestions and contributions toward improving the manuscript as it was being turned into a book under her supervision.

Contents

Part IV. Changing the System

☆

PART I
Surveying the Federal System

The Climate of Opinion

THE question of the relations of the states and the federal government," wrote Woodrow Wilson in 1908, "is the cardinal question of our constitutional system."

The measured words of Princeton University's president came more than a century after relations had been established between the original thirteen states and a central government, almost a half-century after those relations had been tested in civil war. Yet Wilson spoke as truly of 1908 as of 1789 or 1860, and his words are just as applicable to 1955 and any foreseeable future year.

The emphasis has shifted, of course; the specific issues have changed. For brief periods, as during the Civil War, the problem of intergovernmental relations has been charged with deep and sometimes violent emotion. But even in calmer years the problem has always been with us; knotty questions of policy and finance in this area have constantly plagued presidents of the United States, members of Congress and of the Supreme Court, the governing authorities of state and local governments. To government officials, the problems of intergovernmental relations are as inevitable as death and taxes.

Today the whole area is undergoing searching scrutiny. To understand the present concern—and the diverse opinions—among officials at all governmental levels, citizens' groups, and special interest groups, we must keep in mind the swiftly changing world of modern times, which has brought more rapid and more significant changes in intergovernmental relations than ever before. Behind us, between 1933 and 1952, lie twenty years of greatly increased governmental activity, particularly at the national level. New laws, new public services, new taxes, and new expenditures for the benefit of farmers, workers, homeowners, aged and dependent persons, and other groups were piled one on top of another. Along with these came increased governmental regulations affecting industry, labor relations, the stock market, and other facets of the American economy. Governmental regulations and services, budgets and taxes, loomed larger and larger in American life.

The climate of opinion has been both warm and cold toward this increased governmental activity.

Generally speaking, labor unions, farmers' organizations, and associations of leaders in public education, public health, and the like have been in favor of the national government's expanding its services and increasing its financial aids in areas of public interest. Through their national organizations most of these groups have gone on record as favoring increased governmental action in support of the public services of most immediate interest to them.

Labor organizations like the AFL, the CIO, and the railroad brotherhoods have supported measures for better public schools, public health services, employment security, welfare and relief services, public housing, and related public functions. Agricultural organizations like the American Farm Bureau Federation, the Grange, and the National Farmers' Union have favored more support for rural highways, for agricultural research, education, and extension work, and for soil and water conservation, to name a few of their principal interests. The National Education Association, composed largely of school teachers, principals, and superintendents, has naturally concentrated upon better support for public education; the American Public Health Association upon improved public health services; and so on through the numerous national organizations in such major fields as highways, social welfare, housing, land-grant colleges, and conservation.

As a rule these organized groups have not plumped strongly for one level of government as against another, or for one method

4

of getting results in preference to another. They have wanted to keep government as "close to home" as is feasible, by using state, county, city, or school district governments provided the job could be done by such units; but in many cases they have concluded that substantial action by the national government is needed to provide national leadership, to stimulate local action, to raise the level of local service, or to maintain the service at a decent level after it has been initiated.

In short they have in general stood for having each level of government carry its share of the burden and for having effective cooperation among national, state, and local governments and officials. They have not been doctrinaire in support of, for example, the grant-in-aid method as against other methods of producing the desired results in their particular fields of interest. But they have certainly not opposed this method where it seemed to promise results. In a number of cases they have favored direct national action, as in agricultural price supports and river and harbor improvements. But, again, they have on the whole been moderate in their statements.

The voices of protest against increasing national action in many of these fields have, on the other hand, become loud and vehement and have in some instances pointed directly at the entire system of federal aids as one of the evils of our time. These protests have come especially from chambers of commerce, taxpayers' associations, and associations of manufacturers. In December 1952 the National Association of Manufacturers in a revised edition of a bulletin titled *Bring the Government Back Home* outlined its convictions:

The federal government is too big. It is so big and so complex that it cannot be efficiently managed by any man or group of men.

The burden of its cost is now a greater load than the economy can carry and remain prosperous.

The steady pressure for more power to regulate and control is a growing menace to individual and civil liberty.

The increasing concentration of political power and economic control in the federal government is destroying the economic and governmental environment which is essential to the survival of the American system of free enterprise and to the preservation of the American constitutional system of a union of states.

Unless the trend toward ever bigger government is halted, and until it is reversed, the states and private business alike face the prospect of ultimate, complete domination by the federal government. And complete federal domination IS totalitarianism.

To avoid this "totalitarianism" the bulletin offered a program of changes that, its authors asserted, would "establish a better balance of service responsibilities and tax resources between federal and state governments. It will result also in a more manageable and less costly federal government, in the fiscal independence of the states, and in a material reduction of the citizens' tax burdens."

In their opposition to the activities of the national government, associations of businessmen and taxpayers have had official allies in many governors' mansions and in state legislatures. The Governors' Conference (composed of the state and territorial governors) has for many years objected to what it calls encroachments on state rights. Many governors feel that their power and the states' powers are being undermined by the national government. They point to the tendency for federal officials to deal directly with the state agency involved in some program in which the federal government is interested, such as highways or social welfare, thus by-passing the governor's office. The governors, they say, should have administrative authority over programs established and money spent in their states.

Legislators in states that have received back from the federal treasury as grants-in-aid proportionately less than they claim their people have paid in federal taxes, while other states have received more, have become leaders in the denunciation of the grant-in-aid system. A resolution to this effect adopted by the Indiana General Assembly in 1947 has received nationwide publicity:

Indiana needs no guardian and intends to have none. We Hoosiers—like the people of our sister states—were fooled for quite a spell with the magician's trick that a dollar taxed out of our pockets and sent to Washington, will be bigger when it comes back to us. We have taken a good look at said dollar. We find that it lost weight on its journey to Washington and back. The political brokerage of the bureaucrats has been deducted. We have decided that there is no such thing as "Federal" aid. We know that there is no wealth to tax that is not already within the boundaries of the 48 states.

So we propose henceforward to tax ourselves and take care of ourselves. We are fed up with subsidies, doles, and paternalism. We are no one's stepchild. We have grown up. We serve notice that we will resist Washington, D.C., adopting us.

Be it resolved by the House of Representatives of the General Assembly of the State of Indiana (the Senate concurring), That we respectfully petition and urge Indiana's Congressmen and Senators to vote to fetch our county courthouses and city halls back from Pennsylvania Avenue. We want government to come home.

Resolved further, That we call upon the legislatures of our sister States and on good citizens everywhere who believe in the basic principles of Lincoln and Jefferson to join with us, and we with them, to restore the American Republic and our 48 States to the foundations built by our fathers.

(It is perhaps worthy of mention that the Indiana legislature did not follow up this somewhat bombastic resolution by a refusal to accept further federal grants-in-aid, or by granting more home-rule powers to the counties and cities of the state.)

The reasons for these protests from businessmen's associations and from state officials varied somewhat from group to group but they all revolved around a number of related ideas: that there was coming to be too much government, too much centralization of power and functions in the national government; that the rights and the importance of the state governments were being reduced; and that local self-government was being destroyed. These ideas were usually expressed in certain set phrases: the "American way," idealized as a way of "rugged individualism" and "minimum government," was being abandoned; "paternalism," "centralization," "big government," "bureaucracy" were taking the place of individual initiative, personal and family responsibility, local self-government, and states' rights.

Many believed that the Constitution itself was being undermined and would ultimately be destroyed. The states, it was said,

7

were being encroached upon and dominated by the national government to such an extent that in time they would be mere administrative districts. Fears were expressed too that popular control of government would soon end, that dictatorship and tyranny would raise their sinister heads in the United States. Many writers and speakers looked with dismay at the trends they saw and called for a return to the simplicity, the integrity, the personal responsibility, the local self-government, and the states' rights that they believed had once prevailed and could be made to prevail again. Some urged that "all history proves" that when governments become paternalistic, centralized, and powerful the liberties of the people are at an end.

These gloomy forebodings came mainly from state officers and not from national and local officers. Among state officials they came more from governors and legislators than from state administrative officials responsible for carrying out the functions supported more or less by federal aid. They also came more from Republican than from Democratic leaders.

During the years from 1933 to 1952 when the case was being built up against current governmental trends, the Republican party, which had ruled the nation during most of the time from the Civil War down to 1933, was out of power; the Democrats controlled and carried the responsibility for the national administration and its policies. Being thus "on the outside" nationally, the Republican party had done what a party in that situation normally does as a part of its campaign to get back into power. It in large part turned its attention to winning control of the state governments and worked through them to build up its strength, state by state, so as to have firm bases from which to launch its final campaign to regain control of the national administration. At the same time it attacked the party in office for its centralizing and bureaucratic tendencies, and for its alleged destruction of personal liberties and local self-government. The 1952 platform of the Republican party made its case against the Democratic administrations of the preceding twenty years:

We charge that they have arrogantly deprived our citizens of precious liberties by seizing powers never granted.

We charge that they work unceasingly to achieve their goal of national socialism.

. . .

We charge that they have weakened self-government which is the cornerstone of the freedom of men.

. . .

We charge that they have violated our liberties by turning loose upon the country a swarm of arrogant bureaucrats and their agents who meddle intolerably in the lives and occupations of our citizens.

The actions of the Republican party are not reviewed here in any spirit of adverse criticism; quite the contrary. Whenever any party in power in Washington has increased the functions, the taxes, and the expenditures of the national government, it is vulnerable to just such attacks, and the strategy of the opposition party is likely to be successful. It is an important characteristic of the American federal system that all groups and parties have an appeal from the national government to the states and back again.

One consequence is, however, that the "out" party must offer action by the state governments as the preferable alternative to action by the national government. It must in effect make an alliance with those state leaders—governors and others—who want to increase the importance of the states, even at the expense of the national government if that is necessary. Having formed such an alliance, and given the express and implied promises that made the alliance possible, the "out" party, if it then wins control of the national government and becomes the party in power, has to make some effort to carry out its promises to "return" certain functions, powers, tax resources, and even property to the states.

Another circumstance helped make this course of action easier for the Republican party. Powerful elements within the party had taken a strong stand against a number of the measures enacted by Congress during the twenty-year dominance by the Democrats—particularly against those measures that seemed to add up

9

to what was called a "welfare state." The Republican party's candidate himself spoke out against this trend in national policy. His election, therefore, seemed to hold out the promise not only of a *transfer* of functions from the national government to the states, but also of a *reduction* in governmental activities as a whole. In time this may lead to a serious rift in the party; for while certain state political leaders were promising that if the state governments had a free hand they would render more and better services, other elements in the coalition calling for change were and are interested in reducing state and local as well as national activities, taxes, and expenditures.

Since assuming control of the national administration in 1953 the Republican party has in fact taken steps toward both "returning" and "reducing."

The so-called tidelands off the coasts of California, Texas, and Louisiana, out beyond the low-water mark to their "historic boundaries," were promptly returned by act of Congress to those states despite the Supreme Court decision which had declared them to be national properties. The desire to encourage private as against public enterprise in the development of water power and especially in the building of steam plants to supplement water power in the production of electricity has become clearly evident. At the same time ardent conservationists have become greatly alarmed over various moves in Congress to open parts of the public domain to private exploitation.

Furthermore, Congress made substantial tax reductions that were approved by the President, so that the states could have more leeway in increasing their own taxes if they so desired. In the budgets proposed for the fiscal years 1954 and 1955, there were also several proposed reductions in national grants to the states for educational and other purposes although Congress did not go along with all of these.

On the other hand Congress and the President joined hands in authorizing much larger grants-in-aid to the states for highways in the fiscal years 1956 and 1957 and enlarged the nation's direct obligations for social welfare by increasing individual benefits under the Social Security Act, and by extending the coverage of that act to some additional millions of citizens.

On the whole, therefore, the record up to now shows moves in several directions, and it will take more time to reveal how much of a trend there is toward "returning" and "reducing." There is some evidence, in fact, that since taking office the administration has reconsidered and perhaps changed some of its previously announced policies. But there has been no clear-cut change in the basic philosophy of the administration concerning intergovernmental relations. This philosophy was perhaps best expressed by the President's message of March 30, 1953, urging Congress to create the Commission on Intergovernmental Relations. He said in part:

The present division of activities between Federal and State Governments, including their local subdivisions, is the product of more than a century and a half of piecemeal and often haphazard growth. This growth in recent decades has proceeded at a speed defying order and efficiency. One program after another has been launched to meet emergencies and expanding public needs. Time has rarely been taken for thoughtful attention to the effects of these actions on the basic structure of our Federal-State system of government.

Now there is need to review and assess, with prudence and foresight, the proper roles of the Federal, State and local governments. In many cases, especially within the past 20 years, the Federal Government has entered fields which, under our Constitution, are the primary responsibilities of State and local governments. This has tended to blur the responsibilities of local government. It has led to duplication and waste. It is time to relieve the people of the need to pay taxes on taxes.

A major mark of this development has been the multiplication of Federal grants-in-aid for specific types of activities. There are now more than 30 such grant programs. In the aggregate, they involve Federal expenditures of well over $2 billion a year. They make up approximately one-fifth of State revenues.

While by far the greater part of these expenditures are in the fields of social security, health, and education, they also spread into many other areas. In some cases the Federal Government apportions fixed amounts among the States; in others it matches State expenditures; and, in a few, it finances the entire State expenditures. The impact of all these grants on State governments has been profound. While they have greatly stimulated the development of certain State activities, they have complicated State finances and administration; and they have often made it difficult for States to provide the funds for other important services.

The maintenance of strong, well-ordered State and local governments is essential to our Federal system of government. Lines of authority must be clean and clear, the right areas of action for Federal and State governments plainly defined. This is imperative for the efficient administration of governmental programs in the fields of health, education, social security, and other grants-in-aid areas.

The manner in which best to accomplish these objectives, and to eliminate friction, duplication, and waste from Federal-State relations, is therefore a major national problem. To reallocate certain of these activities between Federal and State Governments, including their local subdivisions, is in no sense to lessen our concern for the objectives of these programs. On the contrary, these programs can be made more effective instruments serving the security and welfare of our citizens.

The law establishing the Commission on Intergovernmental Relations repeated the President's basic assumption:

Because any existing confusion and wasteful duplication of functions and administration pose a threat to the objectives of programs of the Federal Government shared in by the States, including their political subdivisions, because the activity of the Federal Government has been extended into many fields which, under our constitutional system, may be the primary interest and obligation of the several States and the subdivisions thereof, and because of the resulting complexity to intergovernmental relations, it is necessary to study the proper role of the Federal Government in relation to the States and their political subdivisions, with respect to such fields, to the end that these relations may be clearly defined and the functions concerned may be allocated to their proper jurisdiction. It is further necessary that the intergovernmental fiscal relations be so adjusted that each level of government discharges the functions which belong within its jurisdiction in a sound and effective manner.

The emphasis on the fiscal element in these official pronouncements by the national administration, and in the statements quoted earlier, might lead some "hard-boiled" political realists to dismiss the whole furor as merely another, if more grandiose than usual, raid on the federal treasury by the states. They might recall the distribution of the federal surplus in 1836–37, the successful state demands for federal public lands to provide schools and internal improvements, and the abortive attempts of the states to tax federal properties and to get all the unreserved federal lands into state ownership.

But much more is involved than just the demand for more state tax resources.

Even this brief survey suggests some of the deep-seated differences of opinion that exist among officials and laymen—differences as to the nature of the American system of government, as to recent trends in the constitutional relations between the nation and the states, as to the dangers of centralization and bigness in government, and as to what are the desirable future relations between national, state, and local governments as these affect human liberties, popular control of government, and the role of the government in society.

Concerning the nature of the federal system and of the Constitution there are in general terms two opposing philosophies. On the one hand there are the states' righters, the bring-the-government-back-home group. To the extent that they hold a theory on the origin of the federal system it is that sovereign states came together to form the union, that even in indissoluble and perpetual union these states retained their sovereignty, and that therefore the central government is the mere creature of the states. They believe that in order to preserve personal liberties and local government the national government must be kept at a minimum, and that the assumption of new activities by the federal government is "unconstitutional." They express fears of "centralization" and of "big government." They want the powers of the various governments "strictly defined and separated." Some of them oppose any suggestion of the "welfare state" at whatever level; others believe that the state governments can handle welfare functions more democratically and efficiently than the national government.

In opposition are those who believe that the people are sovereign; that the people created both state and national governments and that therefore both levels of government are merely the agencies of the people. They believe that the Constitution is a flexible document which cannot be read solely in terms of what the framers of 1787 intended but must be interpreted in the light of changing conditions and needs. They are not afraid of centralization or big government as such, as long as democratic processes are preserved to control government. They do not believe that recent increases in the national government's activities have taken any powers away from the states; on the contrary, they believe that the state governments are stronger and more active than ever before. Finally, they are convinced that it is in the best interests of the nation as a whole not to limit to any great extent the powers of the central government.

Admittedly these contrasts are oversimplified. Not all in either camp hold all the related views. In many cases individuals are not consciously aware of holding one philosophy or the other; they merely react to specific actions and proposals with approval or disapproval. I do not intend to suggest that the differences of opinion are clear-cut and easy to define; rather I would have us use these generalized characterizations merely as convenient points of reference.

Neither do I mean to imply that the nation is once again a "house divided," this time on the issue of intergovernmental relations, and doomed to be rent assunder. Certainly there are significant and basic differences of opinion, as I have outlined; there are tensions and frictions and even animosities among government officials at the various levels; there is a good deal of "viewing with alarm" and shaking of skeletons by numerous nonofficial groups. But there are wide areas of agreement, on purpose if not always on procedure. Excellent cooperation and smooth functioning mark many of the programs in which national, state, and local governments join hands. By no means all governors or legislatures are opposed to financial assistance from the national government. And among those who do voice objections to grants-in-aids, specific projects rather than the system as a whole are as often as not the target.

As we survey the federal system as it operates today and discuss the points at issue, we should keep in mind the very high degree of cooperation that does exist among local units, the states, and the national government. However uneasy their partnership seems at times, it has been remarkably productive for the nation as a whole.

2

The Federal System in Operation

Mᴜᴄʜ of the current discussion about intergovernmental relations in the United States concerns primarily the relations between the national and state governments. This concentration of attention upon one set of relations, however important they may be, is unfortunate.

There is a tendency on the part of many to overlook the full sweep and complexity of the American governmental system, with its national, state, and local levels. Persons who are in public office, and are daily beset by the problems of their particular units of government, can hardly be blamed if they come to think that these problems are the most important ones there are. But to an outside observer it is clear that some public officials seem to lack a sense of perspective and to miss the broad and high view of the system of government as a whole.

A mayor sees the needs of his own city and emphasizes the obvious shortages of money required to meet these needs. A governor of a state hears about and observes the financial and other problems of his own state government. When mayors get together in state and national meetings they quite naturally stress the needs of the cities and combine their efforts and resources to bring those needs to general public attention. When state governors assemble together in their annual Conference of Governors, to compare notes and hear each other's complaints, they similarly adopt resolutions and put forth strong demands for more power and financial resources for the states.

The mayors complain that the states are not giving the cities a fair deal. They point out that the state legislatures are rurally dominated and rural-minded in most cases, and so the mayors carry their pleas for help to Congress and the President. The state governors, on the other hand, although once among the leaders in promoting federal grants to the states, have in recent years made strong complaints against the national government for depriving the states of tax resources and for undermining the states' powers of self-government by making grants-in-aid to particular state departments which then, they allege, fall under national domination. Thus the mayors and the governors are alike in finding the principal causes of their official woes not in the inadequacies of their own governments, but in the level of government just above them.

Mayors and governors are all intellectually aware of the fact that there are other units and levels of government to consider, but it is difficult for them to keep this fact in the foreground while they are pressing their special claims for recognition.

Just as a reminder it is well to put the elementary facts on the record. The American system of government is an integrated, complex structure of more than 100,000 governmental units (1952 census, 116,743). These operate at three distinct levels—national, state, and local—but the three levels are closely interwoven and interdependent. By inspection we are able to see that the different units and levels are distinguishable from each other but we cannot correctly say that they are independent or separate. In the same way we can distinguish the branches and the roots from the trunk of a tree, but it is obvious that they are not separated or independent. They all work together as one system of interdependent parts.

Together the national, state, and local governments conduct a wide range of public functions and services that are, on the whole, generally accepted by the people as being proper for public authorities to perform. These functions are not, in most cases, set off sharply from each other, nor are they strictly allocated, one to this level of government, and another to that (with a few major exceptions to be noted).

At the *national level* there is one national government which

17

alone is responsible for the nation's international relations, national security, the monetary system and central banking, the post office, immigration, naturalization and citizenship, and foreign and interstate commerce.

In addition it provides national leadership, financial and other aid, and some supervision for a number of other governmental services that are conducted almost entirely by the state and local governments, such as highways, public health, social welfare, and some aspects of education.

It supplies, also, some direct services of its own like "social security" (OASI).

Once a weak and puny thing, it has become the greatest single national government in the world. Its roster of civilian employees has recently hovered around two and a quarter million persons— of whom, however, about 1,200,000 are employed in the three branches of the Department of Defense, more than 170,000 in the Veterans Administration, and more than 500,000 in the post office. Only about 350,000 are employed in miscellaneous civilian agencies. In a total annual national budget of about $75 billion, roughly some 80 per cent has gone to pay for defense, past wars, and foreign-aid programs, while about 20 per cent (say approximately $15 billion) has gone into nondefense domestic programs, including more than $2 billion into grants-in-aid to the states.

At the *state level* there are forty-eight states, each with its own government (legislature, governor and other executive officers, and court system). These governments legislate for an exceedingly broad range of public services and private interests, and administer a widely varied array of public functions.

Their rosters of public service employees, practically all engaged in nondefense activities, run to more than 1,130,000, or more than three times as many as the national government employs in nondefense services other than the post office. Their revenues and also their expenditures exceed by a considerable margin the national government's expenditures for comparable nondefense purposes. Although a large part of state expenditures consists of grants-in-aid to local governments, the direct state ex-

THE FEDERAL SYSTEM IN OPERATION

penditures on their own services just about equal federal expenditures for all nondefense purposes.

At the *local level* there were in 1952 more than 3000 counties; nearly 17,000 cities, villages, and boroughs (municipalities or incorporated places); more than 17,000 organized townships, more than 67,000 school districts, and more than 12,000 other special districts. Each of these has its own area and population, an organized government, one or more functions to perform, a number of officers and employees, from a few to many thousands, and revenues to expend that more or less correspond to its needs. Each one is a distinct governmental unit with a political life and responsibilities of its own.

In the total these local governments employ more than 3,500,000 persons to carry out their functions. This is four times as many as the national government employs on all its nondefense functions including the post office, and more than three times as many as the forty-eight states employ on all their services.

The total number of state and local employees, now approaching five million, is more than twice the number of all civilian employees of the national government, more than five times the number that the national government employs on nondefense functions. These ratios of civilian employees give a fairly accurate index of the relative concentrations of national, state, and local governments on nondefense activities.

Among them these three so-called levels of government carry on all the public functions that are performed inside the United States.

Some are performed almost entirely by the units in a single level. Examples at the local level are the furnishing of fire protection and water supplies in cities and villages and the operation of primary and secondary education (grade schools and high schools) in the various types of local school districts. Centered almost entirely at the state level we find the regulation of insurance companies and the licensing of professions. The national government, as already noted, has the sole responsibility for foreign relations,

19

the monetary system, and the postal service and almost complete responsibility for national defense.

Far more numerous, however, are the functions in which there is a joint interest and a sharing or division of responsibility between two or three levels of government. In some of the most important functions there is national, state, and local participation. These functions involve among others the areas of highways, airports, parks and recreation, conservation of natural resources, agriculture, education, public health, social welfare, the promotion and regulation of trade and commerce, civil defense, general law enforcement, and the maintenance of courts.

The work is so divided in many cases that each unit of government carries on some important part of it under its own control. Thus there are separate systems of national, state, and local parks and conservation projects, and separate national, state, and local systems of law enforcement—the FBI, Secret Service, and postal inspectors under the national government; state police and highway patrols under the several state governments; and county sheriffs, city and village police, and town constables at the local level. In these functions there are practically no grants-in-aid. Instead there is a rather clear-cut division of labor.

In a number of other instances the principal administrative responsibility for operating the service rests at one level of government while higher levels provide some financial support (grants-in-aid) and auxiliary services, and set the minimum standards for the service. Elementary and secondary education provide a good example.

In most states local school districts are responsible under state law for providing and maintaining public school buildings, and for operating the schools. The school districts elect their own governing boards and raise their own school taxes. There is a good deal of latitude for local variations in the local school programs.

The state legislatures pass all the basic school laws, set the minimum standards for teachers, school buildings, length of school terms, ages for compulsory school attendance, and programs of

20

studies. In addition the states grant various amounts of financial aid to local schools, and through their state departments of education supervise the work of schools to see to it that minimum standards are met. They also try to encourage improvements in local educational standards.

The national government enters the general educational function only in various incidental ways. The United States Office of Education compiles and publishes school statistics for the entire nation, carries on research on school problems, and issues informational bulletins on a wide variety of educational issues. Congress appropriates money that is distributed to the states and ultimately to the school districts for support of the school lunch program and for vocational education in agriculture, home economics, industry, and distributive occupations. Congress also provides funds and some leadership for agricultural extension work that is carried out by the states among farm families throughout most of the counties in the nation; and it gives some support to teaching and research activities in agricultural subjects to the land-grant colleges in all states, as well as to military training in those colleges and others.

In every instance in which there is national, state, and local participation in an important governmental function, there is a national association of the officials concerned. Once a year or oftener these organizations meet so that the national, state, and local officials can discuss together their common problems and keep themselves informed about how their program of public service is progressing. These associations also issue bulletins and newsletters from time to time, which are in addition to the official bulletins sent out from the national and state governmental agencies that are responsible for administering the various services.

Thus there is no serious failure of communication within the circle of those who are immediately and officially concerned. On the other hand, other officials in the various levels of governments, the state governors for example, are not kept so fully informed about each of the functional programs.

The general public, too, frequently finds itself unable to keep abreast of activities in governmental programs—perhaps because of too much information rather than too little. From the welter of facts and figures that face us almost daily in the newspapers, it is difficult to put together an over-all picture of how a given program operates, what it involves in terms of men and money, and what changes if any would be desirable.

We cannot here deal adequately with all the programs involving more than one level of government; we cannot even cover all the major ones. But even though no two functions are handled in exactly the same way, a brief look at a few of the important functions may demonstrate, in outline at least, how the federal system works—particularly how grants-in-aid are administered. Grants-in-aid are, of course, but one element in intergovernmental relations. But we will be concerned with them again and again because they are at the center of much of the criticism directed at national government activities. A later chapter is devoted to a general consideration of the contention that the grant-in-aid system is undermining the self-government of the states. Here we will simply describe the operation of a few programs under grants-in-aid.

The highway function is one that affects everyone, young and old, rich and poor. It is of special interest to automobile, truck, and bus owners, to road builders, and to manufacturers of all motorized vehicles. Every level of government is involved in it; and because the function is now such an expensive one, every taxpayer also has a personal interest in how it is financed and administered. Any proposal such as has been made to wipe out all federal aid for the highway function should have the most careful scrutiny.

What is the system of federal aid in this function?

From the beginning of American history under the Constitution, the state legislatures have enacted laws concerning the layout, financing, construction, maintenance, and use of highways, roads, streets, and other public ways within their respective state boundaries. This is still true today and no responsible organization has proposed that this be changed.

Although many miles of early roads were built by the army and other national agencies in the territories of the United States, from the western borders of the original states to the Pacific Ocean, as soon as a territory became a state it assumed legal responsibility for all roads and streets within its limits, except for roads within national reservations, national forests, national parks, and other similar national properties, which the national government builds and maintains.

Throughout the nineteenth century the state governments generally avoided building any roads themselves. Instead they placed this responsibility either upon their smallest subdivisions—towns, villages, and cities—or upon their county governments. They authorized these local units to accept, buy, or take land for rights of way for roads, to require able-bodied men to give some days of labor each year on the roads under the direction of local officials, and to do other things to open and maintain the roads. In the modern sense there were at the time no state highway plans, no state highway systems, but there were interconnecting local road systems of varying degrees of passability.

Congress has from the first had the power to provide "post offices and post roads," but aside from certain land grants to the states for "internal improvements" and for railroads, it took no action to establish a general system of such roads. From the 1830s on, the railroads and some canals provided for long-haul service, and the local roads carried people and freight to the nearest railroads and to the market towns.

After about 1890 there came a stirring of demand for change— to "get the farmers out of the mud," to get rural free delivery by the post office to farm homes, to reduce the cost of marketing farm products by providing better rural roads. About this time too the automobile came along, and city people became more interested in rural roads and highways.

Some states responded a little to the new demands, but nearly all were tied down by their reliance on the antiquated, unpopular, and inefficient property tax as a main source of revenue, and by both rural and urban suspicion of a centralized state government. State aid to local governments for highway purposes proved to be more palatable, but even this device was at first employed most sparingly.

To look into the rural road situation Congress in 1893 set up an Office of Road Inquiry, later called the Office of Public Roads, whose officers made extensive, useful investigations and reports, but not until nearly twenty years later, in 1912, did Congress begin to appropriate money to state and local governments to aid in road construction. Even then the states were not prepared to cooperate, but a new act of Congress in 1916, the Federal Aid Road Act, with a more substantial appropriation for aids to the states, finally stimulated the states into action on a nationwide program of highway planning and construction. Every state soon established a state highway department. From that day to this there has been no year without substantial national expenditures for aid to the states in highway construction, and no state for long stayed outside the federal-aid system.

The basic federal highway aid law has been revised a number of times, down to its current version enacted in 1954. Current federal appropriations, through the fiscal year 1955, run to $575 million a year. The annual amount will be $966 million in 1956 and again in 1957. By making its authorization in advance, Congress enables the states to plan carefully their highway construction and expenditure programs for several years ahead.

The grants from the national government can be spent on only those highways, roads, and streets in any state that have been designated by the state highway authorities and approved by the United States Bureau of Public Roads in the Department of Commerce. These roads now include four categories: the interstate highway system (about 37,000 miles of the most important interstate highways); the primary road system (a larger mileage of the next most important highways); the secondary road system (largely so-called farm-to-market roads); and the urban connections with the main highways. Congress has carefully designated specific amounts to be available each year for each of these classes of roads, and smaller amounts for other special purposes.

In the whole United States there are about three and a third million miles of highways, roads, and streets, distributed among the states roughly in proportion to their area and population. Just over one fifth of these miles of public ways are now designated as eligible for federal aid in one or another of the four categories. All other roads and streets, some 2.6 million miles in all, or about four fifths of the total, are constructed and maintained by the state and local governments, without any necessary reference to national laws and standards whatever. The new "turnpikes" and super highways upon which tolls are charged are also strictly state enterprises.

The national Bureau of Public Roads notifies each state highway department well in advance of the amount of federal aid the state will be entitled to for the following year. The amount is determined for each state as its proportion of the amount authorized by Congress on the basis of the formulas set forth in the act of Congress. For example, the federal aid for the primary system is apportioned among the states as follows: one third on the basis of the state's area in proportion to the area of all the states; one third on the basis of its rural population in proportion to the rural population of all the states; and one third on the basis of its share of the national mileage of all rural roads over which the post office carries and delivers mail.

Thus if the total appropriation were $300 million for the primary system for the year, each one third would be $100 million. If then, in a simplified case, a state had 2 per cent of the national area, 3 per cent of the total rural population, and 3 per cent of the rural delivery and "star route" highways of the nation, over which mail is carried, it would get $2 million plus $3 million plus $3 million, or $8 million in all to spend on its primary highway system for that year. In addition it would get its share of the urban system money, based on its proportion of the nation's total urban population; its share of the secondary system fund; and its share of the interstate highway system fund, each figured on the basis of a distribution formula enacted by Congress. The total for any state for a recent year might be anything from two or three million up to thirty million or more, depending on the state's area, population, and so on as weighted in the formulas.

The amount allocated to each state for any year is not sent to it in one lump sum, nor is it sent in advance. Instead the money is held in the national treasury, earmarked for payment to the state concerned. It is to be spent only for highway construction and reconstruction. The state and local governments must themselves pay for maintenance.

Having decided what highways to construct in the year, the state highway department has its engineers make plans, blueprints, and specifications of the work to be done. Those jobs that are to be done on any part of the federal-aid system must be designed in accordance with federal standards as to width and other specifications. This planning is done in consultation with the engineers of the United States Bureau of Public Roads—there are generally one or more in each state. When the plans have been completed they must be approved by the bureau's engineers, locally or at a regional office, and in rare cases in Washington. There is some duplication of work in this process, but the system does provide a double check on highway plans, and agreements are usually reached between the state and national engineers in an informal and routine way.

When the plans have been approved the state highway department takes over the responsibility for the construction, although in some states the actual work is done under county highway departments and the state department merely supervises what is done. The state or county highway department advertises for bids, lets the contract (usually to the lowest responsible and qualified bidders), supervises the work, and pays the contractor from time to time as different parts of the jobs are finished and accepted.

On proof of such performance the representatives of the Bureau of Public Roads are notified; they also inspect the work done and if they find it acceptable they sign the papers that authorize the state to receive payment from the national treasury for the amount that is to come from the federal grant-in-aid. Thus the federal funds are paid to the states from time to time as the various jobs progress. Any money not spent by a state from its allotment within the year is still available to it for some time thereafter.

Each state is required to match with dollars of its own the dollars appropriated by Congress for aid in highway construction. Formerly the matching was dollar for dollar. But under the 1954 act of Congress the states are required to provide only 40 per cent as against 60 per cent of national money for projects on the interstate system. In addition, the so-called public land states, that is, those states in the West and Far West in which 5 per cent or more of the land area is unappropriated national public land, now have their general matching requirement reduced in proportion to national land ownership. For example, Nevada needs to put up only about $1 to every $5 of national funds, Utah a little under $1 to every $3 of national money, and so on. But for any job on any part of the federal-aid system there must always be some state or state and local money to match the federal contribution in some proportion, usually one for one. In practice, of course, the state and local governments put far more money into the road system as a whole than the national government does. In 1953, for example, out of a total of more than $5.5 billion spent on public highways, roads, and streets, less than $600 million was provided by the national government, or about one ninth of the total. The proportion may be higher in 1956 and 1957.

Aside from the matching provision and certain minimum standards for road construction, the requirements imposed upon the states in order to qualify for federal highway aid are not stringent. Each state is expected to have a state highway department for the national Bureau of Public Roads to deal with and to exercise supervision over the expenditure of federal-aid funds within the state. But the federal law does not specify any standards of education or experience for the state highway engineers, and it

27

does not require the state agency to have direct responsibility for road construction.

As to work on secondary (farm-to-market) roads, the present law permits the Department of Commerce, in which the Bureau of Public Roads now is, to accept a state's own certification that the work has been performed according to national specifications. This may be but the first step toward devolving an increasing measure of responsibility upon the states to see to it that federal funds are spent legally and wisely.

Although there have been scattered complaints that federal supervision over state expenditures of federal funds in highway construction has been too strict and has involved unnecessary duplication of work, the cooperation of the national and state authorities in the federal-aid highway program has become an outstanding model for national-state administrative relations.

Besides national grants to the states for highway purposes, there are state grants in the various states to the local governments for highway purposes. To a large extent these are technically called "shared taxes." That is to say, the state levies and collects a gasoline tax or a motor vehicle tax, but under the state law or constitution a certain percentage of the money collected must be turned over to the local governments to be spent by them on certain highways, roads, and streets for which they are responsible according to state law. As a rule no matching of these funds by local governments is required, and there is relatively little state supervision of the spending of the funds.

Public assistance to the needy today includes such well-defined categories as old age assistance, aid to dependent children, aid to the blind, aid to the totally disabled, and general assistance or residual relief for those needy persons who do not qualify under any of the foregoing special categories. There are also numerous smaller or incidental programs in child welfare, institutional care for the sick and needy, rehabilitative services for the handicapped, and health services that impinge on the welfare field.

Here in public assistance there is, then, another broad category of public services in which every American citizen has a real interest, whether he is fully aware of it or not. What the various levels and agencies of government do for the needy—and all levels of government are involved—has wide repercussions upon the moral, social, economic, political, and even religious welfare of the whole people.

Directly involved, of course, are the millions of people who annually receive aid under one or more programs in the public assistance field. Serving them, and also directly concerned, are the tens of thousands of national, state, and local officials and employees who are responsible for administering the public assistance programs. What they do in turn impinges upon the thousands of private social welfare agencies in the country that operate their own programs of welfare and relief; the millions of contributors to private welfare funds; the countless non-aided relatives of those who receive aid—the fathers and mothers, sons and daughters, brothers and sisters, uncles and aunts, cousins and others—who themselves may be unable to assist their needy relatives but are still concerned about their welfare. In this field, too, there is a pronounced taxpayer interest, because the money costs of welfare and assistance services are high even in prosperous times and proportionately higher in depression periods.

In a constitutional sense the primary responsibility for public assistance to the needy has rested upon the states in the Union since the Constitution was established. Congress has had from the beginning the power to tax (and to spend) to provide for "the general welfare," but this authority was at first a vague one and for over a century its meaning was seriously disputed, although Congress did appropriate a little money now and then for disaster relief. The states were, therefore, left to enact the basic laws for relief and aid to the needy.

This legislative responsibility the state legislatures discharged by imposing upon the counties, towns, villages, and cities the duty to levy taxes for relief, if necessary, and to provide the relief needed by the poor through their own officials. Generally speaking the states did not set up state welfare departments for the direct provision of relief and welfare services, although some of them did during the nineteenth century establish state institutions for the needy blind, the insane, the deaf, and other handicapped classes. In practice even the local governments depended largely upon churches and other private groups to provide most of the relief and welfare services. When the local governments did act they often became involved in disputes over the residence of those who applied for aid. Which town or which city or county was legally liable for the support of a particular needy person who had moved from one to another became an important question. The local taxpayer interest in avoiding the tax burden was an important factor.

Before the Great Depression of the 1930s some states had taken steps to assume more direct responsibility for the care of the aged, dependent children, and other classes in need, but the depression struck with such speed and such devastating force in the early 1930s that state and local governments alike found their laws, their public agencies, and their tax-raising abilities totally inadequate to meet even the most pressing needs, while many private relief agencies threw up their hands in despair.

There was a great debate as to whether the national government had any responsibility for human relief in the crisis, whether any action by it would not violate the Constitution by encroaching upon the sphere of the states, and indeed whether any policy of congressional action would not be dangerous paternalism. Sheer necessity seems to have forced the hand of Congress. Several temporizing measures in the early 1930s, including loans by a national agency (which itself had to borrow the money) to states for direct and work relief were superseded in 1933 by direct national grants to the states for emergency relief. Trial and error prevailed for several years as Congress experimented with one emergency program after another, providing grants to state and local governments for direct relief, work relief, loans and grants to farmers, aids for students, and so on. Many will remember the Civil Works Administration, the Civilian Conservation Corps, the Emergency Work Relief program, the Works Progress (later

Projects) Administration (the famous or infamous, as some thought it, WPA), and the Public Works Administration.

As the emergency dragged on and appeared likely to remain a long time, more permanent measures were sought. The report of a national Committee on Economic Security appointed by the President in 1934 was followed by the passage through Congress of the Social Security Act in 1935. This has been the basic law for national, state, and local relations in the social welfare field since then, but it has been amended and expanded by later laws down to and including an important one in 1954.

Under this act the national social welfare and economic security program consists of several major parts, one of which (OASI, popularly called "social security") has none of the aspects of a grant-in-aid program; another, employment security, has very few of the characteristics of a grant-in-aid plan; while several others, often lumped under "public assistance," are definitely grant-in-aid systems.

Social security, better denominated as Old Age and Survivors Insurance (OASI), is a national insurance program for persons over 65 and for survivors of persons who have qualified under the law whether such survivors have reached 65 or not. It provides for stipulated monthly payments. To be eligible for such payments a person must have qualified by being in a "covered employment" including self-employment of certain types, and while in such employment must have contributed to the insurance fund through a payroll tax (deductions from his pay by his employer) and by tax payments of his own into the fund on his salary, wages, or self-employed income up to (now) $4200 per year of earnings. Not all classes of employment are covered; some professions, for example, and national, state, and local government employees are not automatically covered, but under the 1954 amendments to the Social Security Act the coverage has been greatly extended, and state and local employees may now come under the system by an optional procedure. For the survivors of insured workers the insurance features of the system are also important.

Lacking any feature of a grant-in-aid system, and being administered directly by the Social Security Administration in Washington through numerous district and field offices, the social security system has not depended upon the states doing anything and therefore it has developed none of the frictional heat between national and state officials that has appeared here and there in some grant programs. The states have simply been by-passed in this program. Curiously enough, it has succeeded so well and has offered such obvious benefits to those who are covered that many state and local governments now see an advantage in bringing their employees under the protection of this centralized, all-national program.

Employment security is a second major part of the welfare program established by the Social Security Act. This feature is also based upon a national tax on payrolls applicable to the employers of eight or more persons in commerce and industry. Again excluded are large sectors of the nation's economy such as those employed in government, agriculture, and railroading—the railroad workers are under a separate system.

Ninety per cent of the national tax for employment security is waived in any state that adopts a law providing for a corresponding state tax and for a system of unemployment compensation and employment offices that conforms to the minimum standards of the act of Congress. Since the employers in any state were going to have to pay the national payroll tax in any event, every state legislature soon enacted its own employment security law and imposed the necessary payroll tax. Each state has, therefore, an employment security department of its own with a central office in the state capital or in some other large city, and branch offices in all important centers of employment throughout the state. These offices administer the state's employment service, helping to find jobs for the unemployed, and also the system of unemployment benefits for those covered workers who cannot find suitable employment. This program is somewhat unusual in that the local governments in the states have practically nothing to do with it.

The rates of unemployment compensation and the numbers of weeks during which payments will be made vary somewhat from state to state according to state law. In general, however, the system is nationwide and fairly uniform, because it was the act of Congress, to which all states must conform as a minimum, that induced the states to establish their several state systems. About fifty million workers are covered.

The 90 per cent of the national employment security tax waived if offset by corresponding taxes paid or contributions made by employers under the state tax is credited to the state's account in the unemployment trust fund of the United States Treasury, from which unemployment compensation claims are paid on certification by the state. In 1952–53 about four million unemployed persons received an average of 10.2 weekly payments in an average amount of $23.32, the total being more than $900 million. The total trust funds for all states then stood at more than $18 billion.

The other 10 per cent of the tax goes into the United States Treasury. This part was evidently intended to cover all costs of administration, both national and state, but it is not earmarked for that purpose. In fact this one tenth of the total tax has yielded more than has been needed for all administrative expenses, and has caused many more heated disputes than the other 90 per cent.

Up to 1954 no state had any legal claim on this one tenth of the tax collected from employers in the state. Advised by the national Bureau of Employment Security, Congress appropriated each year from general funds the amount it decided the states needed to administer their employment security systems, and this amount the bureau divided among the states according to a formula based on estimates of state work loads, unit costs, and other criteria. This kept the service standards at somewhere near the same levels in all states, but some states received less than the .3¢ tax on each payroll dollar would have yielded them, while other states received more.

Leaders in the states that received less than the local collections demanded a change in the law. Yielding in large part to this demand, Congress in 1954 passed the Reed Act, P.L. 567, whereby

33

35722

the entire proceeds of this payroll tax are in effect dedicated to the employment security system. Congress will still appropriate for state employment security administration, but whatever is left over from the tax will go first into a $200 million revolving emergency fund to help out state funds and second into the separate state unemployment funds held in trust by the United States Treasury.

The two foregoing programs, old age and survivors insurance, and employment security, seem to have been planned to become the mainstays of the entire national social security program. One was to take care of those who could not work because of age, and the other would provide substantial but temporary aid in cases of ordinary unemployment.

At the same time these two plans did not cover all cases of potential need. There would still have to be state and local programs of relief for many persons who could not qualify for OASI or UC, although in time these two programs might cover many more persons. At any rate Congress provided for national grants-in-aid to the states for several public assistance programs and left the administration of these programs to the state and local governments.

The *public assistance* grants provided for in the Social Security Act are clearly within the grant-in-aid category. There were three principal ones in the original act, old age assistance (OAA), aid to dependent children (ADC), and aid to the blind (AB). To these has been added aid to the permanently and totally disabled (APTD). These are all in the general area of what used to be called poor relief because the test is one of needs for food, clothing, shelter, and medical care that the individual is unable to meet by himself. Of course there will also be individuals in need who do not qualify under any of the four assistance programs named. These persons would normally be recipients of general assistance (GA), or "residual relief," from state and local governments if they had no one else to help them. Since the emergency days of the depression in the 1930s Congress has not concerned itself directly with general assistance. This has remained strictly a state and local responsibility.

The four public assistance grants are also based on the assumption that the states have a primary responsibility to care for the needy, but the Social Security Act represents an acceptance by Congress of a national responsibility to assist the states in carrying a burden that is likely to be heaviest in those states where the resources for meeting the needs are inadequate. Consequently Congress provides funds to the states to supplement their own basic provisions.

To qualify for federal aid in the four public assistance programs a state must enact and keep in force a law or laws that will provide a plan for the services, effective throughout the state, to be administered or supervised by a single state welfare agency. The state must also participate in financing the program to some extent, although local units (usually the counties) may be authorized to administer the program and be expected to supply part of the funds. In addition the plan must provide for a merit system of selecting personnel for the program, allow any person who wishes to do so to apply for aid, provide for a hearing by anyone who is aggrieved by a decision in his case, refrain from giving out lists of the names of applicants and recipients to be used for political or commercial purposes, and report to the national Social Security Administration from time to time on its work in public assistance.

This Administration maintains some regional offices and a number of state offices to advise with the state and county agencies that administer the programs, and also some auditors who inspect accounts to see how the federal-aid funds are being spent. The public assistance programs are, therefore, basically state and local programs, heavily supported by federal aid and held up to minimum national standards by a certain amount of national supervision and audit to ensure that the state plan which the national agency has approved is being carried out.

In the fiscal year 1953 more than 2,500,000 persons were receiving OAA; 1,492,000 children in more than 500,000 families were being assisted by ADC; nearly 100,000 blind persons and more than 175,000 permanently and totally disabled were being assisted through state and local agencies that were using substantial amounts of federal grant-in-aid funds. The average OAA recipient was getting more than $48 a month, the average family under ADC more than $82 a month, the blind and the totally disabled $53 and $48 a month, respectively. The federal-aid portion of this money is advanced from the national treasury to the states and by them to the county welfare agencies from time to time as needed.

Although the grants for highways at one time led all others in amount, those for public assistance now account for the largest amounts of such grants. The total amount of such grants in the fiscal year 1953 was $1330 million—nearly a billion and a third dollars—about 48 per cent of all federal grants. OAA alone accounted for more than $900 million in grants-in-aid.

The states made substantial contributions also, but in varying proportions from state to state. Some were liberal in the amounts paid and in the numbers of approved recipients; others stood toward the other end of the scale in both respects. Actually the national government is regularly paying more than half the bill in such a major program as OAA, for example. Under the present law the federal grant is four fifths of the first $25 (or $20), and one half of the next $30 (or $15), making possible a total of $35 per month of national funds for each OAA recipient. In the national average payment of $48 per month in 1953, the federal contribution was more than $30 per month, or about three fifths of the total.

This is what is called an open-end grant, as are the other public assistance grants. All four are on substantially the same basis, although the rates for ADC are different from the others. The state and county agencies decide what persons in their jurisdiction are eligible for relief under the several categories. They also set the total amount to be paid in the light of the individual's needs and his other resources. Having done this they have in effect decided what amount the national government shall pay under the formula. If the amount allowed is just $55 per month, the national government's guaranteed share is at the ceiling rate, or $35, leaving only $20 per month to be paid from state and local funds. Of course anything above $55 per month must come from state and local sources.

It is impossible for either the state or national government to budget precisely under open-end grants. The number of recipients of assistance will rise and fall according to the decisions of county and state relief authorities who have little responsibility for the state budget and none at all for the national. The decisions of lower level authorities thus help to determine the budgets of higher level governments. This is, perhaps, unavoidable if needs are to be met as they arise with changes in general economic conditions and the particular fortunes of individuals and families. The merits and demerits of open-end grants have been debated extensively, but as yet no better plan has been discovered.

What we see then in the public assistance programs is the cooperation of more than three thousand county and city welfare boards, forty-eight state legislatures and departments of public welfare, and the national government, in four different programs that provide substantial relief for needy people. There are countless details that could be explored in all four programs, but the essentials have been stated.

Under the headings of highways and public assistance we have seen a little of how national, state, and local governments join together to provide these major public services. The role of the national government is mainly that of providing substantial sums of money for the state and local governments to spend on the specified functions, setting certain standards (including matching) that they are expected to maintain if they are to receive the money, and exercising a minimum amount of supervision over state and local planning and the performance of these aided functions. The state governments, on the other hand, enact the basic laws and have the primary and direct responsibility for these functions. Some of the functions they administer directly through

37

their own staffs of state officers and employees, but others they delegate for administration to their local units of government.

In reviewing these two major grant-in-aid programs, we have accounted for more than two thirds of the money granted annually by the national government to the states. But there are numerous other grant-in-aid programs—from twenty to more than forty, depending on how minutely one subdivides the field and on what programs are included. The national government's financial investment in some of these is very small, almost negligible, but to the people involved these programs are just as important as those costing many times as much money.

Anyone who wishes to do so can observe and check the facts about these programs, and their detailed operation, in his own state and usually in his own county or other local community. My notes about them here are intended to convey only the minimum of information that a citizen needs to discuss them intelligently.

The Social Security Act of 1935 provided in several ways for the welfare of children. Aid to Dependent Children (ADC), as previously described, should not be confused with Child Welfare Services (CWS) for which a separate grant-in-aid, to be described here, was provided. Through this grant the national government cooperates "with State public-welfare agencies in establishing, extending, and strengthening, especially in predominantly rural areas, public welfare services . . . for the protection and care of homeless, dependent and neglected children, and children in danger of becoming delinquent . . ."

The annual federal appropriation for CWS is far less than for ADC—only about $8 million a year recently as against about $300 million for ADC. Each state is entitled to a minimum of $40,000 annually for CWS, and in 1953 the maximum for any state was about $350,000, the amount being determined primarily by the proportion of a state's rural population to the nation's rural population. The money does not go to the actual support of children, but to the maintenance of state and county social services for the adoption, placement, social and mental adjustment, and protection of children in need of such care. State and local sources supplied about four times as much money as the total federal grant.

Nationally the Children's Bureau in the Health, Education, and Welfare Department supervises the expenditure of the federal funds for the program. It has a regional representative in each of nine regional Health, Education, and Welfare Department offices, so that each regional representative has to serve several states. At the state level the work is carried on through the state welfare department, but most of the actual work with children is done by the county welfare agencies under state supervision. Juvenile courts, state and county institutions, and private welfare agencies all cooperate in the program.

It is reported that in 1951 more than 250,000 children received help from the state and local child welfare services.

A recognition that the nation had been falling behind the needs of the people in the provision of hospitals led Congress in 1946, after extensive public hearings, to enact the Hill-Burton Hospital Survey and Construction Act. This act provided aid to the states for surveying the hospital needs within each state and for developing plans and procedures for meeting those needs.

Under the leadership of their health departments the states made these surveys, and Congress followed up by appropriating substantial funds to assist in the construction of public and other nonprofit hospitals. By September 1954, $631 million in federal funds for hospital construction had been matched with almost twice as much in local funds, both public and private. About 2000 hospital projects have been approved, and more than half of these have been completed. About 100,000 hospital beds have already been made available by the completed projects.

Every state is cooperating in the program. Counties, cities, other local governments, and nonprofit hospital associations present their plans to the state authorities, whose consent is necessary if the federal funds are to be made available. The national funds are allocated to the states on the basis of population and per capita income, so that states with low per capita incomes receive proportionately more in federal aid.

There seems to be almost complete agreement that this program has had remarkable success in meeting an important public need. The act has been extended until 1957, but Congress decides from year to year how much more to appropriate. In 1954 Congress also authorized funds for four new types of projects under the act—diagnostic centers, hospitals for the chronically ill and impaired, rehabilitation facilities, and nursing homes.

The national government's own public health services go back to the beginning of government under the Constitution. Significant grants-in-aid to the states for health purposes began in 1918 with a grant for control of venereal disease, a malady that had increased during World War I. A few years later Congress authorized grants also for maternal and child health services. Both of these acts were relatively short-lived, but in the Social Security Act of 1935 Congress began a broad program of grants to the states for public health purposes. In 1944 Congress enacted a revised and more comprehensive program.

The general objective is to assist the states in establishing and maintaining adequate public health services, but the attack on the problems of ill health has many prongs. Federal grants are made to the states to assist them in their central health agencies, to enable them to train public health personnel, to set up health districts, to conduct health demonstrations, and so on. In addition there are special grants for the control of venereal disease, heart disease, tuberculosis, cancer, and mental diseases. All these grants combined, amounting to more than $30 million a year, are distributed to the state health departments on the basis of state populations, health needs, specific health problems, and financial needs. In the public health grants generally Congress has made a conscious effort to distribute the national funds to the states in accordance with state needs, as reckoned in both financial and functional terms.

The state, or state and local, health departments add the

federal grants to the state and local tax contributions, now substantially larger than those of the national government, and administer their health programs in accordance with state plans that have been agreed to by the national agency, namely, the United States Public Health Service under the surgeon general in the Department of Health, Education, and Welfare. The Public Health Service has a regional representative and several specialists in various health programs in each of its eight regional offices to keep in touch with and to cooperate with the state health agencies.

Under the national School Lunch Act of 1946, and various appropriation acts, Congress has provided for federal grants of cash and farm commodities to the states for use in maintaining a school lunch program in all school districts that wish to cooperate. In 1953 the total grant was more than $130 million, in about equal parts of cash and commodities. To this the state and local contributions and the small sums paid per meal by the millions of children who received the lunches added about three times as much, making a total program of more than a half billion dollars for the year.

The purposes of the program are to safeguard the health of the children by providing a nutritious noontime meal, and to encourage the consumption of agricultural products. Considerable quantities of agricultural surpluses are used up in this way.

To share in this program a state must submit an acceptable plan to the United States Department of Agriculture, the national administrator of the grant. The distribution among the states is determined by the number of school children in the state and the per capita income, the poorer states getting proportionately more than the wealthier. Every state is required to match the federal funds in proportion to ability.

Within each state it is the state department of education that works out the state plan and negotiates the agreement with the Department of Agriculture. Every state is now participating. The actual operations are carried on by the school district authorities and those who are in direct charge of the schools. There is a minimum of national supervision, and that supervision is practically all at the state level.

Some 10 million children are reported to have been under the school lunch program in recent years, but this is only about one third of the total enrollment. The coverage is very uneven—from about one eighth of the children in one state to nearly three fourths in another.

As in all grant-in-aid programs there have been problems of administration, yet this program does meet with considerable public support and is likely to be continued.

Since it enacted the Smith-Hughes Act in 1917 Congress has been making regular grants to the states for vocational education. This program should be clearly distinguished from vocational rehabilitation. The latter provides a smaller grant-in-aid to the states for the purpose of rehabilitating and making employable those individuals who are disabled and need to find a change of employment to help support themselves.

The program in vocational education, on the other hand, is designed for any and all persons, from young people still in school to those of almost any age, who wish to learn some trade or vocation. The classes provided under the program may be full time or part time, and held either during the day or in the evening.

Present federal legislation authorizes grants to the states for vocational education in four fields of employment: agriculture, home economics, trades and industry, and distributive occupations (salesmanship and clerking, for example).

The Office of Education in the Department of Health, Education, and Welfare administers the national grants to the states, approves state plans and budgets for vocational education, and provides for such minimum supervision and auditing of state expenditure of federal funds as the law requires. Acting in accordance with state law, the state departments of education prepare and carry out the state plans for vocational education through separate divisions. Except for audits there is very little national supervision.

Federal payments go to the states and are channeled to the school districts, which provide the actual instruction. Vocational agricultural education receives about two fifths of the congressional appropriation ($10 million out of $25 million in 1953), the field of trades and industry comes next, and home economics receives over one fifth. Education in distributive occupations gets only a small amount. Of course the state and local contributions to all these programs outmatch the federal grants by about four or five to one.

In recent years the number of students in the aided vocational programs has run above three million per year. Thousands of high schools are engaged in these programs, some in every state. The vocational agricultural and home economics programs have a strong hold in the high schools that serve largely the rural areas. The Future Farmers and Future Homemakers organizations show what enthusiasm these vocational courses have developed among the students.

Congress apparently considers the program of great value, for when it was recently proposed that the appropriation for vocational education be reduced, Congress instead increased the amount.

Beginning in 1911 with the Weeks Law which provided for protection against forest fires, Congress has developed a program of cooperation with the states and with private owners of forests and wood lots to protect forests against fire, destructive insects, and blights, to promote reforestation, and to advance forest management and growth. The total amount of federal aid is not very large ($11 million in 1953), but the states provide more than three times as much so that the total program is a very considerable one.

The United States Forest Service in the Department of Agriculture handles the relations with the states, and each participating state has some agency to carry out its functions in the forestry field. A few states, mostly in the Great Plains area, which have little forest area, do not participate. As in other cases, a state that wishes to cooperate makes an agreement with the national agency on the basis of a plan as to what the state will do.

The cooperation in forest fire protection is well known to most citizens. In the national forests the national government has its own rangers and fire protection services but these cooperate with the state forest services in adjoining areas, and in addition federal funds are used in part to help support the state services. Thus there is unified action, and a sharing of the costs between national and state treasuries for the mutual protection of national, state, and privately owned forests.

Somewhat differently administered, but with considerable national aid, leadership, and cooperation, are the projects for the eradication of blights like the white pine blister and of various insects destructive to trees, for the production and distribution of tree planting stock for reforestation, and for the promotion of better forest management. The amount of national supervision over what the states do in this field is reported to be almost insignificant, and the amount of paper work and reporting very small. In effect each state is entirely free to develop its own forestry policy for all state-owned and private forest lands within the state.

The Fish and Wildlife Service in the Department of the Interior is responsible for doing what it can under the law to protect and to help restore and maintain the fish and wildlife resources of the nation for the benefit of all. Each state has its own agencies for the same general purposes, but because the main rivers and other waters in which fish live are interstate, and because important species of game are migratory, it is necessary to have interstate and national as well as separate state action in these fields. There must also be agreement on basic policies of control and propagation.

The national government's interest in these fields goes back very far (Bureau of Fisheries, 1871; Biological Survey, 1885; Migratory Bird Act, 1918). In 1937 Congress provided for aid to the states for wildlife restoration, and in 1950 extended aid for fish restoration. The federal aid is extended on the basis of projects developed by the states and approved by the Fish and Wildlife Service. These projects are of various types including the acquisition by the states of extensive areas of land and water for feeding, resting, or breeding places for wildlife, or for fish, or both; the construction of various facilities thereon; and research into various problems of fish and wildlife management, protection, and propagation. There is a formula for allocating the national funds among the states, but payments are made to the states for specific approved projects. The states must plan and start the projects with their own men and money. Later they receive the agreed-upon amount of reimbursement from the national government.

These projects, and indeed the entire cooperative relationship in this area between the national and state authorities, are of great interest to the millions of men and women who find much of their recreation in fishing and hunting.

The various grant-in-aid and cooperative projects in agricultural colleges, experiment stations, and extension work are too varied and important to be described adequately in a few paragraphs. Taken together they represent in my judgment one of the great achievements of the nation. They have given agriculture a high status, have helped to improve methods of production and marketing in all branches of farming, have by research developed ever-better breeds of cattle, hogs, poultry, and other farm animals and improved varieties of grains, fruits, vegetables, and other farm crops, and have provided leadership, education and informational services for farmers and other citizens in every state.

Although a few states had taken earlier steps toward this goal, it was unquestionably the first Morrill Act enacted by Congress in 1862 that set going the nationwide movement for practical education in farming. This act provided a substantial land grant for every state to help it establish a college for agriculture and

45

mechanical arts. Later Congress provided for annual payments to assist states in the operation of these colleges, to encourage them to set up agricultural experiment stations, and to provide an extension service under state control in every agricultural county in the nation.

Today every state has one or more agricultural colleges, one or more agricultural experiment stations, and a system of agricultural extension workers (county agents) as well as home demonstration agents to carry the messages of better farming and better farm living to every farm home. More than $50 million a year of federal funds channels through the states into these agriculture programs, mostly in the form of grants-in-aid, and of course the states themselves put in a great deal more.

The results achieved under these programs are the fruits of long-continued, intelligent, and sincere cooperation between Congress and the national administration, on the one hand, and the state legislatures, governors, and land-grant colleges, on the other. It would be hard to find any field in which the grant-in-aid principle is more firmly established and more thoroughly justified by its results.

The national government's interest in agriculture and in rural life problems came earlier than its interest in cities. Although urban population began to exceed rural by the early part of this century, it took the Great Depression of the 1930s to bring home to the national administration and Congress the problems of economic insecurity, poor housing, inadequate city planning, and environmental decay that beset daily those who live in cities. The great emergency relief and works projects of the so-called New Deal were directed primarily at the needs of the urban population. As the emergency began to abate, longer-run measures were enacted.

In 1937 Congress passed the United States Housing Act to stimulate the construction of public housing for low-income groups by means of federal grants and loans toward the capital costs and small annual grants thereafter to enable local housing authorities to keep the rents down in such housing. Each participating state passed an act accepting the general terms of the congressional act and authorizing the local authorities in cities and counties to set up housing authorities. Most states participated, many local public housing authorities constructed low-rent apartments, and for some years there was an active public housing program. The housing authorities are state and local agencies, but each one operates under a contract with the federal public housing agency. In recent years the federal aid for constructing new public housing has dwindled to so low a point that it contributes little to the volume of home building throughout the country.

The Housing Act of 1949, now somewhat modified by a new law of 1954, was designed by Congress primarily to help local communities eliminate substandard housing by the clearance of slums and blighted areas. This in turn would assist in the development and redevelopment of urban communities, most of which suffer from decay near their centers as more and more people move out to the suburbs. Since the great financial obstacle to such projects is the high cost of acquiring and clearing the land, the act of Congress provides for capital grants up to two thirds of the cost of a project, and loans for a large part of the rest of the cost. Here again the law goes into effect in any state only when the state legislature has passed a law to accept its terms. Such laws provide for the creation of local slum clearance and redevelopment authorities, and it is these authorities that negotiate agreements with the national housing and home finance administrator for the money needed for any particular project. This is not, therefore, a regular annual grant-in-aid program, but one that depends upon the approval of specific plans and projects.

I have now reviewed, although very sketchily, a number of developments that have taken place in important public services in recent years. Others, such as airport construction and natural disaster relief, I have not touched upon. But even from this brief description of some of the services the pattern of intergovernmental relations emerges.

47

What we see, in broad outline, is an extensive and complex but not uniform system of cooperation "vertically" between national, state, and local governmental agencies supplemented by significant amounts of "horizontal" cooperation between states and between local units of government. The lines of cooperation crisscross in every major function like highways, welfare, and public health and in every region of the country.

In what way do critics want to change this pattern of cooperation in the federal system as it operates today?

As a matter of fact, the changes proposed are not as drastic as might have been anticipated from the sweeping condemnations and dire predictions by some of the more vigorous critics of the national government. One could understandably have expected proposals for revolutionary, root-and-branch social changes. But nothing of the sort has been offered.

Those who favor increasing the importance of the states as against the national government have concentrated their proposals primarily on various federal grants-in-aid they believe should be eliminated, reduced, or changed and on certain taxes they believe the states should have the sole right to collect. For example, most critics would not eliminate governmental activities in highways; but they would have the national government turn over to states sufficient tax resources to allow them to construct their own highways without federal aid or supervision. Those who oppose the "welfare state" want to reduce certain public services and head off some new proposals like compulsory health insurance, but they do not propose to wipe out all social and economic legislation favorable to farmers, workers, the poor, and the handicapped. A little paternalism, more or less, is apparently acceptable.

This is not to minimize the importance of the changes proposed. In particular, what seem to outsiders to be relatively minor reductions or eliminations of grants-in-aid may have profound effects upon certain public services in which hundreds of thousands, even millions, of citizens are concerned—for all the grant-in-aid programs affect in some way the welfare of the entire nation. It is not at all certain that the states, acting individually, would be financially able to take over total responsibility for programs dropped by the national government; or that, without the "prodding" of the national government, the states would keep the programs operating up to even minimum standards.

Even more important than the immediate effects of the changes proposed, however, is the long-run trend they portend. Is the federal government to continue to expand its services as new conditions seem to demand? Or is it to be severely restricted in its activities, with the state and local governments individually determining the need for new governmental activities?

The issues involved in answering these questions may be grouped under two headings, although in actual discussion the lines between them tend to become blurred.

One major problem that turns up in various forms is that of constitutionality. This is the issue raised by Congress when it stated in the law establishing the Commission on Intergovernmental Relations that "the activity of the Federal Government has been extended into many fields which, under our constitutional system, may be the primary interest and obligation of the several states and the subdivisions thereof." Are the relations that now subsist in practice between the national, state, and local governments in large part contrary to the Constitution of the United States? Has Congress passed a number of unconstitutional measures that take over functions properly belonging to the states or that subject the state governments to federal standards and supervision? Has the Supreme Court aided in subverting the Constitution by not declaring such acts unconstitutional? These and other questions of constitutionality require that we pay considerable attention to the written Constitution and to how it has developed and been interpreted.

The second problem or group of problems raises issues of public policy. Thus it is asked whether, even if most of the things now being done by the national government are not unconstitutional, it would not be better public policy for the nation to reverse its course, to reduce the role of the national government, and to increase the roles and the independence of the state and

49

local governments. Here one has to determine the best way to preserve personal liberty and local self-government; weigh the dangers of big government, paternalism, centralization, and the "welfare state"; and decide the merits of handing over to the states complete control of certain functions and specified sources of revenue that would presumably provide the funds needed to support these functions.

These issues cannot be kept wholly separate, but in the interests of simplicity I will discuss first the constitutional questions, in their historical setting, and then turn to the present-day problems of policy and finance.

☆

PART II
Constitutional Problems and Issues

3

Backgrounds of the Constitution

IN THIS chapter and those following I shall try to present in brief compass those aspects of the development of the Constitution that relate to the nature of the Union, the relations among the people, the national government, and the states, and the division of powers and responsibilities among them.

Some readers may wish to skip these chapters on the theory that they are not of current importance and lie too far in the background. My own view is that this would be a mistake. A constitution is not just a written document or a thing of today only. It is a body of ever-changing basic rules of government. It is an essential part of the historic development and traditions of the people. It is developed by the leaders and forces in society that are dominant at the time, in the light of the needs they feel, the ideas they hold, and the intentions they express for improving the government.

A brief survey of the way in which the Constitution of the United States has developed cannot help but improve one's understanding of the issues of today.

Before the independence of the United States was established there were thirteen English-speaking colonies in America from New Hampshire to Georgia. The people in the colonies were not aliens to each other or to England. They shared the same background and traditions and they had a common citizenship, under which they enjoyed the rights of English law. They had separate local governments, but all the colonies were also under a central government—the "crown" or "sovereign" (king or queen) of England and the English Parliament.

With some significant differences, the division of powers and functions between the central government in London and the "local" or colonial governments in America was very much like that outlined in the United States Constitution today between the national government and the states.

The colonies generally recognized that the British government had the right to control the defenses of the entire British empire, to declare and conduct war and make peace, to make treaties and other foreign commitments, to regulate commerce with foreign nations and between the various parts of the empire, to levy duties on such commerce, to regulate relations with the Indians, to conduct the postal system, and to do a number of other things as the highest authority in the empire; and that such acts were binding on all the colonies and the colonists. All the colonies were for administrative purposes under the King's Privy Council, the Board of Trade, and a "Secretary of State for the Southern Department." The crown also appointed the resident governors for most of the colonies, in addition to judges and certain other colonial officers. A few colonies had more extensive rights of self-government, including the right to choose their own governors.

In each colony there was an assembly, elected by the legal voters, which had the power to make laws on a wide variety of subjects according to their several charters or other grants from the crown; to impose and collect taxes for local purposes within their respective colonies; and to control the spending of money so raised and other money in the colonial treasury. The home government in England reserved, however, and exercised the right to disallow and override colonial legislation.

There were numerous conflicts between the legislative assemblies and the royal governors over laws, taxes, and expenditures, but the first important American experience of conflict between central and local governments did not come until Parliament, attempting to raise more money for defense of the empire, tried to impose "internal" taxes in the colonies, especially stamp taxes and a tax on tea. When these acts were followed by the so-called intolerable acts, the colonists revolted. Royal governors were driven out and revolutionary conventions of the people took over the government in one colony after another. Organized in the unauthorized Continental Congress, the thirteen colonies, who now called themselves "the thirteen United States of America," on July 2, 1776, declared their independence and on July 4 adopted and signed the longer and official "Declaration of Independence."

The states acted in unison as "one people" in this declaration, but the delegates from the several state legislatures signed separately under their states' names. They also used the plural form for the states when, near the end of the document, they declared "That these United Colonies are, and of Right ought to be Free and Independent States," as if they may have intended to be independent of each other as well as independent of Great Britain. In fact, however, the states acted unitedly under national leaders in carrying on the war for independence, in negotiating with France and other powers for aid and treaties of friendship, in borrowing money at home and abroad on the credit of the United States, and in providing a little later for the government and development of the common pool of lands held by the United States west of the Alleghenies. Foreign powers like France, Spain, Holland, and Prussia recognized only the United States of America as a whole, and not each separate state.

Thus the states and the people were on the way to becoming truly united in spirit and in action even when the words they used suggested that each state was separately becoming independent of Great Britain. A good many historians, supported by Supreme Court decisions, have asserted that the several states never were separately or disunitedly "sovereign"; that even as they emerged from their tacit union under British rule they kept right on in union under the Continental Congress for all external purposes—for war, finance, and foreign affairs. To the outside world at least they presented a united front, as if they were indeed one nation.

At the same time there were strong forces working against

55

unity. These were centered in the state legislatures where there were many political leaders who were obviously fearful of losing their powers to a central government and jealously protective of their separate prerogatives. Their fears and jealousies had a great influence on the Articles of Confederation, drawn up by the Continental Congress as a framework of governance for the common affairs of all the new states and their people.

The authority behind the Articles of Confederation was an agreement among the thirteen state legislatures, each acting for its own state. The delegates elected by the several legislatures to represent them in Congress drafted the proposed Articles and then sent them back to the state legislatures for approval. When the state legislatures had all given their approval to the Articles and had also authorized their delegates to ratify them formally, the delegates assembled in the next Congress ratified and affirmed them in the following somewhat obsequious language:

And Whereas it hath pleased the Great Governor of the World to incline the hearts of the legislatures we respectively represent in congress, to approve of, and to authorize us to ratify the said articles of confederation and perpetual union, Know Ye that we the undersigned delegates, by virtue of the power and authority to us given for that purpose, do by these presents, in the name and on behalf of our respective constituents, fully and entirely ratify and confirm each and every of the said articles of confederation and perpetual union, and all and singular the matters and things therein contained . . .

There is here no mention of the people of the United States. The Articles did not depend upon or receive any popular sanction or approval. Instead it was the legislatures as the governing bodies of their respective states that authorized the whole procedure and approved the document as an agreement among themselves. Since each legislature spoke for its own state, the Articles became formally a sort of interstate compact. In this respect the document was more like an international treaty or covenant than a constitution, although in its provisions for the powers of government and the rights of individuals it had some characteristics of a constitution.

It is not surprising that this document, authorized at every step by the state legislatures, should provide for a very weak central organization for the United States. There was no provision for a central executive and practically none for a general system of courts. The one organ that was set up was a Congress to be composed of two to seven delegates from each state who were to "be annually appointed in such manner as the legislature of each state shall direct," a provision which, in practice, resulted in appointment by the several state legislatures, not election by the voters except in Connecticut and Rhode Island. The terms of the delegates were limited to not more than three years in any six (a sure way to weaken any responsible body); each delegate was subject to recall by his state; and each was dependent upon his state for his salary and expenses. All these provisions were clearly designed to keep the members entirely dependent upon their state legislatures and to prevent the development of a strong Congress. The very name "Congress" suggested that it was an assemblage of representatives of independent nations rather than a national legislative body serving "one people."

In proceedings in Congress each state delegation had one vote, and for every important action the vote of at least nine states was required. Thus a minority of five states out of thirteen could defeat any measure, while any state whose delegation was evenly divided on a question could not even cast a vote to help make up the requisite nine. But at least there was enough unity and a sufficient scaling down of the claims of "sovereignty" so that it was not necessary to have a unanimous vote of all the states before ordinary decisions could be made.

The people had no direct access to the delegates in Congress; there was no popular voting for them except in the two states mentioned. On the other hand the Congress could pass very few laws binding on or helpful to the people. It could deal, in general, only with the states, and with them only through the state legislatures.

In approving the Articles of Confederation, the states, through their legislatures, solemnly promised to abide by the decisions of

57

Congress and to take the actions needed to carry them out. The states agreed to supply the money Congress needed since Congress had no power to levy any tax, not even a tariff on imports; but in practice they failed rather miserably to do so, and there were many recriminations between states because some failed more than others to meet their obligations. Congress could not raise men to supply the needs of its armies, it could only make requisitions on the states; and here again the record of the states in providing their quotas was a generally shabby one. General Washington complained often to Congress about the lack of men, money, and supplies for his armies, but Congress had no power and no means to coerce the states into action. Congress had no power, either, to legislate on interstate and foreign commerce, and the state legislatures (especially those in the more favorably situated states) imposed tariffs and restrictions that were resented in other states.

There were other features of the Articles that were more favorable to the general welfare. The "sovereignty" of the several states was limited by clauses forbidding them to engage in war or to make treaties with foreign nations. The citizens of each state were to enjoy the rights of free inhabitants in every other state, so that a sort of common citizenship and free migration from state to state were continued; and each state was to give "full faith and credit" to the public acts and records of every other state. To the Congress were granted the rights to regulate the coinage and weights and measures, to regulate trade with the Indians outside of any state, to establish and regulate post offices, and to make rules for the government of the land and naval forces. As already noted, Congress was also authorized to make requisitions on the states for men and money, and to pay out of the common treasury "all charges of war, and all other expenses that shall be incurred for the common defence or general welfare."

But having apparently given considerable power to Congress, the drafters of the Articles asserted in Article II that "Each state retains its sovereignty, freedom and independence, and every Power, Jurisdiction, and right, which is not by this confederation expressly delegated to the United States, in Congress assembled." By this provision even the few meager powers conferred on Congress were to be narrowly and not liberally construed. There were to be no "implied powers" for Congress under the Articles. Only the powers "expressly" granted to it were at its disposal.

Thus under the Articles Congress and the "continental army" led by General Washington struggled along rather precariously, dependent on "grants-in-aid" of men and money from the state legislatures. The state legislatures were in the saddle. Although they had solemnly agreed to carry out the acts and requisitions of Congress, as if they were its agents, in practice Congress was their agent, and dependent on their favors.

The debate concerning the relative success or failure of the government under the Articles of Confederation will probably never end. Due to a combination of circumstances the War for Independence was successful, but no important historian has attributed this success to the Articles or to the system of government they established. There are differences of opinion also as to how bad the economic and governmental situation was after the treaty of peace of 1783.

With the coming of national independence men had apparently had high hopes for peace, prosperity, and tranquillity. These hopes did not fully materialize. There is some evidence that improvements in certain aspects of the economic situation were taking place, but the improvements were more than overbalanced by adverse factors. In 1785–86 there was a serious depression in commerce. The monetary situation was bad, due to a sharp decline in the value of paper money, and the credit of the Congress at a low ebb. There was confusion and uncertainty in business. The unpaid veterans were in a bad mood. Farmers were in hard straits economically and were demanding relief from their debts. Some state legislatures yielded to the demands for the relief of debtors, but when they were slow to act there was organized resistance to government, even armed rebellion such as that led by Shays in Massachusetts in 1786. Congress was for all practical purposes impotent to help.

Writing to Henry Lee and James Madison in October and November 1786, George Washington called for a new super-structure of government "by which our lives, liberties and properties will be secured." He could see through the clouds the rays of a sun of hope for "this rising empire." But a new system of government was needed: "Thirteen Sovereignties pulling against each other, and all tugging at the federal head will soon bring ruin on the whole; whereas a liberal, and energetic Constitution, well guarded and closely watched, to prevent incroachments, might restore us to that degree of respectability and consequence, to which we had a fair claim, and the brightest prospect of attaining."

Later, Washington wrote to Thomas Jefferson in the same tenor: "That something is necessary, all will agree; for the situation of the Central Government, (if it can be called a government) is shaken to its foundation, and liable to be overset by every blast. In a word, it is at an end, and unless a remedy is soon applied, anarchy and confusion will inevitably ensue."

In 1786 a number of leaders from Virginia, Pennsylvania, New York, and other states were already engaged in correspondence and discussions looking toward a revision of the Articles and a strengthening of the central government. A meeting at Annapolis, Maryland, in that year, drew delegates from five states to consider how to improve the regulation of commerce, over which Congress had practically no power. After surveying the hopeless situation of government generally in the United States, they recognized that their numbers were too few and their instructions too narrow for them to make comprehensive proposals for constitutional changes. The delegates therefore adjourned after appealing to their legislatures and inferentially to Congress to arrange for a convention of all the states to meet in Philadelphia in May 1787, "to devise such further provisions as shall appear to them necessary to render the constitution of the Federal Government adequate to the exigencies of the Union . . ."

There is some evidence of the generality of the feeling that a change was needed in the fact that Congress almost immediately took the necessary steps to call the convention, and that every state legislature save Rhode Island's quickly arranged for the election of delegates to a convention to revise the Articles.

It is doubtful whether any convention in history has had its story told more often than the so-called Federal or Constitutional Convention of 1787, which drafted the Constitution for the United States of America. I will not repeat the story here, but instead try only to determine what it decided to do about the basic structure of the Union and about the relations between the states and the central government that it proposed to set up. The question is whether and in what sense the framers planned a federal system for the United States.

The delegates to the Constitutional Convention were all elected by state legislatures and were instructed to bring in proposals for the amendment of the Articles to be passed upon in turn by the legislatures. The instructions varied somewhat, but the general objective was to make the plan of government "adequate to the exigencies of the Union."

The Virginia or Randolph Plan became the principal basis for discussion in the convention. It called for a national government of three branches, with power in the legislative branch "to legislate in all cases to which the separate States are incompetent." This plan was received with general acceptance, but the delegates saw that it involved such sweeping changes in the central agencies of the Union that they could not achieve their goal by mere amendments to the Articles. The large majority determined, therefore, to disregard their instructions and to proceed to draft a complete constitution for the United States that would come closer to providing for "common defence, security of liberty, and general welfare" by means of a strong national government. Indeed, the Virginia Plan spoke of a National Legislature, a National Executive, and a National Judiciary—all capitalized as here given.

This disregard by the delegates of their instructions could be termed an act of revolution; their conviction of the logic of their position carried them even farther along the revolutionary path. The Congress under the Articles was a mere superstructure, as Washington called it, built upon and dependent upon the thirteen state legislatures, without direct connection with the people. If a national government were to be established it would have to rest upon the nation, that is, upon the people. When the Constitution finally appeared it was based directly upon the people in at least four respects:

The preamble declared that "We, the People of the United States . . . do ordain and establish this Constitution for the United States of America." The word "for" seems to suggest a united people standing above the United States and making a constitution for them.

One house of Congress was to be apportioned among the states according to the numbers of their people, and its members were to be elected directly by the voters. Under the Articles there had been no such body.

Congress was to have power to make laws directly for and applicable to the people, including tax laws, which the President and the United States courts in turn were to have power to enforce directly, without the intervention of the states.

The Constitution was to be submitted to special conventions of the people in the several states, not to the state legislatures, and was to go into effect when approved by these popular conventions in nine states, not in all thirteen as was required for the amendment of the Articles.

In all these respects the Constitution simply overrode the Articles of Confederation, by-passed the state legislatures, and brought the proposed central government into direct contact with the people. Since this is so evidently what they did, we may properly assume that this is what the framers intended.

When they were chided for their disregard of their instructions, they replied in various ways. James Madison, often called "The Father of the Constitution," justified their action in *The Federalist*, no. 40, somewhat as follows: The resolution of Congress that called for the convention indicated that the objective or end to be attained was that of "establishing in these States *a firm national government*." But the means or instructions provided for the convention limited the delegates to "the sole and express purpose of revising the articles of Confederation." When the delegates found that these instructions and the purpose for which they had been summoned together were incompatible, which were they to follow? They decided that their duty was to disregard the limitations imposed on them by their instructions, to pursue the end for which they had been assembled, and to submit the best plan of government they could devise.

The establishment of the Constitution upon the basis of popular sovereignty, and the bringing of popularly elected representatives into the national legislature, made, as I have said, a profound and revolutionary departure from the system of dependence upon the state legislatures that the Articles provided for. George Washington took special note of this in a letter to Bushrod Washington when he said: "The power under the Constitution will always be in the People. It is entrusted for certain defined purposes, and for a certain limited period, to representatives of their own chusing; and whenever it is executed contrary to their Interest, or not agreeable to their wishes, their Servants can, and undoubtedly will be, recalled. . . . Furthermore, those who are entrusted with the administration are no more than the creatures of the people . . ."

Madison and Hamilton in *The Federalist* also emphasized the popular basis of government under the proposed Constitution. Madison, in no. 46, in discussing the relative influence of the national and state governments, wrote as follows:

The federal and State governments are in fact but different agents and trustees of the people, constituted with different powers and designed for different purposes. The adversaries of the Constitution seem to have lost sight of the people altogether in their reasonings on this subject; and to have viewed these different establishments, not only as mutual rivals and enemies, but as uncontrolled by any common superior in their efforts to usurp the authorities of each other. These gentlemen must here be reminded of their error. They must be told that the ultimate authority, wherever the derivative may be found, resides in the people alone, and that it will not depend merely on the comparative ambition or address of the different governments, whether either, or which of them, will be able to enlarge its sphere of jurisdiction at the expense of the other. Truth, no less than decency, requires that the event in every case should be supposed to depend on the sentiments and sanction of their common constituents.

This departure from the Articles of Confederation and return of government to the people was in a sense a return to the popular-sovereignty theory of the Declaration of Independence:

We hold these truths to be self evident, that all men are created equal, that they are endowed by their Creator with certain unalienable Rights, that among these are Life, Liberty and the pursuit of Happiness. That to secure these rights, Governments are instituted among men, deriving their just powers from the consent of the governed. That whenever any Form of Government becomes destructive of these ends, it is the Right of the People to alter or to abolish it, and to institute new Government, laying its foundation on such principles and organizing its powers in such form, as to them shall seem most likely to effect their Safety and Happiness.

From this point of view the Articles of Confederation may be considered as a temporary departure or digression from the main course of American constitutional development, and the Constitution may be considered as a return to it.

4

The Original Framers: Their Words and Intentions

THE Constitution of the United States, after it was adopted, soon became a symbol of national unity, strength, and achievement. It took on for prideful Americans some of the aspects of the "crown" of the United Kingdom—that great symbol of British national and even imperial strength and unity. The framers of the Constitution were accordingly praised then and later by many patriotic speakers and writers as an assembly of demigods, or at least of men who were very near that level of ability, high purpose, and integrity. The bickerings, disagreements, and compromises of the Federal Convention were passed over in silence, while the Constitution was exalted into an almost sacrosanct and untouchable symbol of national greatness.

Along with this fetishism arose the feeling that everything about the interpretation and operation of the Constitution must be tested by the touchstone of "the intentions of the framers." This began even before the publication in 1843 of Madison's notes on the debates in the Convention, one of the best sources of evidence as to what was intended. And today, more than one hundred and sixty-five years after the drafting of the Constitution, there are still frequent references to the framers and their "intentions."

Not everyone felt this way about the Constitution and its framers, but certainly the prevailing attitude was one of reverence. The Constitution was supposed to be not only virtually perfect, but also practically complete on all important questions. Every major constitutional and political question was supposed to be answerable either from the Constitution itself or from the intentions of the framers. Had they studied the progress and tribulations of the national government more carefully, the holders of this view would have come in for some serious disillusionments.

In the very first national administration and in the first congresses serious questions arose for which the Constitution had no obvious answer. Has the President alone the power to remove officers whom he has appointed with Senate consent? May he declare the nation's neutrality in a foreign war, when the United States has a treaty of mutual assistance and defense with one of the belligerents? May Congress charter a United States bank, levy a protective tariff, or provide for national assumption of the states' debts? Has the Supreme Court the power to pass on the constitutionality of acts of Congress?

To none of these or various other questions that arose did the Constitution or the utterances of the framers provide any clear and specific answer. As each issue arose the Congress and the President at the time had to work out their own answers. In this way they, and the Supreme Court, too, soon became participants in the continuous process of making and remaking the Constitution to meet the needs of the time. This is a process that goes on today and will continue in the future.

The Constitution simply did not spring forth perfect, complete, and self-explanatory. Most likely it never will be complete and perfect. Men disagreed about it when it was being drafted, when it came up for adoption, and when it was being put into effect. Many of the framers were participants in the early national government and in some of the state governments of that day, and they did not all agree as to what the Constitution meant or what its framers intended. Indeed, it is merely vain imagining to assume that such a thing as "the intention" of "the framers" in the full sense ever existed or ever can be discovered. Fifty-five delegates took part in the Federal Convention, and thirty-nine signed the final document. Hundreds of persons participated in the thirteen state ratifying conventions, while many other citizens engaged in written and oral discussions of the Constitution.

Many questions that came up later probably never were considered by the framers. Consequently they can hardly be said to have had any intentions on these issues. The record of what they did discuss is quite incomplete, obviously, but what is available provides voluminous evidence of differences of opinion as to what was intended and as to what might be expected from the Constitution on the points that men did discuss. There were differences of opinion not only between the proponents of the Constitution and the opponents, but also among the proponents themselves. Even *The Federalist,* the essays published in New York in 1787 and 1788 to help bring about the adoption of the Constitution by the people of New York, displays a noticeably "split personality." In fact each of the two principal authors of these essays revealed within his own writings some vagueness, confusion, and even contradiction—perhaps Madison more than Hamilton.

This is not to say that nothing at all can be determined about the intentions of the framers. There obviously were areas of agreement among the sponsors of the Constitution. That document is itself the best evidence of what they agreed upon. Since it was adopted by the people in every one of the thirteen states within four years, 1787 to 1790, it seems fair to say that the people generally also agreed on the Constitution as far as it obviously went. In short then, although the intentions of the framers were clearly not unanimous, did not cover all points, and where stated show considerable differences of opinion, vagueness, and lack of clarity, some lessons of considerable value concerning what "the framers intended" can be learned from the records they left.

Taking first the original Constitution itself, I find it useful, in order to bring out its meaning, to contrast that document on certain salient points with the Articles of Confederation, which the convention members had before them and which the Constitution was destined to supersede.

67

Madison in *The Federalist,* nos. 39–46, makes much of the fact that the Articles were followed and parts of them used in drafting the new Constitution. It is evident that throughout their work the delegates to the convention made a close study of the Articles, both to avoid their defects and to utilize what was good in them. In view of this fact it is interesting to note what significant words in the Articles were left out of the Constitution and what other words were put in to replace them. It is my assumption that the framers of the Constitution were shrewd, experienced men who knew what they were doing when they used certain words of their own that were not in the Articles, and rejected or at least failed to use others that do appear in the Articles.

United States. Both the Articles and the Constitution utilize this term to designate the organized nation or the group of states taken as a single entity. In fact "United States" became the standard term at the time of the Declaration of Independence to designate the national unit of government and has been used in that way ever since.

There is, however, a subtle difference between the Articles and the Constitution in the way in which "United States" is used. Nearly every use of the term in the Articles is in the phrase "the United States in Congress assembled," as if the United States did not exist except when the delegates from the several state legislatures were assembled in a Congress. Usually the words "United States in Congress assembled" are not even capitalized. Clearly the term "United States" did not as yet mean a fully united nation or a political entity with an established name, a government, and a being of its own.

On the other hand, the framers of the Constitution, just ten years after the Articles were drafted, spoke of the United States and the people of the United States as if they already existed as one nation. "The government of the United States" is recognized as a distinct government, in Article I, section 8, paragraph 18, of the Constitution, and evidently as something separate from and not dependent upon the state governments; while the Congress of the United States is spoken of as such, and never as "the United

States in Congress assembled." In contrast with the term "the United States" the framers used the phrase "the several states" to refer to the separate states and their local or particular governments.

(Foreigners more often than Americans use the full designation, "United States of America," or the abbreviation U.S.A., instead of just United States. Although apparently plural in form the term "United States" is now used almost exclusively in the singular. "The United States is," not "are." It is internationally recognized as one country and one nation, not as a plurality of states.)

Union. The preamble to the Articles designates the agreement reached between the states as "Articles of Confederation and perpetual Union between the States of Newhampshire," etc., while the preamble to the Constitution states one of the objectives of that document to be the formation of "a more perfect Union." In Article IV of the Constitution the term "Union" is used twice: in section 3, "New States may be admitted by the Congress into this Union"; and in section 4, "The United States shall guarantee to every State in this Union a Republican Form of Government . . ."

Thus "United States" and "Union" are the only terms used in the Constitution to designate the national entity as a whole.

Confederation and Confederacy; Federal and Federation. Any term based on the Latin root word *foedus* implies an agreement in the nature of a league, treaty, or compact among states. In general usage the term "confederation" has come to mean a league in which the powers of the member states are superior to the powers of the central authority. The members of the central organ or congress of such a league are dependent upon the separate state governments and they have little or no authority to pass or enforce laws directly upon the people of the several states or to collect their own taxes from the people. A "federal" system, on the other hand, is now usually considered to be one in which a central authority has certain important powers independent of the membership—legislative and law-enforcing powers in a fairly broad area which it exercises directly on the people.

Actually, however, the words "confederation," "confederacy," "federation," and "federal" have always been very loosely and interchangeably used. They were certainly not precisely defined in the period after the Revolution. The Articles, it is true, confined themselves to the use of "confederation" and "confederacy," the first to designate the nature of the agreement between the states and the second to designate the entity created by the agreement. Thus "The Articles of Confederation and perpetual Union" begin in Article I by asserting: "The stile of this confederacy shall be 'The United States of America'." But the men of the time were not as careful in their usage. Some spoke of the United States as a confederation, others as a confederacy, still others as a federation. Because there was no general agreement on the precise differences between these terms, not much weight can be attached to the use of one or the other.

What is significant is that the Constitution contains no term to suggest a treaty or agreement among the ratifying states— neither confederation, nor confederacy, nor federation, nor federal. The complete omission of any and every such word from the Constitution can hardly have been a mere oversight or inadvertence.

The proponents of the Constitution adopted for themselves the terms "federal" and "Federalist" for whatever political advantage this would give them in the campaign for adoption of the new framework of government. (Their opponents came to be called Anti-Federalists, to their evident discomfiture and disgust.)

When men speak of the United States as being a federation, therefore, or as having a federal form of government, whatever they mean thereby, they get no support directly from the Constitution and it is necessary to turn to other key words for direct evidence of the intentions of the framers.

Articles of Confederation and Constitution. The framers of the new plan called it a constitution. The word was already in use among the states to designate the written document that sets forth the framework of the government of a single state. There is in this word no idea of a treaty or of a plighting of faith among various individuals or states; rather it suggests integration or unity.

On the other hand the Articles of Confederation were cast more clearly in the form of a treaty or compact among states. As already noted they were "Articles of Confederation and perpetual Union between the States of Newhampshire," etc. In Article III, "The said states hereby severally enter into a firm league of friendship with each other, for their common defence, the security of their Liberties, and their mutual and general welfare, binding themselves to assist each other . . ." In other parts of the Articles, also, similar language denoting a plighting of faith by the several states gives evidence that the states considered themselves essentially separate and "sovereign" although they leagued themselves together in "perpetual union" for mutual advantage.

Adoption by Legislatures or by the People. The Articles were drawn up by "Delegates of the States in Congress assembled," and were ratified by the legislatures of the several states on behalf of the states as units. On the other hand the famous words with which the Constitution begins are "We the People of the United States . . . do ordain and establish this Constitution for the United States of America." Furthermore, the Constitution was ratified by special conventions of the people in each state, not by the legislatures.

This is surely one of the most significant verbal and structural differences between the Constitution and the Articles.

The "Sovereignty" of the States. One of the most notable clauses in the Articles of Confederation reads: "Article II. Each state retains its sovereignty, freedom and independence, and every Power, Jurisdiction and right, which is not by this confederation expressly delegated to the United States, in Congress assembled."

This seems to imply that the states were separately sovereign and independent before the Articles were adopted, that by their act of confederating they delegated to Congress whatever powers it was to have, and that all powers not expressly so delegated, plus the essence of sovereignty and independence, were retained by the states. This clearly put or left the states in the driver's seat.

The framers of the Constitution left out the word "sovereignty" entirely. It does not appear at all, to describe either the nation or the states. Since other words from the Articles were included in the Constitution, the presumption must be that the framers purposely and deliberately omitted the idea that the states were sovereign. In short, sovereignty was assumed by the people of the United States and this means popular supremacy over both the national government and the states.

Supreme Law of the Land. The only words in the Constitution that imply sovereignty or supremacy, outside of the preamble wherein the people take over the reins of authority, are to be found in the second paragraph of Article VI, "the supreme law of the land" clause, which reads: "This Constitution, and the laws of the United States which shall be made in pursuance thereof; and all treaties made, or which shall be made, under the authority of the United States, shall be the supreme law of the land; and the judges in every state shall be bound thereby, any thing in the constitution or laws of any state to the contrary notwithstanding."

This clause, taken along with other phrases of the Constitution, has the obvious effect of putting the Constitution, laws, and treaties of the United States above the constitutions and laws of the several states. It is reinforced by the requirement that an official oath "to support this Constitution," must be taken by all members of Congress, all state legislators, "and all executive and judicial officers, both of the United States and of the several states . . ." (Article VI, paragraph 3).

Together these provisions illustrate the completeness of the overturn in authority that took place when the Constitution replaced the Articles of Confederation. The former residual "sovereignty" of the states was eliminated, and in place of it the people of the United States established the supremacy of the United States Constitution and of the proper laws and treaties of the United States government.

Reserved Powers, and Powers Expressly Granted. By the "state sovereignty" provision (Article II) of the Articles of Confederation, quoted above, "each state" retained for itself "every Power, Jurisdiction, and right, which is not by this confederation expressly delegated to the United States, in Congress assembled." Under the Constitution as it went to the people in 1787 there was no word of any powers being "retained" by the states, and the national government was not limited to powers expressly granted.

(Several opponents of the Constitution made much of the omission of a reserved powers clause from the Constitution. Alexander Hamilton argued, as did others, that no such clause was needed. It stood to reason, they thought, and was implied in the nature of the Constitution, that the states could and would exercise their former powers and functions to the extent that these had not been granted to the national government by the people of the United States. This did not satisfy a number of critics, and it was apparently agreed generally that a reserved powers amendment would be submitted to the states after the Constitution was adopted. The first Congress carried out this agreement. See Chapter 5, below.)

Necessary and Proper Laws. The drafters of the Articles of Confederation were meticulous in their care to see to it that the Congress should not have any "legislative" or "law-making" powers. They used several subterfuges and evasive expressions like "establishing rules," "making rules," and "regulating the trade . . . with the Indians," but the precious power to legislate or to make laws was denied to Congress. Furthermore, even such treaties and rules as Congress was permitted to make were in several cases not to override the legislation of the states.

In contrast to this the Constitution vests in Congress "all legislative powers herein granted" (Article I, section 1), and closes a list of enumerated powers to tax, to borrow, to regulate, to establish, and to make uniform laws on various subjects, with the sweeping power "To make all laws which shall be necessary and proper for carrying into execution the foregoing powers, and all other powers vested by this Constitution in the government of the United States, or in any department or officer thereof" (Arti-

73

cle I, section 8, paragraph 18). Even under the original Constitution, therefore, Congress had law-making power over the people for all national purposes authorized by the Constitution, and this power it continues to have.

This list of key words emphasizes the importance of the Constitution itself in any attempt to get at the intentions of the framers. But there are also three other valuable sources of information that should not be overlooked:

The debates in the Federal Convention, as reported especially by James Madison and to a smaller extent by other participants.

The correspondence and the other writings of the members put out at the time and later. Of the contemporary writings *The Federalist* essays, already mentioned frequently, are of outstanding importance as campaign documents. Written during the heat of the struggle for the Constitution, they lack somewhat in consistency and objectivity, but for many purposes they are the best discussions we have.

The arguments of the framers when they spoke in the state conventions that were assembled to ratify the Constitution. In these debates, also, political expediency sometimes enters to detract from the merit of other things that are said.

Attention must also be paid to the subsequent speeches and actions of those framers who were elected to Congress or who served in the executive branch after the Constitution had been ratified; to the amendments that were proposed and ratified soon after the Constitution took effect; and to later court decisions on constitutional questions that were rendered by men who had any part in any of the proceedings by which the Constitution was drafted and adopted.

By considering all this testimony we can give the intentions of the framers broader scope than would be possible if we limited ourselves to the Constitution itself. In the summary that follows, which presents in brief what I believe to be the principal intentions of the men who made the Constitution, I have utilized, therefore, the debates and correspondence and other writings of these men as well as the key words of the document itself.

First of all, the framers decided to discard the Articles of Confederation and transform the Union from a confederation of states into a national union of the people under a Constitution which, when adopted by the people in nine state conventions, would completely supersede the Articles of Confederation. In doing this they carried out what Edward Mead Earle has called a *coup d'etat.* The revolutionary character of what was done was recognized by John Marshall and the other justices of the Supreme Court in their decision in Barron v. Baltimore (7 Peters 243, 1833), where they said that "the great revolution which established the Constitution of the United States was not effected without intense opposition."

By this revolutionary act they evidently intended to rid the government of the Union of various serious defects inherent in the Articles of Confederation, notably that of the dependence of the central government upon the state legislatures, and the old principle of legislation only for the states and subject to the consent of the states. (See *The Federalist,* no. 15, by Hamilton.)

I think that they clearly intended to establish the new Constitution on the basis of popular sovereignty (preamble) and to make the Constitution so based "the supreme law of the land" (Article VI, paragraph 2). As Hamilton pointed out (*The Federalist,* no. 15), some of the opponents wanted to eat their cake and have it too. "They seem still to aim at things repugnant and irreconcilable; at an augmentation of federal authority, without a diminution of State authority; at sovereignty in the Union and complete independence in the members. They still, in fine, seem to cherish with blind devotion the political monster of an *imperium in imperio.*" Thus he proceeded to demolish the arguments of the opposition, and to show that national supremacy cannot live with sovereignty and independence vested in the member states. Madison agreed with this, and so did Washington.

I think, too, that they planned to and did create a full-fledged national government, to be based on the people and to legislate for and serve the people, without requiring the consent of the state governments and without being dependent upon them in any way when legislating, taxing, making treaties, and enforcing laws for the nation as a whole. This national government was to be officered by men who held no state offices, and who were not to be delegates of the state governments as such, but whose attachments would be to the Union, to the United States as a whole, and to its national government. So organized, the central government would be able to act autonomously, upon its own initiative, in the national interest, without regard to what the state governments might be doing in their respective territories.

The original framers did not intend that the national government should exercise every conceivable scrap of governmental power. But they did intend to provide for a wide range of power. At one time in their proceedings they voted to authorize the national government to legislate in all cases and matters where the individual states would be incompetent, and James Wilson and Alexander Hamilton seemed to think such a broad grant of power was necessary.

They finally decided to place certain major powers of government in the hands of the national government (foreign affairs, defense, commerce, taxation, naturalization, post offices, and several others). Then they agreed that Congress should have power to levy and collect taxes without limit to provide for the common defense "and general welfare," which presumably included the power to spend money so raised for the general welfare; and they also agreed that Congress should have power to pass all laws "necessary and proper" for carrying into execution any and all powers of the national government, and that all such laws passed in pursuance of the Constitution should be supreme over state laws and constitutions.

All these powers taken together make a very formidable array. In addition the national authorities were not limited just to the powers "expressly" granted, so that evidently a considerable latitude and flexibility in the national powers were contemplated.

76

Madison and Hamilton agreed that Congress would have implied as well as expressed powers.

Despite the broad range of powers granted to the national government, no one, except for Hamilton in the early days of the Federal Convention, seems to have advocated the abolition of the states. The states were to be left, though in a reduced role, and were actually to have some part in helping to conduct the new national government (the state legislatures were to elect United States senators; to regulate elections for the United States as well as for themselves; to provide for appointing presidential electors; and so on). The primary intention was to create a new, effective, autonomous national government for all the people and for the whole territory of the United States, and to set it down over the states to serve the people directly. In effect a dual system of government came into existence, the national government established for the whole country and the state governments left to carry on their local functions within their respective territories.

The framers evidently did not deem it wise to try to list the specific functions and powers of the states. The Constitution granted certain major powers to the national government, mentioned certain powers connected with the national government that state agencies would exercise, and denied certain powers to the states (especially in Article I, section 10), but in general it said nothing about the rather wide range of governmental powers that were not granted to the national government and that presumably would be exercised by the states if exercised at all. In the absence of any express clause in the original Constitution on this subject, it is hard to know what functions the framers generally thought the states would exercise.

Hamilton believed that the functions of the states would be relatively minor and inexpensive. Speaking of the states' needs for revenues he said (in *The Federalist*, no. 34) that ". . . in a short course of time the wants of the States will naturally reduce themselves within a *very narrow compass*" and that after the states' war debts had been eliminated, "the only call for revenue of any consequence, which the State governments will continue to experience, will be for the mere support of their respective civil lists; to which, if we add all contingencies, the total amount in every state ought to fall considerably short of two hundred thousand pounds." In the money of the early nineteenth century this would be about one million dollars for the expenses of all thirteen states combined!

This sounds fantastic in the light of modern state budgets, but the hard fact is that Hamilton's estimate was based squarely on the evidence. The states generally were doing little or nothing beyond supporting their governors, legislatures, courts, and a few central offices. Hamilton could see no reason why the states should need any source of revenue that would yield more than this sum, while on the other hand the national government, always facing emergencies, would need unpredictable amounts and porportionately much more than the states would require.

This certainly suggests that some of the framers did not expect the states to carry on any wide array of services. In truth the states were doing very little at that time except to *legislate* in such areas as property rights, domestic relations, crimes, courts, roads, education, poor relief, state institutions, public health, law enforcement, and the conservation of natural resources. The carrying out of the state laws was left largely to local governments and to the courts acting upon cases brought before them by private initiative.

Because the Constitution says nothing to the contrary, it must have been intended that within the range of the local functions left to them the states were to be free to initiate their own measures by passing and providing for the enforcement of laws without having to get permission from the national government. In other words, the authorities in each state, set up under a state constitution, were to decide initially upon their constitutional powers and duties, and to act autonomously even as the national authorities would do with respect to the national powers.

Since the lines between national and state powers were not precisely drawn, it was recognized that there would be conflicts and that encroachments in both directions would probably result, but more, it was felt, from the states on the national powers than in the other direction. To maintain the supremacy of the national government over the states in any conflict of authority, the original framers took these steps:

They included in the Constitution the "supreme law of the land" clause already quoted, which made the Constitution, laws, and treaties of the United States binding on the judges in all states.

They required all state officers and judges to take an oath to support the United States Constitution, including the supremacy clause.

They provided for a national guarantee of a republican form of government in each state, which implies the right of the national government to intervene in state governments

And they permitted Congress to override state laws for the election of members of Congress.

In addition, judicial review of state legislative acts in the federal courts was evidently expected to help keep the states in line, while the provisions against the states' engaging in war, or making treaties or compacts without the consent of Congress, and other similar restrictions, were clearly designed to keep the states within a range of primarily internal functions.

In addition to the provisions of the Constitution, there are evidences of a general intention to subordinate the states to the national government in Washington's letter transmitting the Constitution to Congress, in the writings of the friends and framers of the Constitution, and in the angry protests of the Anti-Federalists who saw what was coming.

There is a little confusion in the evidence, because even Hamilton and Madison spoke of the "sovereignty" of the states at the same time that they were stressing state subordination (see *The Federalist*, no. 31). Apparently they used the term "sovereignty" rather loosely, sometimes to refer to the position of the states under the Articles, and sometimes to mean no more than their autonomy or right to initiate and carry on their own governmental functions under the Constitution.

In any case the references to state subordination are more numerous and tally more closely with what the Constitution itself provides. Hamilton in *The Federalist* speaks of the states as "the local governments" (no. 23), and mentions the national government as being "a superintending power" with "a general discretionary superintendence" (no. 15) over states and people. Madison refers to the states as "subordinate governments" (no. 14) and "municipal establishments" (no. 45), which he elsewhere hoped would be "subordinately useful" (Letter to Washington, April 1787).

"The consolidation of our Union," referred to by Washington in his letter of transmittal to Congress, was in Hamilton's words to result in "a firm union" (*The Federalist*, no. 9), "a strict and indissoluble union" (no. 11), which would be headed by "a vigorous national government" (no. 11).

The opponents of the Constitution, of course, insisted that what Washington, Hamilton, and Madison were putting forward as the merits and advantages of the Constitution were, in fact, its gravest defects and dangers. Thus there was substantial agreement on the purposes and the probable effects of the Constitution, but not on the desirability of its ultimate results.

In the light of these and other arguments, pro and con, and despite the fears and protests of the opposition, the people in the several state conventions ratified the Constitution.

To assure the people that the loss of powers by the states would not hurt the people themselves, provisions were made to represent the people of every state in both houses of the United States Congress, equally in one, proportionately in the other, and to give the people in each state a corresponding voice in the choice of electors who would choose the President and Vice President. Since the people of all states would be adequately represented within the framework of the national government itself, there would be no need for them to call upon the state governors and legislatures to interfere in their behalf against the national government.

Finally, the framers did not desire that the Constitution they proposed should be rigidly binding on all future generations. It has remained for later protagonists of various political and economic causes, when appealing from the present Constitution—which they think they don't like—to the original Constitution—which they think they do like—to urge that the intentions of the original framers must be respected and obeyed no matter what changes in thought or in circumstances have taken place since then.

This attempt to turn back, as it were, the clock of constitutional interpretation and practice in order to be guided by an earlier view finds little support in the writings and reasonings of the original framers. For one thing, the framers inserted in the Constitution an article that provided for future amendments. This certainly showed that they expected the Constitution might require amendments in the future. Indeed, Hamilton, Washington, and other leading supporters among the members expressed disappointment with various provisions of the Constitution as it went before the people. The existence of the amending article was one reason why Washington thought it best to adopt the Constitution as it was and then proceed to get amendments later.

Whatever praises were heaped upon them at a later date, the framers of the Constitution apparently did not think of their work as perfect. On November 10, 1787, General Washington wrote to his nephew Bushrod Washington as follows:

The warmest friends and the best supporters the constitution has, do not contend that it is free from imperfections; but they found them unavoidable and are sensible, if evil is likely to arise there from, the remedy must come hereafter; for in the present moment, it is not to be obtained; and, as there is a Constitutional door open for it, I think the People (for it is with them to judge) can, as they will have the advantage of experience on their side, decide with as much propriety on the alterations and amendments which are necessary as ourselves. I do not think we are more inspired, have more wisdom, or possess more virtue, than those who will come after us.

The power under the Constitution will always be in the People. . . .

These statements by General Washington relate primarily to the need for formal amendments to the Constitution. They are in harmony with another trend of thought that appears noticeably in *The Federalist* papers. Both Hamilton and Madison realized that there would be need of frequent interpretations of the Constitution. The document clearly was not self-explanatory, nor did it fully reveal the intentions of its framers as to how it should be applied in all situations that would arise from time to time. How could such interpretations be obtained?

Madison in *The Federalist*, no. 39, recognized and approved the idea that in jurisdictional controversies between the national government and a state the United States Supreme Court would decide, and John Marshall in the Virginia ratifying convention expressed the same thought. Hamilton looked upon the courts as peculiarly responsible for interpreting and applying the Constitution in cases where legislative acts impaired the rights of the people under the Constitution (no. 78). But beyond the courts were the "prudence and firmness" of the people themselves, since they, by using their powers of election, by creating public opinion and pressures on the government, and ultimately by revolution, would have the final say in interpreting and enforcing their rights under the Constitution (nos. 28, 31, 33, and 78).

In short, the framers and proponents of the Constitution realized that the Constitution was a man-made and imperfect instrument; that its meaning was not entirely clear but would call for interpretations; that it probably would be found in practice to be deficient in a number of respects, and so would call for formal amendments. They did not claim superhuman wisdom or skill for themselves, or set themselves up as wiser than those who would come after them. They were content to leave the interpretation and the necessary modification of the Constitution to future congresses, legislatures, and supreme courts, and to the people of the United States. They recognized that constitutions are made "for posterity as well as ourselves," and that they must be adaptable to the "exigencies of ages" yet unknown (*The Federalist*, no. 34).

As a matter of fact, in the years since the adoption of the Constitution that document has been changed by amendments from time to time, modified in practice by presidents and congresses, and interpreted and applied in hundreds of cases by the United States Supreme Court and other courts.

Certain general principles like the separation of powers among the three branches of the national government, the division of powers and functions between the national government and the states, and the doctrine of limited government, have changed but slowly, whereas the operating rules by which the principles are applied in practice to particular situations are in process of continual modification.

The legislators, jurists, publicists, newspaper editors, and countless others—including the humblest citizens able to read and write, for in a nation with a written constitution each may be "his own constitutional lawyer"—who have over the years discussed the Constitution, molded public opinion about it, and initiated changes can in a sense as justly be termed framers of the Constitution as the members of the Constitutional Convention. And the decisions of these later framers, discussed in the next two chapters, are as important to an understanding of the Constitution of today as the intentions of the original framers are for an understanding of the original document.

5

The Acts and Intentions of the Later Framers: To the Civil War

THE changes that have taken place in the Constitution since its adoption have not all been in one direction, nor have all been fully consistent one with another. On every constitutional issue that arises there are likely to be two or more positions that can be taken. Which of these will be approved as the basis for action will depend upon a variety of circumstances, of which the political views of those who must make the decision are highly important. It is largely a matter of chance whether those in office when a particular constitutional decision is to be made hold one set of political views or another.

In point of fact, however, there has been from the beginning one dominant trend, at least in the constitutional relations between the national government and the states—a trend toward spelling out and solidifying the supremacy of the national government.

This does not mean that the states have suffered an exactly corresponding loss in authority, or that they are actually less important, less active, or less serviceable than they used to be. It was pointed out in the last chapter that the activities of the states after the Revolution were largely limited to legislating. As the functions and services of government have increased all along the line, and at all levels of government, national, state, and local, I believe and will try to show the states have actually increased in importance.

Of necessity, the account of the acts of the later framers that follows concerns itself with the central constitutional trend, as

84

shown in constitutional amendments, presidential and congressional actions, and Supreme Court decisions. But throughout much of our history there has also been a counter-trend among certain groups—an emphasis on state sovereignty, states' rights, and the Constitution interpreted as a compact among the states. From this counter-trend have come theories on the strict construction of the powers of the national government, the congenital and necessary antagonism between the national government and the states and the struggle for power between them, and the right of the states, separately or in groups, to nullify acts of Congress and even to secede from the Union. These ideas have at times been strongly held, even in high places, particularly in the decades before the Civil War. But, although "states' rights" is still a politically live slogan, it seems to me that the states' rights trend must be considered as a deviation from the central line of constitutional developments. I shall, therefore, discuss it separately in Chapter 7.

One of the first problems faced by Congress under the Constitution was whether or not to establish separate national administration of national functions.

In the discussions before the Constitution was adopted there were various suggestions that state officers should administer the laws enacted by Congress. Some thought that in this way undue expense and duplication of effort would be avoided and conflicts of authority would be prevented, and also that the states would thus avoid suffering the derogation of their "sovereignty" by having to tolerate the operations of national officers within state territorial limits. It was reasoned that the collection of property taxes and excises, if enacted by Congress, and even the collection of customs, for which many of the states already had agents, could be handled for the national government by state officials.

In like manner it was felt by many and urged strongly by some upholders of states' rights that there should be no federal courts of inferior jurisdiction operating in the states, that instead the state courts should handle all cases under both national and state laws arising within the area of any state. They argued that the Congress and the people of the United States should have confidence in the integrity, ability, and justice of the state courts, and should not subject the states to the indignity of having separate federal courts set up within the states to try federal cases.

On the other hand, many felt that there would be a rivalry and a struggle for power between the state governments and the national government; that the states would be unequal in their capacity and in their willingness to support administrative and judicial agencies; that they would follow different policies and procedures in what they did; that their officers would have a primary responsibility and loyalty to their states; that the decisions of some state officers (as in collecting the customs) would affect adversely other states and their peoples; and that appeals to United States administrative agencies and the United States Supreme Court from the decisions made by state officers and courts would cause much friction and yet could not bring about uniformity in administrative actions and judicial decisions. These persons thought it best to have two separate and independent systems of administration and courts, one for the national and one for each of the state governments.

This issue was debated in the Federal Convention, in the campaign for the adoption of the Constitution, in the ratifying conventions, and in the first Congress under the Constitution.

The decision might conceivably have gone either way as far as the terms of the Constitution are concerned. What the first Congress decided was to have separate federal agencies and officers to administer the acts of Congress, and separate United States courts to decide federal cases.

This decision was not an absolute. In a number of minor matters Congress in effect accepted the state laws and the state administration of them instead of enacting national laws and setting up national administration for them. State quarantine and pilotage laws, for example, and state laws and administration for carrying out the election of representatives to Congress were left untouched by the national legislature. Similarly the state courts were left free to decide any cases within their jurisdiction, where federal laws were involved, subject to removal or appeal to United States courts.

In general, however, the decision was to have separate national agencies to carry out the important laws and responsibilities of the nation, and to have separate inferior courts of the United States in every state to exercise the major portions of federal jurisdiction. In this way the states would not be dependent upon the national government for doing their jobs, nor would the national government be dependent upon the state governments.

This general decision by the first Congress was not embodied in any constitutional amendment, and some might object that this is a mere matter of legislative policy, not a constitutional development. In fact, however, the policy thus established has been followed by Congress with respect to most major functions of the national government. Instead of using state agencies and officers for carrying out major national functions, and so working the state administrative organizations into the position of subordinate agencies of the national government, Congress left the states free to work out, and to concentrate their attention and resources upon, their own functions.

This now long-established policy of having the national and state administrations clearly separate and distinct has become a fundamental characteristic of the American system of government. There are some minor deviations from the pattern, but in general this separation prevails throughout the federal system.

Cooperation between national and state administrations is not precluded, of course, and in some areas it has developed extensively as we have indicated, but where it exists it depends upon the voluntary consent of Congress and the state legislatures.

In compliance with a tacit agreement among the leaders both for and against the adoption of the Constitution, a Bill of Rights was drafted and proposed by the first Congress. It became effective as a part of the Constitution when adopted by the requisite number of states in December 1791, soon after the beginning of the government under the Constitution.

Although most of the ten amendments that make up this Bill of Rights are stated in broad language that might apply equally to the states and the national government, the history of the demand for such a bill suggests that it was intended to limit only the national government. Most of the state constitutions, as a matter of fact, already included bills of rights that limited the powers of the respective state governments, and the United States Constitution also imposed definite restrictions on the states (see especially Article I, section 10).

The Supreme Court under Chief Justice Marshall accepted the idea that the federal Bill of Rights protects the people against the national government only and not against the states (Barron v. Baltimore, 7 Peters 243, 1833). The Court has held to this view consistently, but not always unanimously, in the face of many attempts by lawyers to convince the Court to the contrary. (See *The Constitution of the United States of America, Analysis and Interpretation*, pp. 749–52.)

As I note later, however (see pages 102–3), the First Amendment has become an important limitation on the states by reason of the Supreme Court's interpretation of the word "liberty" in the Fourteenth Amendment. Except for this important circumstance the first eight amendments protect individuals against the national government and have little effect directly on the states as such. The Ninth Amendment refers to rights retained by the people, and has no direct bearing on the states.

To many leaders in state government the Tenth Amendment has appeared to be the most important provision among the first ten amendments. Its words and its consequences deserve much attention. It reads: "The powers not delegated to the United States by the Constitution, nor prohibited by it to the States, are reserved to the States respectively, or to the people."

As I have already indicated, some of the proponents of the Constitution thought that an express reservation of powers to the states was unnecessary, since it was patent on the face of the Constitution that the states were to remain in existence and that they would, therefore, continue to exercise powers not delegated by the Constitution to the United States government and not denied by the Constitution to the states.

As I see the situation, if the original states had been content to let well enough alone they might have been able to argue that each original state retained for itself, and by its own authority, the powers not delegated or denied, as seemed to be the situation under the Articles of Confederation. As it was, they desired the greater security that might come from having the reservation made explicit in the United States Constitution by an amendment. But a constitutional amendment like any other provision of the Constitution is ordained by the people of the United States. In seeking a constitutional amendment the states in effect acknowledged the supremacy of the people of the United States and submitted to receiving their powers from the people through the medium of the Constitution.

In drafting the Tenth Amendment, Congress toned down the Massachusetts proposal reserving to the states all powers not "expressly" delegated to the national government by leaving out the word "expressly." This modification is some additional evidence that the states did not, of their own authority, reserve powers to themselves.

The amendment, it seems to me, should be read with the enacting clause of the preamble as follows: "We the people of the United States . . . do ordain . . . [that] The powers not delegated to the United States by the Constitution, nor prohibited by it to the States, are reserved to the States respectively, or to the people."

In other words, it is the people of the United States who, in ordaining the Constitution, delegate some powers to the United States government, reserve other powers to the states or to the people, and place restrictions on both the national government and the states in the interests of the people. This carries out logically the idea expressed by Madison in *The Federalist*, no. 46, that "The federal and State governments are in fact but different agents and trustees of the people."

This view, I believe, is consonant also with the fact that nearly three fourths of the states have been subsequently brought into the Union under the Constitution, and they could not have had any prior "inherent" or "sovereign" powers as states which they could have retained for themselves by their own authority upon admission to the Union. The people of the United States surely are the source of the powers of all the states subsequently brought into the Union, which states had to accept the Constitution as a condition of their admission, so that the Constitution is for them both the means of conveying powers to them and the measure of the powers conferred on them by the "reservation" in Amendment 10. And since all the states in the Union are constitutionally equal, I hold that all the states receive their powers from the people of the United States speaking through the Constitution.

The relationship between the powers granted to the national government and those reserved to the states has provided one of the knottiest problems and has led to some of the most heated debates in the nation's history. The brevity of the Constitution and its lack of specificity not only about the powers of the national government but even more about the powers of the states left many questions open as to what each level of government might constitutionally do.

The men of the time were soon divided into two camps. Those who favored an extensive use of implied powers by the national government came to be called loose or liberal constructionists. Those who wanted to limit the national government largely to the powers expressly granted, allowing the states to exercise all other powers, were called strict constructionists.

The debate began in President Washington's administration, when Alexander Hamilton was pushing his program of making the national government strong and popular. He justified such measures as a protective tariff, a bank of the United States, and national assumption of the states' wartime debts (one of the earliest measures of aid to the states), none of which was specifically authorized by the Constitution, by arguing that the national government possessed implied powers as well as express powers. President Washington and the Federalist Congress accepted this interpretation and passed the measures proposed.

A number of presidents from Jefferson to Buchanan held strict-constructionist views, and Congress during most of this period was also on that side. The Supreme Court under John Marshall, however, adopted the Hamiltonian view when in 1819 it got a case involving the constitutionality of the second United States Bank (McCulloch v. Maryland, 4 Wheaton 316, 1819).

Admitting that the Constitution nowhere expressly authorizes Congress to incorporate a bank as an instrumentality of the national government, Marshall pointed out that Congress does have the powers to levy and collect taxes, to borrow money, to regulate commerce, and to raise and support armies. These functions require the raising of money in some places and the transporting of it to other places where it is to be spent, and for such purposes a bank is a useful instrumentality. Marshall reasoned that Congress, being sovereign within the sphere of its own powers, and possessed of the express power to make "all laws which shall be necessary and proper, for carrying into execution" the various powers vested in the national government, surely has the power to adopt and provide appropriate means to accomplish the authorized ends. He condemned the "narrow construction" views of those who denied the power of Congress to create such an instrumentality as the bank, a view which he thought would in practice render the government incompetent to achieve the great objects for which the people had established it.

And so he and the other justices concluded: "Let the end be legitimate, let it be within the scope of the Constitution, and all means which are appropriate, which are plainly adapted to that end, which are not prohibited, but consist with the letter and spirit of the Constitution, are constitutional."

This liberal-construction view of the nation's powers under the Constitution has been variously interpreted at different times, but has never been abandoned by the Supreme Court. It is one of the

91

most significant and far-reaching of all the contributions that the Supreme Court has made to the development of the Constitution.

But if the national government is not limited strictly to a narrow interpretation of the powers granted to it, what is the Supreme Court's attitude toward the powers of the states? Here the Court has no enumeration of state powers to guide it, and it falls back upon a presumption. The Court will presume the validity of state legislative acts until the presumption is overcome by a clear showing that a piece of state legislation violates some provision of the Constitution (Powell v. Pennsylvania, 127 U.S. 678, 1888). The states presumably have all powers of legislation not granted to the national government or denied by the Constitution to the states.

Thus there is an expansive quality about both national and state powers. As legislation increases in one field and then another, conflicts often arise between national and state legislation. When such conflicts become apparent, what are the constitutional rules for settling them? Several different approaches have been made toward answering this question, illustrated by interpretations of the "police power."

In 1837 the Supreme Court sustained a New York statute which imposed the duty on captains of ships entering the port of New York with aliens aboard to report certain information concerning such aliens to the mayor, the object being the protection of the safety of the people of the place (New York v. Miln, 11 Peters 102, 1837). This was clearly a regulation affecting immigration and foreign commerce, but it apparently did not conflict with any act of Congress. The majority of the Court held:

That a State has the same undeniable and unlimited jurisdiction over all persons and things, within its territorial limits, as any foreign nation, where that jurisdiction is not surrendered or restrained by the Constitution of the United States. . . . That all those powers which relate to merely municipal legislation, or what may, perhaps, more properly be called *internal police,* are not thus surrendered or restrained; and that, consequently, in relation to these, the authority of the State is complete, unqualified, and exclusive.

The phrases "police power" and "internal police" do not appear in the United States Constitution, and, indeed, they appear only incidentally in a few state constitutions. The definitions usually given suggest an almost indefinably broad power to regulate and restrict the conduct of individuals and their use of things in the interests of health, safety, morals, and general welfare of the people. There seems to be little doubt that the states have such a power in a broad sense. The main points at issue usually are these: What limits does the Constitution place on the states' exercise of these powers in protecting the rights of individuals? To what extent, if at all, is the state police power exclusive as against the powers delegated to the national government? It is the second point that is of most concern here.

A popular theory developed in the nineteenth century that the entire power to pass and enforce laws to regulate "persons and things" in order to promote the health, safety, morals, and welfare of the people was vested in the states and no part of it in the national government. Even the decision in the Miln case did not go that far, and the courts never fully accepted this doctrine. Obviously the Constitution had set up a national government with powers to pass necessary and proper laws to regulate the conduct of the people in foreign and interstate commerce, in defense matters, in postal affairs, in bankruptcy, and in a number of other areas. The purposes for which Congress might regulate commerce, for example, were not specified, and Congress passed laws on commerce to forbid the interstate transportation of impure food and drugs (to protect health), of women to be used for immoral purposes, of lottery tickets, and so on. Such laws were obviously regulations of personal conduct for police power purposes, and they were upheld as constitutional. In short, Congress possesses a considerable police power.

A number of laws of the types mentioned, far from interfering with any state police regulations, have been supplementary to the state laws and of aid to the states in enforcing their own regulations. This was particularly noticeable in the federal laws denying the protection of interstate commerce to shipments of liquor into states that forbade the sale of liquor. But when Congress passed an act to deny the privileges of interstate commerce to goods that had been produced by child labor, in order to help the states that were trying to eliminate child labor, the Supreme Court in effect ruled that this was a regulation of production, not of interstate commerce, and so was an infringement on state powers and unconstitutional (Hammer v. Dagenhart, 247 U.S. 251, 1918).

The effect of this and certain other decisions was not only to restrict the concept of the commerce power of Congress by excluding production from commerce, but also to set up the reserved powers of the states as a barrier to the exercise by Congress of the powers granted to it. Said the Court in the Dagenhart case: "The maintenance of the authority of the States over matters purely local is as essential to the preservation of our institutions as is the conservation of the supremacy of the federal power in all matters entrusted to the nation by the Federal Constitution."

This five-to-four decision of the Supreme Court aroused a great controversy. It seemed to make the reserved powers of the states supreme over the powers delegated to Congress. In time both judicial opinion and public opinion swung away from this view to the more traditional one upholding the supremacy of the acts of Congress when passed in pursuance of the Constitution.

In 1941, when sustaining the Fair Labor Standards Act, a commerce act which Congress passed to regulate child labor, among other things, the Supreme Court unanimously overruled the Dagenhart decision and its doctrine (United States v. F. W. Darby Lumber Co., 312 U.S. 100, 1941). It upheld the power of Congress to forbid the shipment in interstate commerce of goods produced under substandard labor conditions. It quoted with approval from Marshall's most famous commerce decision (Gibbons v. Ogden, 9 Wheaton 1, 1824), where the chief justice said that the commerce power of Congress "is the power to regulate; that is, to prescribe the rule by which commerce is to be governed. This power, like all the others vested in Congress, is complete in itself, may be exercised to its utmost extent, and acknowledges no limitations other than are prescribed in the Constitution." Such limitations he indicated are only those which "are expressed in plain terms in the Constitution." The power of Congress over commerce, said the Court in the Darby case, "can neither be enlarged nor diminished by the exercise or non-exercise of state power."

In short, at present, the reserved powers of the state are not a limit on or a bar to the exercise by Congress of the powers delegated to it. Indeed, the Tenth Amendment itself has been held to state "but a truism that all is retained which has not been surrendered" (Darby case). "From the beginning and for many years the amendment has been construed as not depriving the national government of authority to resort to all means for the exercise of a granted power which are appropriate and plainly adapted to the permitted end."

But Tenth Amendment or no Tenth Amendment, the states exercise under the Constitution a wide range of important powers. If state laws lack supremacy over the acts of Congress, they are nevertheless, from the individual's point of view, enforceable laws and laws that must be obeyed, just as fully as any act of Congress, as long as they do not violate any provision of the Constitution or any valid act of Congress.

Following the adoption in a group of the first ten amendments, there were only two others before the Civil War period. Of these only Amendment 11 affects the relations between the nation and the states, and it is the only clearly states' rights amendment ever adopted.

In 1793 the United States Supreme Court took jurisdiction of, and decided, a suit against the state of Georgia that was brought by a citizen of another state (Chisholm v. Georgia, 2 Dallas 419, 1793). There was much protest against this. Those who believed strongly in states' rights and state sovereignty felt that it was an indignity to a state to be subjected to suit in a federal court at the instance of a mere individual from another state. A state could not be sued even in its own courts by one of its own citizens without its consent. By Article III, section 2, of the Constitution,

95

however, the judicial power of the United States did extend to controversies "between a State and citizens of another State."

Following the decision in the Chisholm case, Congress promptly proposed a new constitutional amendment, and the states very quickly adopted it. It provides that "The judicial power of the United States shall not be construed to extend to any suit in law or equity, commenced or prosecuted against one of the United States by citizens of another State, or by citizens or subjects of any Foreign State."

This enactment has had considerable importance in regulating judicial proceedings affecting the states and their officers, but it has not changed greatly the relations between the national government and the states. If this amendment had not been adopted, the Supreme Court might have been involved in one controversy after another, and might have found it even harder than it did to establish its authority as the nation's highest court. Although the amendment does not use the term "state sovereignty," it is based partly on the idea that a sovereign may not be sued without its consent, and it no doubt had some effect not only in soothing the outraged feelings of upholders of state sovereignty but also in perpetuating the idea that the states are separately sovereign.

6

The Acts and Intentions of the Later Framers: Since the Civil War

T HE slavery controversy, secession, and the Civil War let loose a number of forces that changed considerably the relations between the national government and the states. Three new amendments to the Constitution between 1865 and 1870, the so-called Civil War Amendments, embodied some of the more significant changes, but again Supreme Court decisions and the actual practices of government have served to modify the results.

The upholders of slavery before the Civil War took the position that slaves were a form of property, and that the control of property was exclusively a matter for the states. They denied the power of the national government to control or forbid slavery even in the territories. The Emancipation Proclamation, a wartime act of President Lincoln as commander-in-chief, declared the slaves to be free in the states then in rebellion. Lincoln would have much preferred a grant-in-aid or subsidy from Congress to assist each state in a program of gradual emancipation. He saw nothing unconstitutional in such a measure of inducement to the states, as indeed he saw no constitutional objection to the Morrill Act of 1862 to make grants of land to all the states to promote agricultural and mechanical education. But the war in a sense forced his hand in the matter of emancipation of the slaves.

What the Emancipation Proclamation began in the direction of taking from the states the power to legalize and enforce slavery, the Thirteenth Amendment (1865) completed. It provides that

97

"Neither slavery nor involuntary servitude, except as a punishment for crime whereof the party shall have been duly convicted, shall exist within the United States, or any place subject to their jurisdiction," and that "Congress shall have power to enforce this article by appropriate legislation."

Thus a power over the social institution called slavery was taken from the states, and a power to enforce this decision was vested in Congress. The President, Congress, and the ratifying state legislatures had combined to eliminate the powers of the states in a once-important field. And more restrictions were just around the corner.

On July 21, 1868, Congress declared the Fourteenth Amendment to have been adopted as a part of the Constitution. The debate as to the intentions of the framers of this amendment will probably never end. Certain it is that this amendment contains some of the most important restrictions on the powers of the states to be found anywhere in the Constitution. These restrictions came at the end of a bloody struggle over slavery and over the nature of the Union. In a sense the Fourteenth Amendment embodies the decisions made by the victory of the Unionist side in the war in favor of nationalism, national unity, and national supremacy, and against states' rights and the claimed rights of secession and nullification.

The original Constitution left the question of citizenship in the United States somewhat confused and obscure. On the one hand the people delegated to Congress the power to "establish a uniform rule of naturalization" and provided that only "a citizen of the United States" could be elected a representative or senator in Congress, and that "no person except a natural-born citizen, or a citizen of the United States at the time of the adoption of the Constitution, shall be eligible to the office of President . . ." But in Article IV, section 2, we read that "The citizens of each State shall be entitled to all privileges and immunities of citizens in the several States." The relationship between state citizenship and United States citizenship was not made clear.

The Supreme Court decided in Marshall's day that Congress had an exclusive power to naturalize foreigners; that is, to make them citizens of the United States (Chirac v. Chirac, 2 Wheaton 259, 1817). In the Dred Scott decision, which aroused such a storm of protest throughout the West and North (Dred Scott v. Sandford, 19 Howard 393, 1857), Chief Justice Taney recognized as United States citizens only two classes of persons, those naturalized under acts of Congress, and those white persons who were born in the United States as the descendants of persons who had been recognized as *state* citizens at the time the Constitution was adopted.

In other words, under the second category, state citizenship was primary and United States citizenship was derived from it. After the Constitution was adopted a state could still make persons citizens of the state, but it could not under the Constitution make them citizens of the United States. Neither by state action nor by birth in the United States of free parents could a Negro acquire citizenship.

In its first sentence the Fourteenth Amendment radically changed the law of United States citizenship: "All persons born or naturalized in the United States, and subject to the jurisdiction thereof, are citizens of the United States and of the State wherein they reside."

By this provision the people of the United States establish the controlling rule on citizenship in the United States in a new form. United States citizenship is made primary and ascendant, and state citizenship is clearly relegated to a secondary position. To acquire what is called citizenship in any state, all that a citizen of the United States has to do is reside there. Since there is a right of free migration from state to state, beyond the province of any state to forbid or obstruct, state control over citizenship is practically ended. The distinctive privileges that go with state citizenship are also very limited today.

It is my belief that, whether intentionally or not, the citizenship provision of the Fourteenth Amendment is another, and perhaps the final and conclusive step in the constitutional sense, in the progress of the United States toward national supremacy and nationhood. By every definition that I can find, citizenship is membership in a body politic, state, or independent political community. If the citizens are directly and individually members of the United States, as the Fourteenth Amendment makes them, then the "membership" of the several states in the Union is going to be hard to define. I believe that the citizenship clause in the Fourteenth Amendment establishes beyond question the United States as one nation, with one body of citizens, and with national supremacy over all parts of the national territory under national popular sovereignty.

"No state shall make or enforce any law which shall abridge the privileges or immunities of citizens of the United States . . ." This clause follows immediately the citizenship clause that has just been discussed, and apparently much was expected of it by some of the framers. The amendment does not define, however, what are the "privileges or immunities of citizens of the United States," and does not distinguish them from the Article IV "privileges and immunities of citizens in the several states."

Although the privileges or immunities clause still stands in the Fourteenth Amendment for whatever it is worth, its meaning was drastically restricted by a five-to-four Supreme Court decision in 1873 (Slaughter-House cases, 16 Wallace 26, 1873). Certain local butchers in Louisiana, deprived of employment by a state act which gave a slaughtering monopoly in three parishes (counties) to one company, appealed from the state to the federal Supreme Court on the ground that one of their Fourteenth Amendment "privileges or immunities" as citizens of the United States—that is, their claimed right to engage in the business of slaughtering—had been taken from them by the state act.

Broadly considered the issue was a crucial one: Does the Fourteenth Amendment privileges or immunities clause wipe out the "police powers" formerly exercised by the states over local business, and make the right to engage in ordinary lawful callings of any kind a right of national citizenship, not subject to state control? The answer to this question by the majority was No, while the minority of four justices dissented vigorously. The majority thought that the Civil War amendments were intended primarily to give protection to the newly freed Negroes, and not to shift the former general powers of the states to regulate social, economic, and moral affairs within their limits to the national government, or even to change substantially the general division of powers between the national and state governments.

Under this interpretation the privileges or immunities of citizens of the United States were only those specified in the Constitution and in statutes enacted by Congress under its ordinary powers to regulate commerce and so on. But even before the Fourteenth Amendment the states had had no right to abridge these privileges, so that in effect the new "privileges or immunities" clause was rendered nugatory. It forbade no state action that had not been forbidden before. Except for the protection of Negroes, the privileges or immunities clause did not change the boundary line between national and state functions.

But there are other clauses in the Fourteenth Amendment, and the very next one is a restriction on the states that has had a very different history. It provides: "nor shall any State deprive any person of life, liberty or property without due process of law . . ."

Frustrated in their efforts to use the "privileges or immunities" clause as a means of invalidating state laws that they and their clients did not like, lawyers began to argue in the courts that various new state regulations and taxes took their clients' property or liberty "without due process of law." This argument proved to be far more persuasive with the judges, because under this clause every case could be taken up on its own merits, and a piecemeal, gradual development of the law could be engineered, almost in the manner and the spirit of the common law.

In the 1880s and even more in the 1890s and early 1900s state and federal courts began to invalidate state laws and local ordinances under the due process clause. A significant example was a five-to-four United States Supreme Court decision holding unconstitutional a New York statute that forbade any person to work more than sixty hours a week in a bakery or confectionery (Lochner v. New York, 198 U.S. 45, 1905). There were numerous other examples, but here was evidence that the due process clause could be used to check within the states a slowly rising trend toward "social legislation" that might in the interests of health, safety, morals, and general welfare limit the freedom of workers and employers alike.

The Lochner case decision held the sixty-hour law unconstitutional as not a proper police power regulation but "an illegal interference with the rights of individuals, both employers and employees, to make contracts regarding labor upon such terms as they may think best"—a "mere meddlesome interference" for which there was no good reason on the grounds of either public or private health. The dissents in the case were vigorous but temporarily unavailing. Let it be noted that the statute was held invalid not for any defect in legislative or judicial procedure, but for the reason that the Court thought it substantively beyond the power of a state legislature to pass any such law at all.

A number of other state laws fell in the same way, laws providing for wage, price, and rate regulations, and for novel forms of taxation such as so-called progressive taxes, and even laws for certain kinds of public expenditures. The Court's decisions on these are in general lumped under the designation "substantive due process," because the decisions did not deal with procedures, but in effect said that such laws were simply beyond the states' legislative powers, as taking property or liberty without due process. Some state supreme courts went even beyond the United States Supreme Court in invalidating state legislation under the due process clause.

In the late 1930s and the 1940s the United States Supreme Court reversed its position on many of these questions, thus giving the states more freedom, but in one field, that of civil liberties such as freedom of speech, press, and religion, the Court drew even tighter reins on the states. Various lawyers had tried from time to time to get the Court to hold that the due process requirement imposed upon the states by the Fourteenth Amendment demanded that the states observe all the requirements of the federal Bill of Rights, especially in the first eight amendments. The Court in general refused to take this position, holding those amendments to apply only against the national government, but in 1925 it made a major change of position regarding the First Amendment.

A Communist had been convicted under a statute of New York making the practice of anarchy a crime. The convicted man appealed on the ground that this statute deprived him of his right of "liberty" under the Fourteenth Amendment without due process of law. In considering this point the Court majority said: "For present purposes we may and do assume that freedom of speech and of the press—which are protected by the First Amendment from abridgement by Congress—are among the fundamental personal rights and 'liberties' protected by the due process clause of the Fourteenth Amendment from impairment by the states" (Gitlow v. State of New York, 268 U.S. 652, 1925).

Since that pregnant statement was so casually made, many state statutes and local ordinances have been held unconstitutional by the courts under the First Amendment which, although its words forbid action only by Congress, has been transformed by the Fourteenth Amendment and the Gitlow case decision into a restriction also against the states.

What about the other amendments in the Bill of Rights? They deal largely with questions of judicial trials and procedure. Does the Fourteenth Amendment requiring due process affect them also?

One important meaning of process, of course, is procedure, and the Supreme Court and other federal courts have insisted that the state courts must follow fundamentally fair procedure in both civil and criminal cases. A tremendous body of constitutional law, binding upon the states, has been developed primarily by the Supreme Court, under the Fourteenth Amendment, to regulate judicial procedure, especially in criminal cases. Brutal third-degree methods of getting evidence, forced confessions, failure in capital cases to provide counsel, trials that are so hasty, so irregular, or so arbitrary as not to give the defense a fair chance to present its case, are generally held to be unconstitutional. These elementary requirements of a fair and civilized trial are today established restrictions upon the states.

But up to now the Supreme Court has refused to accept the view that all procedural requirements imposed by the federal Bill of Rights upon the United States courts are also fully binding upon the states, although there is much sentiment in favor of this change also. In short, the Bill of Rights holds the federal courts and officials to a more rigid code of fair procedure than is applied by the Supreme Court to the states. The states still have considerable leeway in judicial procedure, arrests, means of getting evidence, and the like.

Another clause of the Fourteenth Amendment says that no state may "deny to any person within its jurisdiction the equal protection of the laws." The framers of this provision must have had the Negroes especially in mind as needing this protection, and in fact the clause has been important (along with due process and other clauses) in protecting the Negroes and other minorities against discriminations in elections, education, the acquisition of property, and accommodations in public places. The Supreme Court has held that the Fourteenth Amendment does not of itself give Congress an independent power to legislate in all these matters directly for the people. What the amendment does is to forbid improper state actions, and it is quite proper for Congress to legislate, as it has done to some extent, to prevent, to forbid, and to punish the persons responsible for any state actions that deprive individuals of their constitutional rights. The equal protection clause is important in racial segregation cases and is likely to become even more important. It is applicable also to some extent in taxation and other activities of state and local governments.

The Fourteenth Amendment includes other important clauses that are potential or actual restrictions on the states, but the four clauses that have been discussed are probably the most important ones.

The last of the Civil War Amendments is Amendment 15, which provides that "The right of citizens of the United States to vote shall not be denied or abridged by the United States, or by any State, on account of race, color, or previous condition of servitude," and that "Congress shall have power to enforce this article by appropriate legislation."

Before the Civil War every state was free to define almost as its government and people saw fit the qualifications for voting in the state. Even aliens who had not done more than state an intention to become citizens were allowed to vote in many states.

The Fifteenth Amendment was designed primarily to ensure to Negro citizens an equal right to vote in all public elections. This amendment has been evaded and ignored in various states in a number of ways. Congress has enacted relatively little legislation to provide for its enforcement, except to establish penalties for state and local election officers who violate it. Many cases of violations of Negro voting rights have come to the federal courts, however, and the Supreme Court has made a number of notable decisions interpreting and applying the Fifteenth Amendment principle. As a result, the states concerned are coming to recognize the validity of the restrictions placed upon them and are moving, at various rates of speed or slowness, toward the goal of equal voting rights for all citizens.

The veterans of the Union and Confederate armies have practically all passed from the scene by now, and there can hardly be any person still living who has a clear recollection from personal experience of the constitutional relations between the national government and the states before the Civil War began in 1861. It is hard to imagine today what the constitutional situation was without the Thirteenth, Fourteenth, and Fifteenth amendments. As a group these amendments forbid the states to legalize slavery or involuntary servitude, to define their own citizenship, to infringe the privileges or immunities of United States citizens, or deprive any person of life, liberty, or property without due process of law, to deny to any person within their jurisdiction the equal protection of the laws, or to deny to any citizen of the United States the right to vote on any such ground as race, color, or previous condition of servitude. Citizenship is now completely under national control.

In addition to establishing national supremacy more firmly by their own words, the Civil War Amendments confer on Congress the power to enforce these amendments by its legislation. Because Congress has used this power very little, it has been left largely to the courts, and especially to the Supreme Court, by the slow and uncertain process of adjudicating the cases that come before them, to interpret and reaffirm the restrictions imposed on the states by these amendments, and to remind the states time and time again of their constitutional duties.

The Supreme Court has become a sort of schoolmaster or mentor to the states, showing them the limits of their powers, where they have gone wrong, and even what they ought to do to discharge fairly their obligations. It has been a lenient and patient teacher, a teacher who is denied the power to apply the rod. Nevertheless there is evidence that its teachings and admonitions are having some effects in raising the legislative, administrative, and judicial standards and practices of the states.

The composition and the procedures of the two houses of Congress are such that it is difficult for Congress to pass laws to enforce the Civil War Amendments. Perhaps it is wiser policy not to try to do this except in emergencies, and to rely instead upon the slow process of education to bring the states that are below the standards set by those amendments up to standard. But anyone who thinks that Congress has no power in the fields of the social and economic policies of the states should read the Civil War Amendments again in the light of the tremendous range and variety of cases that have already arisen under them.

More than forty years elapsed after the Fifteenth Amendment before another formal change was made in the Constitution. The progressive forces of the late nineteenth century and the early twentieth suggested various changes in the Constitution affecting national-state relations, but only three of these made their way into the constitutional document, the Sixteenth and Seventeenth in 1913, and the Nineteenth in 1920.

For a few years during and after the Civil War there was a national income tax whose rates were uniformly applicable over the entire country. Enacted by Congress, this tax was accepted by the Supreme Court, although its favorable decision did not come until after the tax had expired (Springer v. United States, 102 U.S. 586, 1880).

The basic issue raised about a federal income tax at that time was whether it was a duty, impost, or excise tax which, when levied under the Constitution (Article I, section 8, paragraph 1), "shall be uniform throughout the United States," or whether it was a "direct tax." If it were the latter it would come under Article I, section 9, paragraph 4, which provides that "No capitation, or other direct, tax shall be laid unless in proportion to the census or enumeration herein before directed to be taken."

If the latter rule applied to an income tax, the national government would almost have to set a fixed total amount to be collected, say $10 per capita in each state, and then, because incomes would vary from state to state, set a different scale of rates for each state to get the desired amount. This would be practically unworkable, and if tried at all it would result in great inequalities of federal tax burdens from state to state. Persons of small incomes in some states would be paying more than persons of higher incomes in wealthier states for the support of the same central government.

In the Springer case decision, the Supreme Court held that an income tax was not a direct tax, and hence did not have to be apportioned by population among the states. Fifteen years later, Congress having in the meantime (1894) enacted a new nation-wide uniform income tax, the Supreme Court reversed its former position (Pollock v. Farmers Loan and Trust Co., 157 U.S. 429, 1895). Concentrating its attention upon income that is derived from property, like rent, the Court ruled by a five-to-four vote that a tax on such income is equivalent to a direct tax on the property itself; consequently it had to be apportioned among the states and could not be levied by Congress uniformly throughout the United States. Because the majority of the justices thought that other parts of the law could not or should not stand by themselves, the whole act was declared unconstitutional.

In the years between the Spanish-American War and World War I, the need of the national government for more revenues than could be provided by the tariff and existing excises became acute; and those political leaders who wanted the burden of supporting the national government distributed throughout the nation in accordance with ability to pay, which many of them believed was also in accordance with benefits received, continued to demand a federal income tax law. In 1909 Congress enacted an excise or income tax on corporations only, and at the same time proposed a constitutional amendment to authorize a general income tax without apportionment among the states.

The necessary ratification from three fourths of the state legislatures was obtained by early 1913. All told, forty-two states approved it, despite the arguments of the opponents that an income tax is socialistic and inequitable. The Sixteenth Amendment reads as follows: "The Congress shall have power to lay and collect taxes on incomes, from whatever source derived, without apportionment among the several States, and without regard to any census or enumeration."

A modest personal income tax with moderately progressive rates was promptly enacted (1913) by Congress. Since then the individual and corporate income taxes combined have become the main source of the national revenue.

The nationalizing effect of the income tax can hardly be doubted. Since the shackles of the Pollock case decision have been removed by the Sixteenth Amendment, Congress is able to tap the income of all individuals and corporations in the United States and subject to its jurisdiction as no combination of states could possibly do. In World War I, in the Great Depression, in World War II, and in the "cold war" and the Korean war that followed, the national government has been able to raise money in unprecedented amounts for the nation's defense and welfare. It makes no difference in what states the concentrations of individual and corporate income may be located; Congress has the power by means of geographically uniform income tax laws to raise the revenue where it is to be found, and the power to spend the money where it is needed for the nation's welfare and defense.

The next amendment to be adopted concerned the direct election of senators.

All the state delegates to the Congress under the Articles of Confederation were elected, paid, and controlled by the state legislatures. The framers of the original Constitution deferred to some extent to those who favored such dependence of the central Congress on the state legislatures by arranging to have the state legislatures choose the two United States senators to represent each state in Congress. The other conditions were changed, however; the senators were guaranteed six-year terms; they were not subject to recall by the legislatures; they were to be paid from the national treasury; and they were to vote as individuals in the Senate and not as two-man, state-unit delegations under state legislative instructions. In fact, therefore, the Senate came to represent the nation in much the same way that the House of Representatives did—with due allowance for the fact that all members of Congress are rooted in the states and have to look after their political fences in their states and districts.

The demand for direct popular election of senators arose in the nineteenth century partly in response to a general demand for more popular control over government and partly as the indignant reaction of the people against the influences of great wealth that were known to have swayed some legislatures when electing senators. Furthermore, the sessions in which a state legislature had to choose a United States senator were frequently so tied up with this responsibility that the legislature's work for the state itself suffered neglect.

The state legislators themselves generally came to recognize the need for a change, and in one way or another popular referendums to express the people's choice for senator had been developed in a number of states before Congress in 1912 proposed a constitutional amendment for the direct election of senators. Between May 16, 1912, and May 31, 1913, enough state legislatures had ratified the amendment to place it in the Constitution as the Seventeenth Amendment.

This amendment was an important step in disentangling the state and national governments from each other, so that each could operate in its own field with as little dependence upon the other as possible. It was also an important step toward placing the responsibility for, and the power of control over, the national government directly in the hands of the people themselves. This change may be interpreted, therefore, along with the United States citizenship clause of the Fourteenth Amendment, as a part of the broad movement toward popular control of government on a nationwide basis.

Although they are chronologically out of place at this point, another pair of steps in this direction should be mentioned to help round out the story. The original Constitution provided that "Each State shall appoint, in such manner as the legislature thereof may direct, a number of electors equal to the whole number of Senators and Representatives to which the State may be entitled in the Congress . . ." (Article II, section 2). These electors, popularly known as presidential electors, were to carry out the election of the President and Vice President every four years.

Alexander Hamilton apparently reflected the prevailing opinion of the times that the intention was to have the *people* of the states choose the presidential electors and to do this anew before each presidential election. Speaking of the office of President in *The Federalist*, no. 68, he said:

It was desirable that the sense of the people should operate in the choice of the person to whom so important a trust was to be confided. This end will be answered by committing the right of making it, not to any preestablished body, but to men chosen by the people for the special purpose, and at the particular juncture. . . . Another and no less important desideratum was, that the Executive should be independent for his continuation in the office on all but the people themselves.

In Hamilton's view, the state legislatures might designate the method of election, but the actual election of presidential electors would be by the people every four years. Four states (Massachusetts, Pennsylvania, Maryland, and Virginia) carried through popular election of the electors at the very first choice of a President (1788). Other states tried different methods, including election by the legislature itself. From 1832 on, only South Carolina clung to election by the legislature, and it changed to popular election at about the time of the Civil War.

In the meantime the nomination of presidential candidates by state legislatures and even by party groups in Congress was under severe attack from democratic forces. In 1831 the Anti-Masonic party held a national convention of the people to nominate its candidates for President and Vice President. This method quickly spread to other political parties, so that soon the candidates did not owe their nominations to either congressional or state legislative caucuses. The people who were members of the party made the nominations in national party conventions. In recent decades efforts have been made with some success to bring the nominations more fully under popular control through the device of presidential preference primaries held before the conventions.

Here then we see that the process of separating national from state political processes has gone far. Although the presidential electors are chosen and their votes are counted by states, the choice is not by the state governments but by the states considered as people. The nominations have been taken out of congressional and state legislative hands, and the national nominating conventions have practically no connection with the state governments. Moreover, the system of direct popular election of presidential electors has become so thoroughly established that to many persons it would seem to be downright unconstitutional for any state legislature now to change the system.

The long-agitated question of votes for women, answered only in part by individual states which enfranchised them, came to a head in 1919 when Congress proposed a constitutional amendment to the effect that "The right of citizens of the United States to vote shall not be denied or abridged by the United States or by any State on account of sex."

Submitted to the states on June 4, 1919, this amendment was adopted by three fourths of the states and declared in effect on August 18, 1920. Here was another act expressing a national democratic feeling that the states had separately been too slow to sense and respond to, yet which was passed quickly once Congress had made the proposal.

Like the Fifteenth Amendment, the Nineteenth is in the form of a restriction or prohibition upon the states, which otherwise have control over suffrage qualifications. Both amendments carry also the clause that "Congress shall have power to enforce this article by appropriate legislation," a power that Congress has found no occasion to use in the case of the Nineteenth Amendment.

A curious states' rights argument against the amendment has, however, been considered by the Supreme Court. Maryland not having ratified the amendment, some citizens of that state who opposed woman suffrage tried to have the amendment itself declared unconstitutional (Leser v. Garnett, 258 U.S. 130, 1922). As paraphrased by Justice Brandeis in his opinion for a unanimous court upholding the amendment: "The first contention is that the power of amendment conferred by the federal Constitution . . . does not extend to this amendment because of its character. The argument is that so great an addition to the electorate, if made without the state's consent, destroys its autonomy as a political body."

Pointing out the similarity between the Fifteenth and the Nineteenth amendments, and noting that the Fifteenth Amendment, which had been in effect for fifty years, had been sustained by the Court in several decisions, the Court simply brushed aside the contention. Had any such proposition been accepted by the Court, that there are absolute limits in favor of states' rights even on the power of constitutional amendment, then one of the admittedly worst features of the Articles of Confederation would have been written into the Constitution, because a single state by refusing to ratify the amendment could then, at least within its own territory, defeat or nullify an amendment to the Constitution of the United States.

The prohibition of the liquor traffic by the Eighteenth Amendment to the Constitution in 1920 was an act so unique in the history of the nation as to be hard to characterize. The closest parallel to it is the Thirteenth Amendment with its prohibition against slavery and involuntary servitude; but the slavery issue was far more fundamental—it had been agitated far longer, and slavery had in effect been outlawed in large part as a war measure before the Thirteenth Amendment was adopted to clinch its abolition. Both amendments reveal, however, that if the states fail to achieve an adequate measure of social control or justice in a matter that the dominant national sentiment deems highly important, it is in line with national precedents to amend the United States Constitution in order to abate the evil and to transfer predominant control over it from the states to the national government.

The counter idea that there are some functions that so thoroughly inhere in the states as to be beyond national decision even by constitutional amendment, as argued against the woman suffrage amendment, was brought up also against the prohibition amendment, only to be rejected by the Supreme Court (National Prohibition Cases, 253 U.S. 350, 1920; see also United States v. Sprague, 282 U.S. 716, 1931).

The idea of national prohibition of the liquor traffic came to its practical end as an experiment when the Eighteenth Amendment was repealed by the Twenty-First Amendment in 1933. In addition to repealing prohibition the new amendment includes one substantive provision which has not yet been adequately explored: "The transportation or importation into any State, Territory, or possession of the United States for delivery or use therein of intoxicating liquors in violation of the laws thereof, is hereby prohibited."

In a sense this provision merely embeds in the Constitution a provision that Congress had much earlier enacted as a statute to help the "dry" or prohibition states to enforce their laws, by denying the protection of interstate commerce to liquor shipped into such a "dry" state. In fact, however, in the absence of congressional laws on the subject under the commerce power or some other power, the states began almost at once to set up their own strict barriers against liquor brought into their jurisdictions in order to enforce their highly variable liquor policies, and the Supreme Court upheld one act after another. This clause appears, therefore, to be an extension of state powers over the liquor traffic beyond what they had had even before the Eighteenth Amendment.

It is not yet certain what would happen if Congress should start to legislate on the interstate shipment of liquor. It is clear that the Twenty-First Amendment does not of itself exempt the liquor traffic from the Sherman Anti-Trust Act, an act of Congress under its commerce power, and it is certainly to be doubted that the amendment wipes out, as to liquor, the commerce power, the war powers, the postal power, and other pertinent powers of Congress. In the meantime, however, with the indulgence of Congress, the states seem to have a freer hand in the regulation of the liquor traffic than they probably ever had before under the Constitution.

The acts of the "later framers," especially as they appear in constitutional amendments, have now been passed in review. These changes have been accompanied by changes in state and national laws and policies, and also in the constitutional decisions and doctrines of the Supreme Court, which is the most potent single agency for the development of American constitutional law.

One thing is certain, namely, that the Constitution as it stands today is far different from what it was when it came from the hands of the original framers. And, following a brief chapter on

"The States' Rights Deviation," I shall try to summarize the relationships between the national government and the states as I see them at the present time, say in 1954. This summary will deal not alone with constitutional law, but with that blending of constitutional law and governmental practice which characterizes the system as an operating whole.

7

The States' Rights Deviation

THIS chapter is something of a digression. But there is enough of states' rightsism in many of the adverse criticisms directed against the national government in recent years to warrant the use of a few pages to throw a little light on that subject of unhappy memory, states' rights.

/ The struggle for states' rights—as against the supremacy of the national government—has been like a fire that smolders for a time and then flares up anew, in new places and with new combustibles, but which never really dies out.)

There seems to have been a short period of good feeling after George Washington took office as the first President in 1789, but even in his administration there were local and sporadic outbursts against national authority. There were occasional strong words on the subject in the halls of Congress. Treaties continued to be ignored by the states, and in some cases federal courts were obstructed by state authorities. It took much time and patience on the part of President Washington and other national authorities to begin to govern the country within even the narrow range of functions that Congress at first provided for. But the Federalist party, which grew out of the movement for the Constitution and stood clearly for a national program, was the leading political party by the end of Washington's administration, and it brought about the election of John Adams as the second President.

In the meantime Thomas Jefferson, first in President Washington's cabinet and then as Vice President during John Adams's administration, was building up the original Republican party among "strict constructionists." Jefferson had been in France during the framing and adoption of the Constitution, and was not at first well informed about it. Nevertheless he developed strong views on the subject. In the end he accepted the document but with the reservation that a Bill of Rights must be attached to it. When this was done he praised it highly, although as a non-author he remained free to interpret and even to attack it as he saw fit.

As early as 1791 Jefferson strongly opposed Hamilton's elastic construction of the powers of the national government. "I am not a friend to a very energetic government," he had once said, and he objected vigorously to such measures as the establishment of a national bank.

By the enactment and enforcement of the Alien and Sedition Laws in President Adams's term, with apparent disregard of the rights of the people as specified in the First Amendment, the Federalists gave Jefferson and his party a fine opportunity to attack them for violating the Bill of Rights and for bringing about federal usurpation of state powers. In the Kentucky Resolutions of 1798 Jefferson declared the Constitution to be a compact among the states, denounced various congressional acts for their encroachments on states' rights, and called upon other states to adopt similar resolutions to lay before Congress. His words suggested that the states had reserved to themselves a right to nullify acts of Congress that they believed to exceed the national powers.

James Madison, drafting a parallel set of resolutions for Virginia, went even farther than Jefferson in asserting that it is the duty of the states "to watch over and oppose every infraction" of the principles on which the Constitution was founded, including a strict construction of the national powers; urging that the Constitution is a "compact to which the states are parties"; and insisting that the states, as the parties to the compact, "have the right and are in duty bound to interpose for arresting the progress of the evil, and for maintaining within their respective limits the authorities, rights, and liberties appertaining to them."

These doctrines thus enunciated by Madison were, in effect, the assertion of a right of state nullification of acts of Congress and, indeed, of annulment by state legislatures, because it was to the state legislatures and not to the people that he and Jefferson appealed for action.

Madison's views in the Virginia Resolutions represent a most surprising reversal of his former position. Between 1786 and 1788, while Jefferson was in France, and when the Union under the Articles appeared to be going to pieces, Madison could not say enough about the ineptitude, selfishness, and irresponsibility of the states, and the failure of the Articles of Confederation. Before the Federal Convention met in 1787, he wrote a letter to Washington in which he outlined his ideas for constitutional reform:

I have sought for middle ground, which may at once support a due supremacy of the national authority, and not exclude the *local authorities* wherever they can be *subordinately useful* [my italics] . . . I would propose next that in addition to the present federal powers, the National Government should be armed with positive and compleat authority in all cases which require uniformity . . . Over and above this positive power, a negative *in all cases whatsoever* on the legislative acts of the States, as heretofore exercised by the Kingly prerogative, appears to me to be absolutely necessary . . .

Other points urged by Madison in this letter were that the national government should be free to operate by itself, without the intervention of the state legislatures, and that the national government should have the right to coerce the states if necessary.

After the drafting of the Constitution Madison was an active "federalist" in the struggle for adoption. As one of the principal authors of *The Federalist*, he wrote extensively, and approvingly, on the powers granted to the national authority. He referred to the states as "local or municipal authorities," and he left no doubt that a branch of the national government, the United States Supreme Court, would be the tribunal to settle controversies between the national and state authorities.

But whether he intended to do so or not, Madison gave some support to the states' rights view, and some basis for later arguments for it, by his complex and involved arguments in *The Federalist* and elsewhere. He was apparently trying to be balanced, moderate, middle-of-the-road, and to avoid undue shock to the states rights' supporters in 1787–88. In fact he was somewhat confusing to his readers and self-contradictory in what he said.

Essay no. 39 of *The Federalist* in particular caused considerable subsequent confusion. Madison was replying to the adversaries of the Constitution who said that the Constitutional Convention should have preserved the *federal* form of government, "which regards the Union as a Confederacy of sovereign states," instead of which a national government had been framed, "which regards the Union as a consolidation of the states." These adversaries "asked by what authority this bold and radical innovation was undertaken." Considering in response to this issue the "foundation" on which the proposed Constitution was established, Madison went on to say:

On examining the first relation, it appears, on one hand, that the Constitution is to be founded on the assent and ratification of the people of America, given by deputies elected for the special purpose; but, on the other, that this assent and ratification is to be given by the people, not as individuals composing one entire nation, but as composing the distinct and independent States to which they respectively belong. It is to be the assent and ratification of the several States, derived from the Supreme authority in each State,—the authority of the people themselves. The act, therefore, establishing the Constitution, will not be a *national*, but a *federal* act.

That it will be a federal and not a national act, as these terms are understood by the objectors; the act of the people as forming so many independent States, not as forming one aggregate nation, is obvious from this single consideration, that it is to result neither from the decision of the *majority* of the people of the Union, nor from that of a majority of the States. It must result from the *unanimous* assent of the several States that are parties to it, differing no otherwise from their ordinary assent than in its being expressed, not by the legislative authority, but by that of the people themselves. Were the people regarded in this transaction as forming one nation, the will of the majority of the whole people of the United States would bind the minority, in the same manner as the majority in each State must bind the minority; and the will of the majority must be determined either by a comparison of the individual votes, or by considering the will of the majority of the States as evidence of the will of the majority of the people of the United States. Neither of these rules have been adopted. Each State, in ratifying the Constitution, is considered as a sovereign body, independent of all others, and only to be bound by its own voluntary act. In this relation, then, the new Constitution will, if established, be a *federal*, not a *national* constitution.

The rest of this essay was devoted to an analysis of the various federal and national features of the Constitution, as Madison viewed them, and he closed with the comforting assurance that "The proposed Constitution, therefore, is, in strictness neither a national nor a federal Constitution, but a composition of both."

Without questioning Madison's sincerity in this analysis, and with the admission that I see a certain logic in it, I still feel that Madison was merely making a special effort to give assurances to the state-sovereignty advocates who were against ratifying the Constitution. Actually the distinction Madison makes is a somewhat metaphysical one. Chief Justice Marshall rejected it in the famous McCulloch decision (1819) already cited. After outlining the steps by which the Constitution was drawn up and "submitted to the people" he went on to say:

They acted upon it, in the only manner in which they can act safely, effectively, and wisely, on such a subject, by assembling in convention. It is true, they assembled in their several states; but where else should they have assembled? No political dreamer was ever wild enough to think of breaking down the lines which separate the states, and of compounding the American people into one common mass. Of consequence, when they act, they act in their states. But the measures they adopt do not, on that account, cease to be the measures of the people themselves, or become the measures of the state governments.

From these conventions the Constitution derives its whole authority. The government proceeds directly from the people; is "ordained and established" in the name of the people; and is declared to be ordained, "in order to form a more perfect union, establish justice, insure domestic tranquility, and secure the blessings of liberty to themselves and their posterity." The assent of the states, in their sovereign capacity, is implied in calling a convention, and thus submitting that administration to the people.

But the people were at perfect liberty to accept or reject it; and their act was final. It required not the affirmance, and could not be negatived, by the state governments. The Constitution, when thus adopted, was, of complete obligation, and bound the state sovereignties.

It has been said, that the people had already surrendered all their powers to the state sovereignties, and had nothing more to give. But, surely, the question whether they may resume and modify the powers granted to government, does not remain to be settled in this country. Much more might the legitimacy of the general government be doubted, had it been created by the states. The powers delegated to the state sovereignties were to be exercised by themselves, not by a distinct and independent sovereignty, created by themselves. To the formation of a league, such as was the Confederation, the state governments were certainly competent. But when "in order to form a more perfect union," it was deemed necessary to change this alliance into an effective government, possessing great and sovereign powers, and acting directly on the people, the necessity of referring it to the people, and of deriving its powers directly from them, was felt and acknowledged by all.

The government of the Union, then (whatever may be the influence of this fact on the case) is emphatically and truly a government of the people. In form and in substance it emanates from them, its powers are granted by them, and are to be exercised directly on them, and for their benefit.

Madison himself, in no. 45 of *The Federalist*, warmly acknowledged the importance of the people in the formation of government. He chastised the states' righters who, he said, had left the main issue of the debate over adoption, as to the degree of power needed by the central government to achieve what was essential for the national security and for the general welfare, and had entered into a "secondary inquiry" as to the effects of the proposed change on the states:

But if the Union, as has been shown, be essential to the security of the people of America against foreign danger; if it be essential to their security against contentions and wars among the different States; if it be essential to guard them against those violent and oppressive factions which embitter the blessings of liberty, and against those military establishments which must gradually poison its very fountain; if, in a word, the Union be essential to the happiness of the people of America, is it not preposterous, to urge as an objection to a government, without which the objects of the Union cannot be attained, that such a government may derogate from the importance of the governments of the individual States? Was, then, the American Revolution effected, was the American Confederacy formed, was the precious blood of thousands spilt, and the hard-earned substance of millions lavished, not that the people of America should enjoy, peace, liberty, and safety, but that the government of the individual states, that *particular municipal establishments* [my italics] might enjoy a certain extent of power, and be arranged with certain dignities and attributes of sovereignty? We have heard of the impious doctrine in the Old World, that the people were made for kings, not kings for the people. Is the same doctrine to be revived in the New, in another shape—that the solid happiness of the people is to be sacrificed to the views of political institutions of a different form? It is too early for politicians to presume on our forgetting that the public good, the real welfare of the great body of the people, is the supreme object to be pursued; and that no form of government whatever has any other value than as it may be fitted for the attainment of this object. Were the plan of the convention adverse to the public happiness, my voice would be, Reject the plan. Were the Union itself inconsistent with the public happiness, it would be, Abolish the Union. In like manner, as far as the sovereignty of the States cannot be reconciled to the happiness of the people, the voice of every good citizen must be, Let the former be sacrificed to the latter.

Elsewhere in *The Federalist*, too, Madison was vigorous in his support of the supremacy of the national good.

In short, Madison the Constitution-maker and Madison the Republican partisan of ten years later were rather different people; and his ideas of 1798 about the Constitution being a compact among the states, and about a state power to nullify acts of Congress, do not square with the main tenor of his arguments when the Constitution was being presented to the people for adoption. Both Hamilton and Madison recognized the right of the state governments to agitate against any federal laws that might encroach on the states, but in *The Federalist* they did not propose, and the Constitution did not provide for, any means of state nullification of acts of Congress. The doctrines of the Kentucky and Virginia Resolutions were a later development and not consonant with what Madison had argued earlier.

It is interesting to notice, too, that outside of Virginia and Kentucky the 1798 "resolves" of these two states fell on deaf ears in the other southern states, and were vigorously condemned in the states north of the Mason and Dixon line. The Federalists opposed the resolutions strongly, and they actually gained in political strength in 1799 at the expense of the Republicans. Both Madison and Jefferson dropped the idea of state nullification as the means of wiping out the Alien and Sedition Acts, and returned to their more congenial and constitutional political weapon, the attempt to get the people to elect Anti-Federalists to Congress.

Although both Jefferson and Madison were successively elected to the presidency (1800 and 1808), this fact cannot be attributed to their utterances in the Virginia and Kentucky Resolutions. And by 1830 Madison was clearly once more in the antinullification camp.

Another claim to the right of nullification arose a generation after the Virginia and Kentucky Resolutions, when South Carolina claimed the right to nullify a tariff law passed by Congress. Actual nullification was prevented by President Jackson's stern position against it. Nevertheless the slavery controversy soon thereafter raised a similar issue, and the conflict over federal control of slavery in the territories led on to southern secession and civil war.

Southern historians have discovered in the publications and utterances of some of the secession leaders statements that were almost lyrical in praise of states' rights. John C. Calhoun and other theorists of the South accepted as a historical fact that each of the thirteen original states had at the beginning been completely independent and sovereign in the full international sense of sovereignty. Calhoun further claimed that this sovereignty was by nature inalienable and indivisible, and that the Constitution was therefore only a compact among states, each of which continued to be fully sovereign.

123

(It is interesting to notice that in Connecticut at a later date some lawyers representing certain towns that had existed, they claimed, before the colony was organized once claimed substantially the same right of sovereignty for those towns as against the state of Connecticut.)

This theory was made explicit in the constitution of the Confederate states. As a practical matter the framers of that document followed rather closely the Constitution of the United States, but they began the preamble differently: "We, the people of the Confederate States, each State acting in its sovereign and independent character, in order to form a permanent federal government . . ."

Ironically, the recalcitrancy of some of the states, which even in wartime pursued their theories of states' rights, is considered by many historians to be a major cause of the Confederacy's defeat. President Jefferson Davis himself felt keenly the lack of state support:

Complaining that his own troubles were sufficient, he wrote when the war was drawing to a close, "but these difficulties have been materially increased by the persistent interference by some of the State Authorities, Legislative, Executive, and Judicial, hindering the action of this government, obstructing the execution of its laws, denouncing its necessary policy, impairing its hold upon the confidence of the people, and dealing with it rather as if it were the public enemy than the Government which they themselves had established for the common defense, and which was their only hope of safety from the untold horrors of Yankee despotism." *

These conclusions about states' rights in the Confederacy are stated even more emphatically by Frank Lawrence Owsley, the southern historian who wrote the principal monograph on the subject:

There is an old saying that the seeds of death are sown at our birth. This was true of the southern Confederacy, and the seeds of death were state rights. The principle on which the South

* Quoted from E. Merton Coulter, *The Confederate States of America, 1861–1865* (volume 7 of *A History of the South*), pp. 400–1, with the permission of the publishers, Louisiana State University Press. Copyright 1950 by the publishers.

based its actions before 1861 and on which it hoped to base its future government was its chief weakness. If a monument is ever erected as a symbolical gravestone over the "lost cause" it should have engraved upon it these words: "Died of State Rights." We are in the habit of ascribing as the causes of the failure of the Confederacy the blockade, lack of industrial development and resources, breakdown of transportation, inadequate financial system, and so on, all of which are fundamental; yet, in spite of all these, if the political system of the South had not broken down under the weight of an impractical doctrine put into practice in the midst of a revolution, the South might have established its independence. If the leaders had been able to bury their differences as to the theory of government, if they had allowed the Confederate government the same freedom as that of the Federal (harassed though the Federal government was by internal strife) during the space of the war, it would have been almost an impossibility for the South to suffer defeat. But the Stephenses, Toombs, Browns, and Vances could not wait till after the war to try out their theories and air their differences . . . they sowed dissention among the people and destroyed all spirit of co-operation, finally, between the states and the Confederate government, and, at times, arrayed local against central government as if each had been an unfriendly power.

In using the term "state rights," both state sovereignty and state rights as used in the days of Jefferson and Calhoun are included for the leaders were seldom consistent in their claims: one time they would act upon the Calhoun theory of the absolute sovereignty of the state, while at another time the same man merely insisted upon the rigid division of powers between the state and central governments in accordance with the Jeffersonian doctrine —insisted with the tenacity and spirit of Shylock. But whether they acted upon the state-rights or state-sovereignty theory the practical results were the same: the state assumed or tried to assume functions whose exercise must of necessity devolve upon the central government, in any successful war against a strong antagonist; and the Confederacy was paralyzed, and, as we have already seen, the whole people were demoralized and embittered against each other and their governments by the controversies involved.*

* Quoted from Frank L. Owsley, *State Rights in the Confederacy*, pp. 1–4, with the permission of the publishers, the University of Chicago Press. Copyright 1925 by the University of Chicago.

Constitutional Problems and Issues

Since the Civil War, the states' rights doctrine—based on what Hamilton called "the inordinate pride of state importance"—has not led to bloody violence. As we have seen, however, it has in one form or another remained a factor in the politics of this nation. Although the Union victory in the War of Secession pretty well laid to rest Calhoun's theory of *absolute* sovereignty of each state, the "state-sovereignty theory," as Owsley termed it, which insists on a rigid reservation of powers to the states, is resuscitated regularly by those who oppose some extension or other of national powers.

But I believe and have tried to show that there is no constitutional basis for this theory. The people cannot be assumed to have undone with the left hand what they did with the right, to have reserved to the separate states powers that would defeat the powers conferred on the national government to promote the national security and the national welfare. If in the original Constitution they were not sufficiently clear about national objectives and national supremacy, by their subsequent actions they have done much to remove the uncertainty and doubt.

☆ 8

National-State Relations Today: The Constitutional Essentials

THE Constitution, in all its provisions, looks to an indestructible Union, composed of indestructible States."

This statement in a Supreme Court decision of 1869 sets forth succinctly the basic fact about national-state relations under the Constitution of the United States—the importance and permanence of both the national and the state governments.

It is true of course, as we have seen, that the national government has been established as supreme. No state may constitutionally nullify or obstruct the acts of the national government. Every state stands under the compulsory jurisdiction and process of the nation's Supreme Court to decide on the state's rights and duties under the United States Constitution and laws. The constitutional acts of Congress are also binding on the states. National citizenship is the primary citizenship for all the people in the United States—above state citizenship—and the national government may reach with its laws any and every citizen (as well as all aliens and other persons) in any state. The national Constitution is the highest written law for all the people of the United States, for the nation as a whole and for each of its parts—for the national government and for the state and local governments as well. The Constitution is without qualification the "supreme law of the land."

It is true also that the activities of the national government have increased manyfold in the century and a half since the nation's beginning. These activities are not all specifically mentioned in the Constitution. But that document has proved to be a very

127

flexible and adaptable instrument. It can, when necessary, be formally amended—and has been, twenty-two times. More important perhaps, it contains "implied powers" which can be interpreted by the Congress and the Supreme Court in the light of new needs. From the war powers, the commerce power, the postal powers, and the taxing power, all granted explicitly to the national government, Congress has, by implication, drawn the authority to do many things.

A power that has been especially adaptable to new needs is the power of Congress to tax (and, *ergo*, to spend) for the "general welfare of the United States." It merits special attention.

The Constitution does not mention a separate or distinct "spending power," although it does regulate congressional appropriation of funds out of the treasury. It is recognized, however, that from taxation and other sources the national government will have revenues, and that the taxing power is used primarily though not entirely to provide revenues. This being the case, the power delegated to Congress "To lay and collect taxes, duties, imposts, and excises; to pay the debts and provide for the common defense and general welfare of the United States" is widely interpreted in practice to imply a power to spend the money so raised "for the common defense and general welfare." There is no point in raising a revenue unless it is to be spent for such public purposes as the common defense and the general welfare.

This has not always been the favored view. But in 1936, in a case involving an attack upon a taxing law, the Supreme Court accepted the broad view of Congress's power to spend for the general welfare. In the decision in United States v. Butler (297 U.S. 1), Justice Roberts (conservative, Republican, a former Philadelphia lawyer) wrote:

Since the formation of the nation, sharp differences of opinion have persisted as to the true interpretation of the phrase "general welfare" in the taxing power. Madison asserted it amounted to no more than a reference to the other powers enumerated in the subsequent clauses of the same section; that, as the United States is a government of limited and enumerated powers, the grant of power to tax and spend for the general welfare must be confined to the enumerated legislative fields committed to the Congress. In this view the phrase is mere tautology, for taxation and appropriation are or may be necessary incidents of the exercise of any of the enumerated legislative powers. Hamilton, on the other hand, maintained the clause confers a power separate and distinct from those later enumerated, is not restricted in meaning by the grant of them, and Congress consequently has a substantive power to tax and to appropriate, limited only by the requirement that it shall be exercised to provide for the general welfare of the United States. . . . Mr. Justice Story, in his Commentaries, espouses the Hamiltonian position. We shall not review the writings of public men and commentators or discuss the legislative practice. Study of all these leads us to conclude that the reading advocated by Mr. Justice Story is the correct one. While, therefore, the power to tax is not unlimited, its confines are set in the clause which confers it, and not in those of section 8 which bestow and define the legislative powers of Congress. It results that the power of Congress to authorize expenditure of public moneys for public purposes is not limited by the direct grants of legislative power found in the Constitution.

Even so, as Justice Roberts said for the Court, the power is not unlimited. The tax and the expenditure must be for the general welfare, for national as distinguished from local welfare.

The question remains, then, what is for the general or national welfare? This is for Congress, not the Court, to decide.

In recent decades Congress has, in the interests of general welfare, appropriated money for many functions and services not mentioned in the Constitution—public housing, for example, a wide range of other public works, emergency relief for the unemployed, old age and survivors' insurance, the support of agricultural prices, research in a wide range of subjects.

Congress has entered the field of education, too. Without adequate basic education a people cannot long preserve or wisely use their system of self-government. Furthermore, the defense of the nation depends upon having a citizenry with the essentials of education to understand and to use properly the weapons of modern warfare. The national safety and security may depend upon having enough men and women adequately trained in science, technology, economics, and public affairs. A surprising number of men have had to be rejected from the draft because of the lack of an adequate elementary education. The maintenance of the nation's productive capacity and its commerce also depends upon education, both literary and vocational.

In short, there are important national interests in having all citizens educated up to at least a minimum standard, and in having a large number trained and educated beyond the minimum level for scientific work, the professions, business, and public affairs. And Congress, under its general welfare power, has provided land grants, money grants, and direct services to education, a considerable stimulation to public schools, land-grant colleges, and instruction in particular vocational fields—notably in agriculture.

The Constitution says nothing about how to maintain reasonably full employment in the land or about how to ensure the economic health of the nation by protecting basic industries like agriculture or by making possible at least a minimum of income for the unemployed, the aged, dependent children, and other handicapped classes. These are functions that seem to invade the time-honored roles of families, voluntary groups, local governments, and the states, but nevertheless they are functions that have been accepted by the national government because they are national in their scope and their impact, they affect the nation's commerce and welfare, and they are far beyond the powers of forty-eight states individually to plan, finance, and administer. The maintenance of the economic health of the nation is now recognized as having a close relationship to the nation's security.

The commerce power is another that, alone and in combination with other powers, has enabled Congress to enter areas not specifically mentioned in the Constitution. For example, in order to protect and regulate commerce, Congress has found it necessary or expedient to regulate such matters as industrial disputes, wages and hours, and the production of coal, oil, and agricultural products.

Public health is linked to interstate commerce and to the postal system. Deleterious foods and impure or fraudulent drugs have been sent far and wide through interstate commerce and by mail. Railroads, steamship lines, airlines, and truck and bus systems, all interstate carriers under congressional regulation, may easily become carriers of contagion. And so Congress has enacted various measures to safeguard the nation's health.

For interstate commerce, for postal purposes, and for national defense, all of which are authorized national functions, a good modern highway system throughout the land is essential. And, as we have seen, the national government has become very important in planning and financing the construction of roads.

The original framers intended, I believe, that the powers they granted to the national government should be expanded "by implication" as national needs arose. And the later framers have by and large accepted the implied powers. Both major parties have had a hand in their development. Presidents of both political parties, and not a few state officials as well, have proposed various of the measures that Congress has passed. Congress has approved and passed the various laws, usually with bipartisan support and in many instances by large majorities. The Supreme Court has accepted a broad interpretation of the commerce power, has upheld a broad federal spending power for the general welfare, and has declined to interfere with grant-in-aid measures. The state legislatures have accepted the federal grant-in-aid laws, all forty-eight state legislatures in many cases, by passing laws of their own to put the services into effect. State administrations have taken up the work of administering the grant-in-aid laws, and no governor has resigned in protest against the unconstitutionality of what was being done. The people also have generally accepted the laws.

But the original framers, no less than their successors, were well aware of the dangers in unrestrained governments, and they worked out a system of government that is unusually complicated and replete with various "checks and balances." Certain powers, for example, are reserved to each of the branches of the national government, and no one branch may act with impunity against the will of the others. The division of powers between the states and the national government is another "check." The framers also placed effective limits on the powers of all government in favor of individual liberties—and further restrictions were imposed by the Bill of Rights and later amendments.

All things considered, there is no country in the world that imposes as many and as varied written constitutional restrictions on government action as are to be found in the United States. The underlying principle is that the freedom, the responsibility, and the moral and intellectual development of individuals constitute the primary purpose for which governments exist.

Those who sometimes criticize the United States system of government for its great complexity should be reminded that the purpose of this complexity was largely to protect the liberties of the people. They should not overlook the fact that the American system provides more freedom and more varied opportunities for the citizen to bring his ideas and influence to bear upon government than any other known system of government in the world. This is a characteristic feature that is not often emphasized. To bring out this fact it is almost necessary to go outside the formal constitutional rules and documents, and to summarize the whole system.

Practically all adult men and women may vote. Popular elections are frequent at all levels and in all units of government, and through them the voters choose not only legislative and executive officers but in most states they elect the judges as well. Education is free and widespread though not universal. There is freedom to get information from a wide array of communications media. All persons have a right to criticize public officials and their acts; to assemble and to associate together freely for all lawful purposes; to organize political parties, committees, and other groups; to speak and publish their views without any prior restraint; to petition government for the redress of grievances; to run for and hold public office. Grievances can be directed against particular units and officers of government with considerable ease and accuracy. People on each side can appeal from the legislature or the executive to the courts, from the courts to the legislature, and even back to the courts. If state services are deemed unsatisfactory, the people can appeal to the national government; or appeal for state action if national services do not satisfy. Within each state there can be appeals from local governments to the state legislature, or to the state executive, or to the courts. If the party in power does not give satisfaction the voters can turn to its major rival, and through it get new persons into government. If anything unconstitutional is done or proposed it can be attacked at elections, in legislative bodies, and in the courts.

By these and other related devices and procedures an alert citizenry can play one part of the governmental system against another, or one political party against another, and so keep the various parts of the government "on their toes," alert, active, and responsible, while also keeping the entire government under fairly effective control.

This apparent looseness in the governmental system, with its many opportunities for appeal from one center of power to another, is perhaps the outstanding characteristic of government in the United States, and it has a significant effect on national-state relations.

For one thing, it prevents any single official or department or branch from speaking finally and conclusively for the government, either national or state. The "tidelands" issue mentioned earlier is an excellent example. The states appealed from national executive action to the Supreme Court, and then to Congress when an election brought a change in administration.

Something like this happened also in the Southeast Underwriters insurance case. After the federal Justice Department had won from the Supreme Court a decision that certain insurance companies, operating under state laws, were engaged in interstate commerce and were subject to the nation's antitrust laws, the states appealed to Congress to protect state control over the insurance business. This Congress and the President obligingly did, but on condition that the states themselves would take certain steps to prevent monopolies and private rate-fixing in insurance.

Thus the states again appealed successfully from one branch of the national government to another.

One aspect of this complex system of government that many foreign observers and perhaps many Americans also do not understand is defined approximately by the terms "autonomy" and "free initiative." Congress and the President, the national policy-making authorities, may go ahead and act for the general welfare upon their own interpretation of the national powers without consulting or getting the consent of either the United States Supreme Court or the state governments. Each state government may do the same in acting for the welfare of its state without consulting the President, Congress, or the Supreme Court. If not sovereign the states are at least autonomous.

This apparent looseness of governmental structure strengthens the importance of each part of the system: each part, though subordinate to the whole, has certain "checks" on the other parts and on the whole. At the same time, paradoxical though this seems, it also ties the nation and its parts permanently together. For the threads between the President and the Congress, Congress and the Supreme Court, the Supreme Court and the state legislatures, the state legislatures and the Congress, Congress and the state governors, state governors and national executive agencies, national executive agencies and state divisions, state executive divisions and state legislatures, and so on, are so intricately interwoven that a break at any point would only temporarily snarl the threads; it cannot unravel the whole.

The relationship between the states and the nation that emerges from the complex governmental structure of the United States is sometimes called a partnership. I have used the term "partners" in the title of this volume, and in a way I believe it is a very apt term. But I want to make perfectly clear the sense in which I am using "partners" and "partnership."

It seems to me that there is between the nation and the states nothing like an ordinary business-partnership arrangement in which the partners have equal status and voting powers. Each state, being but a part of the entire people, is not an equal partner of the nation; at the same time, all the states combined *are* the nation and cannot be called its partners.

On the other hand the national government and the state governments are the agents of the nation to perform their respective functions and responsibilities for the nation and for its several parts, the states. They share the responsibility to promote the general welfare of all the people. In this sense they form a partnership, though not a partnership of equals, and not a partnership in any transient sense.

For what I have in mind it would be hard to find a more eloquent expression than that of Edmund Burke when he was criticizing the contract theory of the state. Said he:

Society is, indeed, a contract . . . [B]ut the state ought not to be considered as nothing better than a partnership agreement in a trade of pepper and coffee, calico or tobacco . . . to be dissolved by the fancy of the partners. It is to be looked upon with other reverence . . . It is a partnership in all science, a partnership in all art, a partnership in every virtue and in all perfection. As the ends of such a partnership cannot be obtained in many generations, it becomes a partnership not only between those who are living, but between those who are living, those who are dead, and those who are to be born.

As the distinct and separate agents of the people of the United States, a great nation among nations and one that we hope will endure to promote human welfare through many generations(the national government and the state governments have a joint responsibility to respect each other, to consult with each other, and to cooperate with and assist each other to promote the national security and the general welfare.)t is in this broad meaning that I speak of a partnership in national-state relations.

(An "indestructible Union" of "indestructible States" is, then, the constitutional pattern of our government. It makes a certain amount of controversy inevitable—even desirable, so far as it protects individual liberties by bringing every major public action up for discussion before the court of public opinion.) While the constitutionality of the activities of the Union, acting through the national government, cannot, as I think I have shown, be seriously challenged, there is a broad area in which the deciding factor is one of policy.

It is largely because the constitutional powers of the national government are now so great that the questions of policy are so important. To be sure the people want their public services well administered, and want to have them available and as nearly uniform as possible throughout the nation. In many cases direct administration by the national government is the best way to achieve these results.

But there are other values also, other things that people want. Among these are the maintenance in full vigor of suitable state and local governments under local popular control. They desire a considerable amount of local freedom to conduct their public services and the ability to vary them and adapt them to local ideas and conditions. When Congress considers any new measure, therefore, it needs to consider carefully whether it is necessary or even desirable to push national action to the limits of national power. In many situations it may be better, as a matter of public policy, to assist and induce the state and local governments to perform the service up to at least a minimum standard.

The following chapters will present varying points of view on some of these issues of policy and finance.

☆

PART III
Issues of Policy and Finance

9

Dividing Up the Functions of Government

ONE of the usually unstated assumptions in any discussion of the allocation of governmental functions is the idea that there is a fixed number of public functions, and that any addition to the functions or activities at one level of government must result in a corresponding subtraction from the functions or activities at other levels. This is not in accordance with American experience or with reason.

The smallest rural units of government, townships and the smallest school districts, have, indeed, been losing functions to larger governmental units above them, to counties and consolidated school districts, for example, and many of the little units have passed from the scene. They lost out because they were losing population, they did not have adequate tax resources, and their jurisdictional limits were too small for the provision of modern roads, modern health and welfare services, modern graded schools, high schools, and the rest. These little rural units simply did not have the capacity to generate new public services to replace those which they proved progressively incapable of handling.

But has the disappearance of thousands of these small units of government meant a decline in public services and functions? Quite the contrary, I think. The people are now simply acting in and through larger local units of government, and these units are actually doing more than the eliminated small units did. The educational programs of the consolidated school are more complete than the one-room ungraded schools could provide. The county highway, health, and welfare departments are far more active in their respective functions than the townships could possibly be. The functions are still local, but they are local in larger and more effective units, and the people are thinking and acting in larger units and with wider horizons.

So much for the bottom local levels of the governmental pyramid. With variations, however, the conclusions are much the same at higher levels. National regulation of some aspects of labor organization, labor-management relations, and wages and hours for workers has been accompanied by increased state activity in these fields, where formerly the states were doing but little. Many states are showing a competitive spirit, to prove that they can regulate labor relations better than the national government, and Congress through the Taft-Hartley Act helped to open the way for more state activity.

Similarly, the federal grant-in-aid programs in highways, old age assistance, aid to dependent children, public housing, employment security, and numerous other fields have obviously resulted in increased state activities in these fields, just as they were intended to do. There is hardly any denial of this fact, and indeed the figures are hard to dispute. While the national government has been increasing its functions, there has been no subtraction from state activities and functions, but instead a considerable increase.

The fact of the matter is that the total amount of governmental activity has increased tremendously in the past fifty years in the United States, and is still going up; and that all levels of government, from counties, cities, and school districts up through the states to the national government, have shared in the increase. If we take expenditures as an index and, putting defense functions and expenditures on one side, consider only nondefense functions within the United States, it is obvious that the states and localities have increased their functions and activities far more than the national government has.

Nevertheless, as we have seen, there are from time to time protests that the national government has increased its activities too much, that it should "return" certain functions to the states. (Historically, of course, there is room for considerable doubt that the states ever exercised many of the functions in question.) The reasons advanced for "returning" the functions are several.

Let us consider first the argument that the smaller and more local government is always to be preferred to the larger and more central one. It is "closer to the people." It is more democratic. It permits big problems to be broken up into small ones, so that people can see and understand them, and then act according to their local needs and wishes.

There is obviously a continuing American prejudice (though not shared by all people) in favor of the small, relatively weak, and local, and against the larger, stronger, and more "distant" government. It is a fact, however, that increasing numbers of problems are big ones that cannot be broken up into small ones for local decision. Giant corporations and giant labor unions cannot be regulated and controlled by townships, counties, or even by single states. A government of ample size and power is required, one that encompasses all the major elements of the problem. Similarly a nationwide or even a statewide highway system cannot be left to townships or counties to construct and maintain according to their own standards and wishes. These examples are, perhaps, sufficient.

A second argument is that the more local governments will do a better, a more economical, and a more efficient job—alone—than a larger or more centralized one.

The argument has been made, for example, that townships should construct and maintain roads, assess property for taxation, and provide poor relief, in preference to having the counties or states do these things, and that small school districts should operate one-room ungraded schools in preference to having larger school systems in large consolidated districts or counties.

One factor that is often omitted from such arguments is that of the standard or quality of service to be rendered. Another commonly neglected factor is how anything like statewide uniformity of service can be obtained by such a method. It has long since become obvious in American experience that an expanding private economy with rising standards of living and education simply cannot be maintained without constant improvement and expansion of the public services, or without the planning and provision of many of those services on statewide, regional, and national bases for as much uniformity as can be obtained.

Horse-and-buggy government obviously will not suffice for handling the problems of a modern technological civilization. The high-powered automobile, the jet airplane, atomic power and atomic bombs, the advances in chemistry, in agriculture, in medicine and public health, and in science and education generally, for populations and areas as large as those of the United States, require adjustments in civilization and types of control and public service that simply cannot be fully provided by the small old units of government.

There remain many small and local problems that do not call for action by big government, but there is nothing to be gained except injured toes by kicking against the necessity of our times for large-scale government—government that can utilize the great technological and industrial advances of the age to best advantage, and also guard most effectively against their abuse with consequent dangers to the people.

A third contention is that where the national government has entered upon a service or function previously within the state sphere, confusion and wasteful duplication result.

In the labor relations field the confusion consists in having divergent state and national laws regulating collective bargaining and strikes, with resultant uncertainty among employers and employees as to which law applies to them. There is also some duplication of state and federal labor relations administration.

In a grant-in-aid field like highways the duplication consists in having federal highway engineers and inspectors in the states making their own checks and inspections of state highway plans and construction, together with an Office of Public Roads in Washington that may duplicate to some extent the work of state highway departments and that presumably would not be needed at all if the states had sole responsibility for the roads. Some state highway departments are today so well staffed, it is argued, that they could get along very well without the federal highway engineers and perhaps even without the United States Office of Public Roads.

As to the confusion between state and national regulatory laws, as in the labor relations field, this appears to be an unavoidable consequence of having a federal or two-level system of government. It is most noticeable in periods of change and when new laws are first being put into effect. After the preliminary shaking-down process the confusion is greatly diminished, as a rule, and the lines between national and state jurisdictions become fairly well known.

In the regulatory functions, there need be hardly any duplication of effort once the lines of authority are known. Indeed, as a source of information, research, and advice, the national agency often saves the state agencies a tremendous amount of duplication of each other's efforts. In addition to this there have been a number of significant experiments showing how national and state agencies can cooperate successfully even to the extent of using the same staff in performing common services, as in the enforcement of fair labor standards laws and in game-law enforcement.

The duplication that arises under grant-in-aid programs consists largely of the check and double-check varieties. Indeed the question may be raised whether it is not worth all it costs to have, for example, both national and state engineers pass on the plans for interstate highways, and to have both federal and state welfare administrators pass upon the annual plans and budgets for administering welfare programs. A federal post-audit of state expenditure of federal funds seems to be just good sense. Up to now there have been no adequate studies to show that anything is lost by such "duplications" of effort. What we do know is that the standards of performance in the federally aided state services are generally among the highest in the state administrations. May there not be some fairly obvious relationship here?

The charge of duplication against the national government by the state is obviously a two-edged sword, though it may have some value against a few federal activities. If the service to be rendered is one of national concern, and one in which some uniformity is desirable, the administration of it by some forty-eight separate states without any central coordination would obviously result in the maximum of duplication. The duplication is the least when the central government handles the function alone, without any reliance on the states. Compare, for instance, the management of the postal service, or social security, or the Veterans Administration, by the national government alone, with what it would be if divided up among the forty-eight states. If each state had to negotiate and keep in touch with each of the other forty-seven, keep full records of all "cases" that move from state to state, do all its own research and publishing of rules and forms, and so on and on, the duplication of labor would be almost infinite—if, indeed, it could be carried on at all even by the larger and wealthier states.

Intermediate between complete national administration and complete state administration of any service are two other methods: one, state control and administration with federal financial aid and subject to minimum uniform federal standards and supervision, and the other, a division of the service into separate activities some of which are performed nationally and the other and more local services carried out by the state and local governments. Public health falls under both these latter categories, because some state health services receive federal aid, while others are divided and performed partly by the national administration and partly, like environmental sanitation, largely by the states. The conservation of natural resources and other functions also fall more or less in both these intermediate classes.

Through the years in a number of these fields there has been so much common planning and conferring between national and state officials that the amount of duplication and of confusion has probably been reduced to a relatively low point. In general these wastes and duplications are such that they can be discovered by study and that reasonable men in legislative and executive departments are willing to eliminate them as they come to light. Unfortunately there are no satisfactory studies available to prove much one way or the other about the extent of the alleged wastes and duplication.

Implicit in the arguments for a "return" of functions to the states is the idea that there should be clearly established lists of mutually exclusive state and national functions under the Constitution. The original framers of the Constitution were wiser than to make any such attempt, and I submit that any lists that could be made up to show national and state functions separately would be unrealistic and unworkable. My reasons are essentially two.

In the first place no important broad function of government can be defined with such explicitness that it will not overlap or have some effect upon one or more of the other functions in the list. The experience of the United States has shown that national defense affects and is affected by health, education, science, technology, agriculture, natural resources, highways and transportation, and so on. Interstate commerce in the broad sense of intercourse affects or is affected by highways, health, safety, law enforcement, morals, and property rights, to name but a few functions. Education affects every function of life and government. To put education and health into separate categories raises many questions about who will handle health education, the sanitation of the schools, the authority of the health department over school children with contagious diseases, and so on. In short, human relations and activities constitute a web so intricately and closely woven that to touch a thread at any point is to be in contact, directly or indirectly, with every other point in the fabric. Actually there are no "walls of separation" in any real sense.

Secondly even if the functions of government could be put into certain crudely defined categories it is practically impossible to define at one time what the national, state, and local interests in any function will be even the day after the lists are made up. For example, it is conceivable that in the case of all-out war, and the invasion of the United States by an enemy, the role of the states in defense might have to be increased at once although today that role is very small. At present the national security interest in science education may be such as to warrant substantial national aid to step up the teaching of science in all secondary schools and colleges. American society and world conditions are both so dynamic, so full of the forces of fateful change, that any attempt to tie particular functions of government down to specific levels of government would soon prove out of date and harmful. Time and circumstances must be controlling factors in deciding what functions shall be performed by what governments.

With the exception of foreign affairs, most of defense, the coinage, and a few other almost exclusively national functions, American experience shows that in general we do not face here an "either/or" question—that a function must be *either* state *or* national. Many persons are enamored of the idea that education, for example, is entirely a state and not a national function. As a matter of fact, this has never been so, and simply cannot be. Education in its various aspects is a national *and* a state *and* a local *and* a private function or responsibility. The same is true of public health, law enforcement, and several other so-called functions of government.

Another idea that has a certain deceptive attractiveness about it is that some functions are primarily state or primarily national, with the implication that the *primarily* should control the allocation. There is a pleasing symmetry about such an idea, beginning with the *exclusively national* and running down through the *primarily national* to the *joint national and state* to *primarily state* and ending with the *exclusively state or state and local*.

Again this is not in accordance with American experience. In public health, for example, there have been from the beginning some national aspects and activities, some state, and some local. Public health work did not begin as a comprehensive program at any level of government, but instead began at different levels of government with specific activities like the quarantine of ships, the regulation of burials, and the location and cleansing of slaughterhouses. It was only after many of these had been started at different levels of government that the broad concept of modern

public health work was developed and that people began to ta
of public health as *primarily* a state function.

I think that the *primarily this or that* approach is of relatively
little value also because it provides no objective standard and indeed hardly any historical standard to guide one in applying it.
The application depends unduly upon tradition, feeling, and opinion factors. That under the powers reserved to them by the Constitution the states have broad responsibilities for the protection
of the public health is an accepted fact, and I think as it should
be. But there are some things, especially in environmental sanitation in urban places, that city governments can deal with more
effectively than the states, and there are others that are jurisdic-
tionally and perhaps financially beyond their powers, that only
the nation can deal with adequately.

Once we recognize that where the national interest in correct-
ing some evil or in further advancing the nation's welfare is important enough the national government has a duty to act, we are
on the way to laying down some principles for the allocation of
functional activities. It is my considered judgment that there is a
national interest in a function and a duty of the national government to act either to remove or prevent an evil or to promote a
good when any of the following aspects of American life are significantly affected:

The external relations of the nation, so-called "foreign affairs"

National defense against any possible foreign enemy

Internal security against sedition, subversion, large-scale violence, threats to the republican form of government

The preservation of complete internal free trade throughout
the nation

The protection of civil liberties, equal protection of the laws,
and due process of law

The national economic health, including high levels of employment, control of money and credit conditions, prevention of excessive inflation or deflation, aid to large-scale "sick industries" of

permanent national interest (mining, textiles, agriculture, etc., have all been in this condition at times)

The conservation of natural resources

An adequate system of national transportation and communication, including transport by air, water, railroads, and highways

The education, health, and welfare of the people in all respects that seriously affect other national interests, including welfare aid to people and areas stricken by major disasters

The preservation of the Constitution, the national government, and the national political processes, such as free elections, freedom of political participation and discussion, and a free press

The preservation of a strong system of state and local government for all the useful purposes of such a system

Because the states are also constitutional agents of the people of the United States, each within its own area responsible for promoting the welfare of the people, I hold that there is also a state, or state and local, interest in all the major functions of government, and a state duty to act, except where the national government has exclusive control or has "occupied the field," to promote the security, health, and welfare of the people. Every state has a special interest in those conditions that are more or less peculiar and local to it, but the states also have wider and more general interests. To the extent, therefore, that the national government has not "occupied the field"—and the non-occupied areas are wide indeed—the states have a duty to act.

These general principles of allocation do not, of course, solve the practical problem involved. Believing as I do that it is unrealistic to try to lay down in advance a comprehensive allocation of all internal functions of government among national, state, and local governments, how would I have the necessary day-to-day decisions made?

I think there is no better way than the one that is now followed. When any proposal comes up for a new state or national function, have it studied thoroughly by persons competent in that field. Provide for adequate publicity of the evil that is to be remedied, the facts that bear upon it, the bills that are proposed to remedy it, and other pertinent data. Let the opinions of the best experts available, both inside the various levels of government and in private life, be heard.

If the proposal is for national action, let Congress debate the matter fully before acting. In the two houses of Congress will be found representatives of all state and local interests and of many points of view. Because there is no scientific way of deciding such questions, this full consideration of the issues offers the best practical substitute. If the members of Congress are willing to pass the bill, knowing full well how they probably will be attacked in their home states for their actions, one can be reasonably sure that there is a sufficient national interest in the new function to justify it, at least on a trial basis.

If the function is one that is proposed for a particular state, let it there go through the same democratic process of study, hearings, and debate, and a clear-cut vote in both houses of the legislature. If it passes, there is reasonable assurance that the measure is one that informed and responsible officials and legislators believe to be in the interest of the people of the state. If the measure later proves to be undesirable, it can be repealed.

The fact that the national government has the power to act in some field or function does not mean that it needs always to act, or that it needs to cover the entire field when it does act. Its action should go far enough to protect and promote the national interest effectively, but that is all. Beyond that it is more in the national interest, I believe, to leave matters to private action and to state and local action. Thus, many needs will be taken care of privately, as I think they should, and others will be provided for by various combinations of national, state, and local action, a result I believe to be desirable.

To achieve the maximum goal of public welfare, there is need to utilize the services and the resources of every level of government, and in every part of the nation. On grounds of greater efficiency one level or class of units may be chosen for this or that particular service or part of a major function, but all are likely to have some contribution to make. This can be illustrated from national defense, law enforcement, conservation, public health, and many other fields.

In every field then the question is this: What specific division of labor and what combination of national, state, and local authorities working together will produce the best results in administering the function without endangering the essentials of the United States constitutional system or sacrificing any other recognized national interest?

The arrangements that I visualize, therefore, are not based upon the assignment of this whole function to one level of government exclusively, and that whole function to another level exclusively (beyond what the Constitution already prescribes), but the progressive development of better and better ways for all levels of government to cooperate in performing functions.

This is the course upon which the American system of government has already embarked, and I hold its results in general to have been good.

10

Tax Sources and Overlapping Taxes

Money is, with propriety, considered as the vital principle of the body politic; as that which sustains its life and motion, and enables it to perform its most essential functions. A complete power, therefore, to procure a regular and adequate supply of it, as far as the resources of the community will permit, may be regarded as an indispensable ingredient in every constitution."

These are the words of Alexander Hamilton in *The Federalist*, no. 30, the first of seven essays (nos. 30–36) in which this master of public finance made the initial analysis of the respective taxing powers of the national government and of the states under the Constitution. The lack of an effective power to raise money for national purposes was one of the chief defects of the Articles of Confederation, and the framers of the original Constitution of the United States had seen to it in their draft that this defect in national power would be overcome.

From the days of the Revolution down to the present the relative powers of taxation of the national and state governments have been something of a bone of contention; and in times of crises, like wars and depressions, when taxes are increased and multiplied, the debate over taxing policy usually develops considerable heat. Instead of heat I hope that this chapter will contribute a little light.

At the very beginning of government under the Constitution, the national government's revenues exceeded those of all the states combined and probably exceeded both state and local revenues. The state governments were doing very little and had but small need for revenues. The local governments were more active in performing functions, but, instead of resorting entirely to taxation and the cash support of government services, they required the citizens to perform some services directly, like road repairs and jury service, with little or no compensation, while for other services the citizens paid fees to particular public officers instead of paying taxes into a local treasury. Certain public services were performed by private companies—toll road, toll bridge, and ferry companies, for example—and others by local citizens acting individually or in groups, like volunteer fire companies. The national government, on the other hand, had to have money. It had a war debt to pay, including the state debts it had assumed, it had war veterans to pay off, an army and a navy to recruit, support, and train, a foreign service to support, and other functions for which neither chartered private companies nor volunteer local services would do.

The national government under the Constitution relied largely upon import or customs duties as a source of revenue, but it also introduced an excise tax on alcohol and later a few other taxes from time to time. State and local governments relied mainly on a group of taxes that impinged on property owners and that in the course of time became consolidated more or less in every state into a sort of general property tax. There was some state and local experimenting with other taxes, but by and large both the states and their local units relied on the general property tax for revenue down through the nineteenth century and until about World War I. In short there was a largely unplanned "separation of tax sources" between the national government on one side and the state and local governments on the other. Overlapping of taxes was exceptional and relatively unimportant.

Except during the Civil War, when national taxes increased substantially and a national income tax was used, the taxes levied during the nineteenth century by local governments, which had been steadily increasing, were generally greater than those of the state and national governments. The states were usually in third place. So small were the expenditures and taxes of the state governments that the local governments led them all the way. The needs of the national government were also ordinarily so small that, with customs revenues and a few selective excise taxes such as those on liquors and tobacco, plus some revenues from the public lands, the national budget showed frequent surpluses both before the Civil War and again toward the end of the century.

This almost idyllic state of the public finances (as seen in retrospect, of course) was due for a rapid change. Industrialization, urbanization, numerous technological changes of great social consequences, the increased travel and mobility of the population, scientific discoveries, the spread of education, and a rapidly rising standard of living brought with them increasing public demands upon the public services. National, state, and local governments all began to respond to the new demands. Public budgets became harder to balance. More revenues had to be sought. Neither the old revenue system of the state and local governments, dependent primarily upon general property taxes, nor the traditional revenue system of the national government, with its reliance upon customs duties and a few select excise taxes, would any longer suffice.

In the depression of the early 1890s a number of experiments with new taxes were made by both the state and national governments. In 1894 Congress imposed a new income tax with rates that were geographically uniform throughout the nation, but the national government was rudely shocked in 1895 when the Supreme Court ruled that the tax was unconstitutional. Some of the states also were rebuffed, though mainly by their state supreme courts and under their state constitutions, when they attempted to impose taxes that did not conform to the property-tax pattern. A period of indecision ensued while one experiment after another was tried.

By 1913, however, a great change was in the making. In 1909 Congress imposed a corporation excise or income tax, and by 1913 three fourths of the states had approved the Sixteenth Amendment to the United States Constitution, as submitted to them by Congress—an amendment that opened the door to national taxation of all incomes. Congress promptly enacted a personal income tax. Since that time the two national income taxes, corporate and personal, have become the main sources of the national government's revenue. But in times of depression and even more in times of all-out wars, these too have been found insufficient. As a result Congress has also enacted a series of selective excise taxes, such as those on motor fuels, automobiles and their parts and accessories, estates, gifts, telephone bills, admissions, transportation, and luxuries.

While the national government was thus reaching out for new sources of revenue the states were doing the same. Every state was to some extent getting away from excessive reliance on the property tax and was broadening its tax base and diversifying its tax system. Each state has autonomy in these matters so long as it stays within constitutional limits. As a result, every state pursues a different policy, as it has a right to do, and no two states have the same tax system. Even when two states tax incomes, for example, or tax motor fuels, tobacco, or liquor, no two states will have exactly the same law or the same rates of tax. Furthermore, no state is likely even to adopt the same definitions as Congress has enacted for a cognate national tax. This is what must be expected in a federal system where the member states have real autonomy.

The net result is that Congress, moving in with a solid front from one side, and the state legislatures, advancing in broken and uneven ranks from the other, have come to occupy to some extent but in varied ways a number of the same tax "fields." By 1953, *in addition to the taxes imposed by the national government,* 47 states had "death taxes" (estate, inheritance); 12 states had gift taxes; 48 states had motor fuel taxes; 32 states had corporate income taxes; 31 states had individual income taxes; 29 states had distilled spirits taxes, while 17 others had liquor monopolies; and 41 states had cigarette taxes. State general sales taxes in 32 states also overlapped to some extent various national selective excise taxes. The bulk of the revenues of both the national and state governments come from these overlapping levies.

This, in short, gives a rough sketch of the "problem of overlapping taxes" that has been discussed in many conferences and official bodies for the past generation.

At least two other factors have tended to create discontent and a feeling of frustration at the state level in the overlapping of taxes.

During World War I and its immediate aftermath, during the Great Depression of the 1930s, during World War II, and then during the "cold war" and the hot war in Korea, the demands for revenue for national defense and security, and for national relief measures, were so great and so overriding that the state legislatures felt they had to hold back the expansion and improvement of state services. To some extent these fell behind during the period when national services required most of the revenue that the people could be induced to part with. At the same time the national revenues from taxes came to exceed by a wide margin, especially in war and defense periods, the total amounts of taxes collected by the state and local governments combined. This was a great reversal of positions.

Along with these defense and depression crises came inflation, in spurts and jerks that could not be predicted or provided against. While inflation and war-stimulated prosperity caused state and local revenues to go up to some extent even at the old tax rates, the prices of materials and of personal services rose even faster, so that state and local budgets got out of balance and had to be adjusted even in times of evident prosperity. Taxpayers were getting more income, and at most times were enjoying a rising standard of living, but state legislators held back on tax increases, fearing that the people could not be induced to accept tax increases as fast as state and local officials felt there was a need for them. Except for a short time in World War II state and local budgets increased from year to year, state budgets more than local ones, but they never seemed to cover all the needs and demands.

It was in this sort of setting that leaders in state governments began to complain of the "encroachments" of the national government upon the "proper" tax sources of the states, and to denounce the national "usurpations" of such tax fields.

The outcry against overlapping taxes has been directed mainly against the national government as the alleged encroacher and usurper. It has been voiced primarily in the interest of the states, while the local governments, which have had an even harder time trying to make ends meet against state competition for revenues, have received relatively less attention and sympathy.

State officials have not been alone in presenting objections to overlapping taxes, however. Most taxpayers' associations, chambers of commerce, and similar groups have been active in raising the issue. They represent private interests that object to the burden of tax payment in general, and to the extra compliance costs that are involved in some cases—like the payment of income taxes to both the national and state governments but under different laws that require quite different calculations of taxable income.

Let us look first at the general tax situation, and then take up a few specific cases and proposals for change.

There is no serious allegation that the United States Constitution puts unjustifiable restrictions upon state taxing powers. The taxing powers of the states under the Constitution are, with a few relatively unimportant and justifiable exceptions, concurrent with those of the nation. That is a major reason why there can be so much overlapping.

The states are expressly forbidden to tax either imports or exports, and also to levy "any duty of tonnage," which means a tax upon ships according to tonnage each time they enter or leave a harbor. In the interests of freedom for interstate and foreign commerce these are surely defensible restrictions.

In addition the Supreme Court has consistently held that the states may not tax the property, functions, and instrumentalities of the national government, and that they may not impose *discriminatory* or *unduly burdensome* taxes upon interstate commerce or on those who engage in such commerce. These restrictions are justified on the ground that the power to tax may be the power to destroy, and that the states have no right to destroy the national government or the commerce and other interests that it was set up to protect. But it is within the power of Congress to relax these restrictions upon state taxing powers, and Congress has done so in a number of instances, some of which I shall mention below.

In cases that involve state taxing power the Supreme Court has always kept in mind the needs of the states for revenues. In recent decades it has been noticeably liberal in upholding state tax laws— but this is not the place to go into the details on this complex subject.

Neither is it often or seriously charged that the national government has acted unconstitutionally in enacting taxes that overlap upon state taxes. Of course there are individuals who think of every tax or law that does not conform to their ideas of what is right and proper as being unconstitutional. Even taxes that merely depart from traditional ideas of the "absolute right of property" are sometimes denounced as violations of the Constitution.

To repeat the pertinent constitutional provision: "The Congress shall have power to lay and collect taxes, duties, imposts, and excises, to pay the debts and provide for the common defense and general welfare of the United States . . ." A broader statement of the power of Congress to tax might have been possible, but was hardly necessary. The power as stated is without limits as to the types, rates, or amounts of taxes that may be imposed by Congress. The power is comprehensive and plenary, and the acts that Congress passes under this power are supreme over those of the states. There is today no substantial doubt about the basic validity of the national taxes now in effect.

In enacting national tax laws Congress has uniformly considered the national government's needs for revenue, and the productiveness, feasibility, and justice from a national point of view of one tax as against another. All its voting members come from states and they unavoidably think also of the effect of a new or increased national tax upon state sources of revenue, and upon any industry or interest affected, and whether it is going to carry a disproportionate tax burden.

Congress probably has made mistakes in its selections of tax sources, and in other provisions of its tax laws from time to time, but such mistakes are not the result of either thoughtlessness or deliberate intent to encroach upon and to hamper the states. There is probably no class of bills that receives more careful scrutiny in the committee rooms and the halls of Congress than bills to impose or to change taxes.

On the other side there is a considerable body of evidence that the members of Congress are solicitous about the preservation and the strengthening of the state taxing powers. For example, although national banks are instrumentalities of the national government and were once held immune from state taxation, Congress many decades ago passed an act, still in effect, to permit states to tax the capital of such banks on the same basis as other monied capital. Congress has likewise enacted laws to permit states to tax as income the salaries of national officers and employees who are resident in the states, and to extend their taxing powers over persons and private property on federal reservations. With the tacit or express consent of Congress certain activities of nationally owned government corporations and of contractors doing work for the national government are also subject to state taxation under Supreme Court decisions.

The effectiveness of state taxes is in some instances endangered by competition between states for revenues, and also by the possibilities of private evasion through interstate commerce and the postal system carrying goods into states without payment of the state tax.

In the development of their estate and inheritance taxes the majority of the states found that they were handicapped because a few states refused to enact such taxes and instead advertised themselves as havens for those who wished to avoid paying such taxes. "Move to State X. No Inheritance Tax. No Income Tax." But in 1926 Congress imposed a nationwide estate tax and allowed a reduction or credit of 80 per cent to anyone who had paid a corresponding state tax in the amount necessary. Although Nevada still has no inheritance or estate tax (at the present writing), no taxpayer can save anything on estate tax merely by residence in that state. All other states fell into line with the national law, and

158

so all states can have effective death taxes. However, there is one quirk to the present situation that will be mentioned later.

State cigarette taxes illustrate the jurisdictional difficulty. It is easy to send cigarettes from any state into a cigarette-taxing state in such a way as to evade the tax. In foreign commerce this is called smuggling. Congress only recently passed the so-called Jenkins Act to make it a federal offense to do this with cigarettes, and prosecutions under this act have already begun. Other examples of congressional acts to help the states overcome jurisdictional difficulties could be cited. All that the states have to do, as a rule, to get national protective legislation for their tax laws is to present facts that reveal a substantial evil and to propose a reasonable law to overcome it.

Another evidence of the solicitude of Congress for protecting state and local revenues is found in various specific laws by which national government agencies that take over previously taxable property in any place are authorized and in effect required to make payments to the local governments "in lieu of taxes." The property is not then subject to direct local taxes, but a reasonably equivalent payment is made. Federally aided public housing falls within this rule. The present laws on this subject do not cover all situations as yet, but various comprehensive bills are now receiving favorable attention in Congress.

The difficulties in the tax field of which the states complain are not, therefore, that the Constitution is too restrictive on their taxing powers, or that Congress and the Supreme Court have been ungenerous in their treatment of state taxing powers. The difficulty as I see it is primarily that both national and state governments have been increasing their functions and activities and their needs for revenue at the same time and at a fairly rapid rate. The states collectively and the national government have to get their revenues out of the same people and the same national economic system.

The states have been unfortunate in that they have had to increase their revenues in a period when national defense needs have been almost overwhelming. Even in unitary countries like Great

Britain the needs of war and defense take precedence over non-defense functions. State and local governments at such a time necessarily have to yield to the nation's prior claims for revenue for defense purposes. In recent years from 65 to 90 per cent of national government expenditures and taxes have gone into defense activities. Had the nation been equally prosperous and without war, I believe the fiscal story of the states would have been entirely different, but this is a proposition that I could not really prove.

Because national dominance over tax revenue sources in times of war and defense is hard to attack directly, the arguments of the states have turned largely against overlapping as such and a few related points. But if overlapping is bad as such, then a *separation of sources* must be considered better, and this is the direction in which the states' arguments have tended.

One argument seems to be that certain taxes are more "proper" for the states than for the national government, and that therefore these taxes should be left exclusively to the states. A tax may be more proper for the state than for the national government because it is a tax upon some essentially local activity (like a tax on admissions to theaters, on local telephone bills, and on club dues); or because the tax can be more effectively administered by state and local governments than by the national government, or at least equally well administered, which may be especially true of taxes on essentially local activities; or because the states, all or some of them, employed the tax first, and successfully, and that therefore it should be left to them, for otherwise the national government would be usurping a proper state and local tax.

The arguments as to priority in time are not, it seems to me, of great importance for public policy. Whether the national government, or one or more states, first taxed incomes, inheritances, tobacco, or motor fuels, can hardly be determinative of what is best for the national interest, which must always come first. Under the Articles of Confederation the states alone levied customs duties, but the Constitution put an end to that and assigned this revenue source to the national government in the interests of national unity and internal free trade. Otherwise the Constitution establishes a condition of almost completely concurrent taxing powers for the nation and the states, and the fact that one has entered a field is no bar to the other's doing so. There have been "encroachments" of this nature from both sides, and any attempt to establish which had temporal priority would be as futile as it would be inconclusive.

The important question is what is best for the country as a whole when a specific tax allocation is being discussed. Should the national government alone, or only the states, levy taxes in a certain field; or should the national government levy what it wants in its own way, leaving each state free to levy what it wants in its own way or to make no levy at all? The latter system (free choice for both levels, with resultant overlapping for any tax, in anywhere from one to forty-eight states) is the system that now prevails, and it provides substantial autonomy or freedom of choice for both levels of government. If real self-government for the states is what is desired, this free-choice arrangement on tax sources should not be lightly changed.

From the national viewpoint the free-choice system is an important factor in national security. "When the chips are down," when the nation is engaged in all-out war for its existence, there should be no restrictions and no limits on the national taxing power. Alexander Hamilton made this point in *The Federalist*, no. 31: "As the duties of superintending the national defence and of securing the public peace against foreign or domestic violence involve a provision for casualties and dangers to which no possible limits can be assigned, the power of making that provision ought to know no other bounds than the exigencies of the nation and the resources of the community."

But the fact that the national government needs to have an *unlimited power to tax* when the nation stands in greatest peril is no reason why it has to use all its taxing powers all the time. The policy of Congress has been to impose additional taxes in times of war and during great efforts to prepare for defense, and to relinquish some of these taxes, especially the minor ones and such as overlap or duplicate state taxes, when the nation no longer needs them. There is no point in holding onto all the wartime sources of revenue, with their administrative costs and difficulties, when the need is no longer urgent; but the right to impose such taxes again when needed should always be retained.

If the United States is now entering upon such a postwar period, an issue that is still doubtful, this may be a time to relinquish temporarily certain taxes.

If and when this is to be done the question of what are "proper" or appropriate taxes for state administration should enter into the calculation—because a number of states on the prowl for new sources of revenue may wish to take up what is relinquished. Also the elimination of overlapping taxes should be considered. Certain wartime taxes on activities of a local rather than interstate nature (club dues, local telephone bills, admissions to theaters, etc.) are of this character, and they are also of such a nature that any states not having such taxes already could enact state taxes to replace the national tax, and could also successfully administer them. This tapering off of national taxes and corresponding increases in state and local taxes in postwar periods is a normal occurrence in the United States and in other countries. For the time being it may result in more separation of tax sources and less overlapping.

Certain other general objections to having both national and state taxes in the same field are worthy of brief mention.

When the taxpayer has to prepare both a national and a state income tax return, or estate tax form, he will have more difficulty and spend more time and money than he would if he had only one to make out. Along with this goes some additional expense to the public in the maintenance of separate national and state agencies to administer the tax. These extra costs and expenses seem burdensome, but as arguments for abolishing either the national or the state tax concerned, where the tax yield is substantial, they fall short of the mark. They may point to the possible desirability of joint collection, or a single collection with a division of the revenues, or some such arrangement, but the state governments, I think wisely, show no enthusiasm for giving up their present tax autonomy just to make the tax administration easier or compliance less time-consuming and expensive.

Of course in some fields of overlapping taxes, so called, the situation is quite different. The national tax on motor fuels, for example, is collected from the producers at the refineries and such places, while the state tax is collected primarily from the first importers into the state or from road users at the pumps where the tanks of trucks, buses, and private cars are filled. The two collections are from different groups of payers, at different places, on different quantities, and under different conditions. There is here no such double compliance problem as the individual payer of income tax faces. Most other national excise taxes are also collected from the producer, while state and local sales taxes are collected by the retailers. Double compliance costs are, therefore, not a necessary concomitant of all so-called overlapping taxes. Indeed some taxes that are classed as overlapping are so only in part.

The idea that overlapping taxes cause reductions in tax yields is not usually pressed very strongly. Any tax that is passed along to and must be paid by the buyer of the product no doubt has some effect in reducing sales and thus also reducing tax yields. Whether the tax is in one bite or two should hardly make much difference, if the total tax is the same and the price is otherwise unchanged.

But this raises the question of "taxes on taxes." The gasoline one buys for his family car reaches the pump at the filling station with the 2¢ per gallon national tax already paid and included in the base price at the pump. The state tax, let us say 4¢, is then added to the base price to make the full price to be paid. The two taxes add up to 6¢, but the second or state tax includes no tax *upon* the 2¢ national tax.

On the other hand, if a *percentage* tax is applied by the state, as in the case of most general sales taxes, then a tax upon a tax may result if the national excise tax is included in the base price on which the retail price and the state's sales tax are figured. Of course any state that wishes to do so can provide a remedy for this difference by placing its tax upon the wholesale price of the article less the national tax or on some other tax-free basis. If it does not do this the state treasury is the beneficiary to the extent of the state tax upon the national tax on this article.

All in all, the objections to overlapping taxes on the grounds of compliance costs, yields, and "taxes on taxes" do not get to the central issues between separation and nonseparation of sources of revenue.

Another objection to overlapping taxes is that national and state legislatures, acting independently in taxing the same subject, may impose unduly heavy burdens upon it, while other tax subjects escape taxation or carry lighter loads. This certainly is a possibility, but the thoroughness with which tax measures are discussed in Congress and in state legislatures, the interchange of information between them, and the ability of pressure groups to present facts and exert influence, make it unlikely that relative burdens on this and that tax subject will not be considered. Indeed if national and state governments were constitutionally restricted to separate tax sources, and one, say the national government, suddenly had to increase its revenue greatly, as in the case of a war, that one would certainly have to put severe burdens upon its taxable subjects, while the tax subjects of the states would be spared important increases.

Some commentators have noted that in the range of the overlapping national and state taxes, the national government gets most of its revenues from progressive income taxes, with higher rates on higher incomes, based on ability to pay, while the states now put most of their emphasis on the more regressive taxes, or taxes that weigh more heavily on poor people, notably on general sales taxes. This is not something that has been forced upon the states by the national government but is a matter of state choice. By their own decisions one third of the states have no personal income taxes, while those that do have them do not have rates as steeply progressive as the national rates are. Congress has made all state income taxes paid in a year deductible from a person's income in figuring his national income tax. Thus the states have much to gain and little to lose by having their own income taxes, but many of them cling to more regressive tax systems. The principal overlapping of taxes is therefore in the middle reaches of the tax scale, between the most progressive and the most regressive.

Let us consider now proposed specific shifts in taxes.

Although much has been said by state governors against national and state overlapping of taxes generally, and about national encroachments on the proper spheres of state taxation, the governors' demands have not been extreme. They have not advocated a complete separation of national and state tax sources. In recent years the resolutions of the Governors' Conference, which may be taken as some evidence of what the state governments would like, have related primarily to three specific fields of taxation—inheritance and estate taxes, the national tax on motor fuels, and the national share of the payroll tax for employment security.

Various committees of citizens and individual tax authorities have made more systematic proposals, some of which go much farther in the direction of separating national from state tax sources. One of these plans, submitted by Roswell Magill of New York to the Committee on Federal-State Relations of the first Hoover Commission in 1948, and reissued in 1953 by the Chamber of Commerce of the United States, proposed that the states get out of the taxation of individual incomes, tobacco, and liquors (except for license taxes), and that the national government relinquish its estate tax, gasoline tax, taxes on admissions and club dues, and taxes on retail sales like those on jewelry, furs, and other items. This plan, which included also proposals to discontinue federal grants-in-aid for highways and to end the national government's retention of any part of the unemployment compensation payroll tax, was clearly aimed at a substantial elimination of overlaps in taxes at the points of greatest irritation without seriously altering the potential revenues of either the national or the state governments. The governors in their resolutions have not gone this far and have not proposed that the states relinquish any present taxes.

The 1953 resolution of the Governors' Conference on estate

165

and inheritance taxes reads: "The federal estate tax imposed in 1926 has been amended by supplemental increases which result in great inequity to the states. This tax should be simplified, integrated and modernized."

Under the 1926 national estate tax each state could get as much as 80 per cent of the total proceeds of the national tax imposed upon estates within its jurisdiction, but, leaving this law intact and unchanged, Congress later enacted supplemental rates of taxation from which the states get nothing. As a result in 1953 the national treasury received practically 80 per cent of the proceeds (more than $881 million) and the states 20 per cent (about $222 million). Thus the revenue positions of the two levels of government under this tax have been almost reversed, owing to no important decreases on the state side but to great increases on the side of the national government.

No one seems seriously to doubt the need for some national law like that of 1926 in order to keep the states in line and to prevent any state from again becoming a haven free from estate taxes, but the states want more of the revenue from the estate tax, up to 100 per cent.

The reasoning on the basis of propriety is that the states make and enforce the laws by which property is transferred at death and therefore are entitled to taxes imposed on such transfers. Unfortunately this argument proves either too much or too little. The states make the basic laws on many other taxable subjects like the payment of wages and salaries, corporate distribution of dividends, and the manufacture and sale of products like liquor, tobacco, and automobiles. To give the states priority in taxation on any such ground would raise serious questions about a number of sources of national revenue.

That the states may need more revenue and that the estate tax is one source from which they could get it without greatly reducing the national revenues is a frank statement with which hardly anyone could disagree. If the time comes when the national government can afford to do so, it should share a larger portion of the estate tax revenue with the states, or reduce its own rates and leave each state to increase its own rates as it pleases.

Another resolution of the 1953 Governors' Conference reads: "Gasoline taxes are peculiarly appropriate for imposition by states to finance the construction and maintenance of their highway systems. The federal government should withdraw from this field, with accompanying adjustments in the federal aid highway program."

As an emergency measure to produce a national revenue in the hard times of the Great Depression, Congress imposed its first tax upon gasoline in 1932. This tax has been continued through several changes and renewals since then as a source of general revenue for the national treasury. It is collected without great cost from the producers. The current rate of 2¢ per gallon is applied to most of the gasoline produced and not merely to that portion which is used upon the highways.

The national revenue from this tax is not directly related, in law or in fact, to the federal aid given to the states for highways. Congress appropriated money for highway aids from general funds for more than fifteen years before the gasoline tax was imposed, and the revenues from the tax have never been dedicated by Congress to highway aids, nor have the aids even been equated in amounts with the revenue from the tax.

Nevertheless the idea exists in the minds of many persons that all the gas tax revenue *ought* to be dedicated to road purposes. Many reason that the need for roads is so great, and the motor fuels are to such a large extent used in vehicles on the highways, that there is a natural connection between the tax and the highways.

This may be taking too narrow a view of the problem of financing government services. The need is great for national defense, also, and for education, health, and welfare services. Who can say which need is the greatest at any one time? And can it not be argued that all persons, businesses, and activities have an obligation to assist in the support of all the services of government?

167

Why should not the gasoline industry pay something toward other functions of government, as liquor and tobacco do?

When a particular tax is dedicated or earmarked to be used exclusively for one service, that service may easily become overexpanded in comparison with others. Those services, like health and education, with which no particular revenue or tax is directly connected may suffer from neglect. The whole idea of tax dedications to particular functions is, therefore, condemned by most authorities on public finance. They feel that a government should get its revenues wherever it can, and by the fairest general rules that can be devised, and should put all the revenues into a general fund. Then the needs of all the services should be balanced against each other and the money for each be appropriated from the common treasury. Only in this way can there be effective budgeting and adequate legislative control over public revenues and expenditures. When this course is not followed there is competition among pressure groups to get sales taxes, income taxes, and other revenues, as well as gasoline taxes, dedicated to particular services. In some states this has reached the point where the planning and budgeting of state revenues and expenditures are largely ineffective.

When the national government does not need all the present revenue from the motor fuel taxes, it should consider reducing the rate of the tax. I believe, however, that it should keep its hand in this field as long as it maintains a policy of selective excise taxes on tobacco, liquor, and other products. If it ever adopts a general manufacturers' excise tax, motor fuels should come under it along with other products.

If selective excises such as the United States government imposes can be justified, it is hard to find one better than the 2¢ United States motor fuel tax for reaching practically everybody in the nation. Even families and individuals who do not own and operate automobiles are affected, since they use bus transportation and receive deliveries of goods by truck. Thus this is in a sense an excise or sales tax of the widest possible incidence. In addition it is a tax on pleasure and on luxury expenses, since much travel by automobile comes in this category.

If and when Congress reduces its tax on motor fuels it should not be expected either that all the states will take up the slack and impose a state tax to equal that relinquished, or that the states that do impose an additional 2¢ gas tax will acquire additional revenue in the proportion of their highway needs or any other needs. Two things we positively know about the states are these: They never all do the same thing, or do anything in the same way; and revenue potentialities are never distributed among all the states in proportion to their service needs.

Admissions, club dues, and local telephone taxes are taxes of a type that the state and local governments can effectively administer. Whenever the national government no longer needs the present revenues from these taxes it should reduce them (as, indeed, it is already doing). The states have always had the power to levy such taxes, and they can do about them as they please— and perhaps more easily when the national tax is reduced or eliminated.

Unemployment compensation taxes present a unique problem. To make the problem clear, it is necessary to review briefly the situation described in Chapter 2. When Congress enacted the Social Security Law twenty years ago, it provided for a 3 per cent national tax on payrolls out of which to pay unemployment compensation. But in any state whose legislature enacted an approved law and tax for an unemployment compensation system, the tax-paying employers would not have to pay both the state and national tax. Instead an offset or credit up to 90 per cent of the national tax would be allowed to any employer who had paid or was liable to pay the state tax. Thus 2.7¢ per dollar of payroll would be credited to the state from each 3¢ of the national tax, and only .3¢ was to go to the national treasury for national purposes. By agreement between each state and the national government, the state would administer the employment security system, while the national government would serve as custodian of all the funds and would also pay the reasonable administrative expenses of the state unemployment compensation agency. Every state in the Union soon passed the necessary laws.

The national agency charged with supervising the state administrative agencies reviews their budgets and Congress sets the amount of money to be granted to each state agency for administrative purposes. For some states the amount allowed is less than the revenue of the .3¢ that the national government collects from employers in those states, while in other states it is more. The total amount allowed in any year to all states for administration of these laws is regularly less than the total amount received by the national treasury from the .3¢ tax. The difference each year, usually more than $100 million, has been retained in the national treasury and used like any other money for several purposes. This has been described as "shortchanging" the states and as depriving them of some revenue that "belongs" to them.

The national government needs to keep a hand in the unemployment compensation system in order to ensure that the system will be nationwide in scope. In times of war and other great emergencies this may be of signal national importance. But a payroll tax is an unfortunate type of tax for general revenue purposes, and the amount gained for the national treasury is not significant in this instance. Many have felt that a way should be found to credit the state employment security funds with the net surplus after all administrative expenses, both national and state, have been paid.

Recently such a way has been found. Under the so-called Reed Act of 1954 after state and national administrative expenses connected with the employment security system have been paid, the balance of revenues from the national government's .3 per cent tax on payrolls will go first into an insurance fund to protect all state unemployment compensation systems, and second into the state funds from which benefits are paid. No part of the revenues will be available for general national expenditures.

Although there is some difference in emphasis, I think that the tax allocation propositions I present below are in line with the general position taken recently by the Governors' Conferences.

Some of my propositions, however, have little or no reference to the limited and specific proposals in the resolutions of the Governors' Conferences. I have in mind also various proposals from other sources—proposals that are not only more sweeping but are also in some instances, I believe, contrary to the best interests of the nation. These other proposals must be dealt with if the background of national-state financial relations is to be understood.

Putting the needs for national security and national welfare ahead of all other political considerations, I think the American people would be wise to resist every effort to place constitutional limits on the national taxing and spending powers. The Governors' Conference has wisely proposed no such limitation, but other persons have done so, and some of them have set forth their proposals in the name of states' rights and the preservation of the states. Alexander Hamilton in *The Federalist* (nos. 30, 31) proved irrefutably that a national government whose responsibilities for national defense and welfare are illimitable and utterly unpredictable needs an unlimited power of raising a national revenue. The national taxing power was so hardly won and has been so indispensable to the national safety and well-being that any substantial limitation of the power would, in my opinion, be a dangerous backward step.

I believe also that flexibility of taxes with overlapping is preferable to a separation of sources. The present allocation of taxing powers under which both the national and state governments have a wide range of free choice to levy various taxes has proved to be a strong feature of the American federal system. Not only is the national government with its priority and supremacy able to protect and to utilize its essential tax sources, but in addition each state is able to have its own structure of state and local taxes in accordance with its own policies, needs, and circumstances. In matters of taxation each state is truly autonomous and not dependent upon any acts of Congress or agreements with the national government such as a comprehensive constitutional or even statutory separation of major sources would entail.

The present system is flexible and viable to a high degree, whereas a general constitutional or contractual separation of sources would be rigid and restrictive, and would probably lead to unforeseen results. (For various minor taxes a certain amount of practical separation of sources is, of course, more helpful than harmful.) Among other points in favor of flexibility at present is the ease with which there can be greater concentration of taxing powers in the national government in times of war and other dire emergencies, and a return to more state and local taxation when each emergency is over.

The danger that with both national and state governments taxing the same subjects (e.g., gasoline, estates, incomes, tobacco, liquor) serious injustices will occur can be avoided by more careful study and more ample consultation between the national and state taxing authorities. Indeed, having both the state and national governments interested in a particular tax means that it will be more carefully watched for injustices.

The expense and inconveniences of compliance under overlapping taxes can be similarly reduced. But in fact when national excise taxes are collected, as they should be, at the source of the product (the oil refinery, the whiskey distillery, the automobile or tire factory), and the state taxes are collected at the point of importation into the state or of retail sale, there is no serious problem of compliance. It is mainly in income and inheritance taxes that the compliance problem is important, and here the inconvenience can be greatly reduced by state and national agreement upon forms, definitions, and times of tax payment.

Except for certain pension and retirement trust-fund purposes, where the individual's tax contribution builds up a special fund for him, I believe that the dedication of taxes to particular expenditure purposes is undesirable. Congress has in general avoided such dedications of national taxes, and this policy should be continued.

On the other hand Congress has yielded to the pressure of certain special interests to the point of requiring the states to dedicate some of their tax revenues (e.g., gasoline tax for highways, game and fish licenses for conservation work) as a condition for obtaining federal grants-in-aid. Congress should repeal all such earmarking requirements now imposed on the states and permit the states to match federal grants in definite amounts with funds from any lawful state source. Each state should also work to eliminate tax dedications as far as possible, to the end that state tax revenues can be used more flexibly and adaptably and be stretched farther and more evenly over the various state functions according to relative needs from time to time. It is to some extent because certain large tax funds are dedicated that the states must impose additional taxes to meet other state needs.

The state and national governments now have separate tax collecting departments, each one for its own taxes. Proposals are made from time to time to have the national government collect all taxes of a certain type (e.g., income or inheritance taxes) and distribute the states' respective shares back to them. There is a plausible suggestion of greater economy and efficiency in such proposals and an implied promise to the taxpayer of less compliance cost. To be most effective such a system would require that each state conform its own tax laws and ideas more or less to those of the national government. This would be a denial of the very autonomy of the state governments that the United States federal system implies. In time of all-out war or other great emergency such a centralization may be unavoidable, but for ordinary times the states would be wise to retain their separate tax-collecting agencies to look out for their own revenue interests.

Finally, I believe that mutual assistance in tax administration can go a long way in solving problems created by overlapping taxes. By laws and by administrative practices the national government already renders great assistance to the states in the collection of state taxes. The states give a certain amount of help in return. Many states fail, however, to make full use of the assistance and information that is available to them from national sources. This shortcoming seems to be due in part to the short-handedness of many state tax departments, and in some states to the indifferent standards used in selecting state tax department personnel.

There are great improvements yet to be made in many state tax departments.

Because state and national tax departments have a common interest in better tax administration, the efforts toward more mutual assistance and exchange of tax information need to be continued.

11

Grants-in-Aid and Centralization
of Government

T HE second phase of the fiscal relations between the national and state governments that arouses controversy is the system of federal grants-in-aid to the states. Are these grants a boon or a bane? Do they encourage a dangerous centralization of government?

Since many persons and organizations have written and spoken about grants-in-aid in a condemnatory spirit, the following chapter is oriented to a large extent toward what the critics have said, but I shall try also to give a broad picture of the whole system.

While national or central governments in all countries usually have very extensive if not unlimited powers of taxation, regional and local governments usually lack the revenue resources and taxing powers needed to finance adequately the functions they are expected to perform. Furthermore, such local governments usually differ so much among themselves in tax-raising ability that it would be unfair to ask them all to raise from local resources the money needed to provide locally any one of the national services. The idea of a central government giving aid to local governments to supplement and to help to equalize their local revenues for services of a nationwide interest is therefore found and practiced in many countries. The term "grant-in-aid" apparently originated in England, where such aids to local governments have been in use for a long time. In the United States we usually speak of "federal aid" to state and local governments, and of "state aid" to local governments within the state, but the term "grants-in-aid" covers both federal and state aid.

The present-day American concept of a grant-in-aid is a rather technical one.

There were various forerunners of the federal aid of today, including the early assumption by the national government of the Revolutionary War debts of the original states, the grants of public lands to the states for schools and internal improvements, and the distribution of the federal surplus among the states in 1837. There have also been emergency grants for public relief and public works, as exemplified extensively in the New Deal phase of the Great Depression in the 1930s, and in recurrent instances of national disaster relief. Then there are numerous cases, especially in the states, of so-called shared taxes, wherein the state government, as a rule, imposes and collects a tax on, for example, gasoline, cigarettes, general sales, or incomes, and by law assigns some percentage or other calculable part of the revenue to counties, school districts, or other local units. All these must be put aside here, because they are not true grants-in-aid in the modern sense.

There is still another category of "subsidies" or aids granted by the national government, and in some instances by the states, to private producers like farmers, gold and silver miners, and others to encourage production or to pay for the limitation of production. There are also disaster relief grants and loans to individuals, and other types of subsidies. Sometimes these are listed along with grants-in-aid, by mistake or for some ulterior motive. But true grants-in-aid are intergovernmental, from one public treasury to another, and usually from the treasury of a higher level, more central government, into the treasuries of the local governments included within the central government's area.

Regular, non-emergency federal grants-in-aid to state and local governments are the ones primarily before us here. These vary so much among themselves that only the state and national experts in each field can know them fully, but in general they have the following characteristics:

Each separate grant relates to a single function or activity of government, like highway construction, old age assistance, or vocational education; or to a few closely related ones.

Each is covered by a standing act of Congress that lays down, usually, the nature of the service to be rendered, the amounts to be appropriated for it annually, the formula for distributing these amounts among the states, and the conditions the states must accept to receive the funds, including usually a matching provision.

Each state that wishes to benefit from the program must pass its own law accepting the conditions, including the matching clause, but no state is required to accept.

The states administer the function or activity according to a plan agreed upon between state and national authorities, but there is some national supervision and an audit of expenditures by an appropriate national agency.

The states receive the national payments according to some time schedule in the law or regulations, or when approved work has been done, but the national government reserves the right to withhold payments for failure of the state to comply with the rules of the agreement.

State grants to local governments are exceedingly varied, but many of them follow the national pattern except that the requirements are in many instances more simple and informal.

Of the fifty-two distinct federal grant-in-aid programs operating early in 1954, four were begun before 1900, the earliest (1879) being a grant to assist public institutions in the education of the blind, a program carried on in connection with the American Printing House for the Blind. There were no new programs begun between 1901 and 1910; eight came between 1911 and 1920; one between 1921 and 1930; fifteen between 1931 and 1940; twenty-three between 1941 and 1950; and one in 1951. The rapidity with which these programs have increased in number has been a cause of real concern to many critics of modern political trends.

The acts of Congress establishing grant-in-aid programs usually offer the states a sufficient financial inducement so that within a few years practically every state "joins up." In the less wealthy states there is no doubt a feeling that the state will get something it could not afford to pay for alone, whereas in the wealthier states the legislators probably reason that this is one way to get back into the state some of the money that the state's taxpayers have contributed above the national average to the United States government. In every case, however, the program to be financed must be one that the state legislature approves; otherwise it would hardly accept it.

Congress has been severely criticized for offering the states such strong financial inducements as it does in federal-aid laws. Usually Congress offers dollar for dollar, but in a number of instances the ratio is two dollars of federal money or even more for each dollar of state money. The states then are said to be coerced, "bludgeoned," or seduced into conforming with the congressional policy, to be "selling their birthright" of self-government "for a mess of pottage."

I have sometimes thought that some congressional offers have been rather high, but I have no way of knowing whether any lower offer would have achieved the desired result. It seems to me that Congress should never pass a federal-aid law unless and until the members are convinced that there is a substantial national interest in establishing a nationwide service. When Congress is so convinced, after careful study and full debate, surely Congress should offer enough financial inducement to get all or the great majority of the states to accept the offer. Otherwise no nationwide service could be established.

The ways in which state legislatures are brought into line usually involve first some persuasive activity on the part of state and national administrative officers in the field to be aided (health, highways, etc.) to persuade members of Congress to pass the desired act, and then further persuasion directed at state legislators to get them to approve. This sort of activity by state functional administrative officers in conjunction with their appropriate pressure groups may by-pass the governor's office completely and get the state practically committed to a program without the state's chief executive having consented at any preliminary stage. Many governors are naturally resentful of this slight to them, and concerned about the splitting up of the state administration into a series of separate administrative departments, each with its direct contacts with a national agency.

At any rate, within a few years after congressional enactment practically every federal-aid law has been adopted by all the states, and it is rare for any state later to withdraw from a program, although the exit is always legally open.

The fields in which federal aid is important have already been mentioned, in Chapter 2. The list is impressive. It has been said to include nearly all the major fields of state administration except general law enforcement, insurance regulation, and state parks. Actually, this is misleading. The state judicial system is untouched, and the basic fields of state legislation such as property law, marriage, divorce and family relations, wills, estates, and trusts; corporations and partnerships, industrial safety and workmen's compensation, eminent domain and taxation, general police regulations over business and personal conduct, political parties and elections, local government, penal and correctional systems and institutions, and certain other fields, remain almost entirely outside the federal-aid programs.

Even in the major fields that are touched by federal aid, the extent of federal penetration is not as great as it might seem to be. State control over primary and secondary education, and over colleges and universities (with the exception of the land-grant colleges), is hardly touched by federal aid at all. Similarly, environmental sanitation in public health, residual relief and institutional care of the needy in welfare, and a tremendous mileage of rural roads and city streets in the highway field—these are not directly affected by federal aid or federal regulations. In some fields the state activities that are affected by federal aid and federal standards are relatively minor and peripheral.

One measure of the importance of the several aided functions is found in the amounts of money involved. These amounts have, of course, increased greatly since about 1900. In the fiscal year 1953 the total of all federal grants-in-aid was $2780 million, or just over $17 per capita. This was less than 1 per cent of the gross national product, and just over 1 per cent of the national income. It was also less than 3 per cent of all public expenditures—national, state, and local. Ninety-two per cent of this total went into six major programs:

Public assistance (mainly old age assistance)...$1330 million
Highway construction .... 501 million
School lunches (cash $83 million; commodities
$134 million) .... 217 million
Employment security (administration)....... 202 million
School operations and construction in defense
areas .... 200 million
Hospital construction .... 109 million

Looked at in another way, federal aid in 1953 amounted to about 4 per cent of all federal expenditures and to about 9 per cent of all state and local expenditures. Federal aid to welfare services amounted to 42 per cent of the money spent by all governments in welfare; in highways the ratio was 9 per cent coming from federal aid; and in education it was only 5 per cent. Except in the welfare field, the portion that comes from federal aid is certainly not dominant or overwhelming although important. If the states generally were greatly exercised about federal domination through grants-in-aid they could in most instances supply the extra money from local sources and reject the aid voted by Congress.

As a matter of fact, instead of confining themselves merely to matching the federal-aid funds, the states in most major fields of public service spend considerable additional amounts of their own money. If state and local funds are considered together, the margin of excess over what is needed to match federal aid is greatly increased. Note that all federal aid in 1953 amounted to only 9 per cent of all state and local expenditures. Of the 91 per cent difference only 9 per cent at the most would be needed to match federal aid, which leaves 82 per cent as voluntary state and local expenditures from their own funds for both the aided and the non-aided functions. Even if the national government could be said in some sense to control the spending of the 9 plus 9 or 18 per cent, the remaining 82 per cent would fall outside the controlled area. And the records show that since the end of World War II state taxes have been increasing and state expenditures have been going up sharply over practically the whole range of state functions, with great increases of state aid to local governments.

With every grant of money to the states comes national control over them, the critics say, and they add that when there is national control the states lose their self-government. Because there has been much criticism of federal control "in some of the aided services," the question is what is meant by the control and how extensive and effective is it?

This is an intricate subject and one about which there is much difference of opinion. I do not pretend to have the final answer, but I have a feeling that the ogres of federal control and federal bureaucracy employed by the opposition to frighten people have been marched out a little too often.

In a sense every proposal for a federal-aid program has come from the states, because the people of the states make up more than 99 per cent of the nation. Fewer than 1 per cent of the people live in Washington, D.C. The proposals have not all or perhaps many come from the governors or from the legislatures as such, but they have come from good roads associations, health organizations, and countless other groups that are seated in the states, and from various state officials, local officials, and organized groups of officials in the various fields to be aided. Their pleas have been heard in Congress by senators and representatives who represent the states there, and substantial majorities of such representatives have passed the laws.

The terms and conditions set by Congress for the receipt of federal aid have been no more than the proponents have considered reasonable. Thereupon the acts of Congress have gone back to the state legislatures and have been approved by majorities there, in nearly every state, and in the few states where not approved the programs have not gone into effect. Subsequent changes in the rules for each program have had to be within the terms of the act of Congress, which is by acceptance of the states a sort of contractual agreement between the nation and the states, and even these changes have in most cases been discussed and cleared between the national administration and the state administrators through correspondence, annual meetings, and otherwise. When state protests against some of the national requirements have become sufficiently insistent, Congress has not been averse to relaxing the requirements or giving additional protection to the state administrators.

Questions of federal control aside, what have been the effects in the states of the federal aids that have been increasing so much lately? The Commission on Intergovernmental Relations carried out "impact" studies in a number of states to determine what the effects of the various federal-aid programs had been on the welfare of the people, on the state and local governments, and on state and local finances, among other things. The results of these studies were almost doomed to be disappointing. The time, the financial resources, and the personnel available for such studies were simply not adequate, no matter how competent many of the investigators may have been. Only by long and searching historical, statistical, economic, social, and other studies could any impacts or effects have been isolated, identified, and measured. Even then it could not be said with authority what the situation in the states would have been had there been no grants-in-aid. The influences upon the people and the governments of the states during a few decades of fluctuating expenditures would be almost impossible to isolate and measure. Too many other variable and unmeasured if not unmeasurable factors were at work concurrently.

Nevertheless by a cautious use of the reported data we may venture a few tentative conclusions. For example, many persons in the wealthier states have thought of federal aid as a device to drain off income collected by national taxation in the wealthier states in order to give it to the people in the poorer states. The proposers of various federal-aid programs evidently did not think of federal aid as a means of redistributing income from the rich to the poor states, and all the federal-aid programs combined could hardly have much effect in this respect. Only a fraction of the 1 per cent of the national income involved each year is shifted from state to state, because much of the money is granted to the governments of the wealthy states, from whose taxpayers the money is largely collected.

The extreme differentials in the distribution of federal aid among the states in favor of the poorest states and against the richest is in a ratio of about 4 to 1, on a per capita basis—and in between these richest and poorest states at the ends of the scale are many that are not greatly affected one way or the other by any equalizing effect of grants-in-aid. When contributions to national tax revenues are figured out state by state on a per capita basis, and federal aid received is calculated on the same basis, it can be seen that some of the poorer states show plus signs (more aid received in proportion to taxes paid), while the wealthier states show minus signs. This fact is of some significance. However, much of the money so distributed has gone into public works like highways, which presumably help to promote community welfare but add no measurable amount to the wealth of individuals or of the states. In short, federal aid has had some equalizing effect, but it is obviously small, uneven, and practically unmeasurable.

We can say, however, that along with federal aid to the states has come the establishment of new state functions and services, the improvement and expansion of others, and the raising of the standards of service and of the personnel engaged in rendering such services.

Watered and nourished financially from two sources, and held up, by agreement, to fairly high standards, the federally aided and state-administered functions have grown and improved steadily through the years. The states have, accordingly, increased from time to time, and by substantial amounts, their own expenditures on these functions, just as they have on the functions that receive no federal aid. Thus the state governments have become more active and alert in the service of the people. They have drawn more and more trained and competent persons into their employment, and have greatly expanded the numbers of their staffs of employees. State government and administration have become increasingly strong and important, not only in the functions that receive federal aid but in other functions as well.

One other change that has been noticed in this process is that functions that were formerly local, in the counties, townships, and other units, have been increasingly drawn into the immediate orbit of state administration. This is true in highways, public welfare, and public health, for example, where state services and state controls over the local services have both increased. At the same time the demands on local governments for services have also increased, without corresponding increases in their taxing powers, so that the states feel and respond to a rising need to give state aid to their local governments, especially for education, for highways, for welfare work. State aid and state centralization have been growing at the same time as federal aid and national centralization. These are, perhaps, only evidences of the increasing integration of American society in modern times. Grants-in-aid may be more an effect, or a method of meeting new demands upon government, than a cause of anything.

From the point of view of Congress and the national government, of course, the grant-in-aid system is not the only one for achieving a nationwide public service in which there is a genuine national interest. One clear alternative is suggested by the Old Age and Survivors' Insurance. This system was put into effect as a complete and direct national operation at the same time as the Old Age Assistance program and other public assistance plans were put on a grant-in-aid basis. The results in achievements and in public attitudes have indeed been surprising. The direct national OASI system, which by-passes the states entirely, has been a great success, so great, indeed, that now many state and local governments are trying to find ways to bring their own employees directly under this system. It has caused none of the frictions and irritations that have accompanied the federal-aid public assistance programs. Yet, if the national government were to install more such direct services to the public, the states would indeed begin to lose out in the competition for public favor. By using the grant-in-aid method in highways and other fields Congress has clearly strengthened the states.

If my general analysis of federal aid, short as it is, comes anywhere near being correct, someone might question why there is opposition to such aid. I now turn to this question, for obviously there is a great deal of objection in certain circles and certain sections of the population. This book is being written on the assumption that most people are not adequately informed about national-state relations, including the subject of grants-in-aid. Therefore, I believe, most people have not made up their minds upon the issues in the controversy over federal aid. As I see the evidence, the opposition to grants-in-aid is most fully revealed in certain publications of various commercial and industrial organizations, both national and state, such as chambers of commerce and manufacturers' associations, and in the publications of taxpayers' associations and public expenditure councils, national, state, and even local. For their own reasons many state governors have taken the same side.

There is no particular partisan explanation of why certain governors who in recent years have gained leadership in the Governors' Conference have led in the fight against federal aid, as they have led in other agitation against various phases and exercises of national powers in the domestic scene. Certainly the "Dixiecrat" governors of the States' Rights party of 1948 had some share in the drive along with certain other Democratic governors of conservative tendencies. On the other hand the anti-centralization movement in the Governors' Conference gathered strength and momentum as the number of Republican governors in the Conference gained upon and outstripped the number of Democratic governors, a trend that was reversed in 1954.

Whatever the reason, governors—supported by the groups mentioned above—have been specific in their objections to federal aid. They point out that the operation of a large number of federal-aid programs within a state causes certain difficulties in state administration. The governor has difficulty in coordinating the joint

national-state services with each other and with other branches of
the state government. There is extra difficulty in budgeting federal funds and working them into a complete state budget. There
may be unnecessary waste and delay due to the need for national
inspections and approvals of projects. Some critics feel that the
matching requirements are unreasonable, and that they serve to
distort state spending too much in the direction of the federally
aided functions. A few also suggest that there should be more attention paid to the equalization of burdens among the states, so
that the poorer states would not be so heavily burdened—a suggestion that seems to approve of the principle of federal aid.

Most of these questions are such as can be dealt with after specific studies and recommendations in the different fields. I touch
upon a few of them in the next chapter. But leaving the governors and their special problems aside for the moment, I want to
turn to what I think lies at the bottom of much of the opposition.
Here I must deal with a broader and more general problem of
current politics, of which federal aid is only one facet. I refer to
the problem of centralization and decentralization, which is usually closely linked to grants-in-aid by the critics of that device.

Putting aside partisan interpretations, and all charges of ulterior
motives against the opposition to federal aid, I think their views
stem from a basic complex of fears about the condition of the
world, and fear is often very close to hatred. For many persons,
and for the interests by which they live, the world has been changing too fast, has been moving in wrong directions, and is becoming too big and complex. Fears of change, fears of bigness, of
centralization, of "distant government," fears of "too much government," of bureaucratic domination, of dictatorship and of socialism, are all apparent in the literature of protest against recent
developments in United States government.

The writings against federal aid are full of plausible, picturesque,
and rather appealing phrases. "We sold home rule in return for
grants-in-aid." "The dollar that is raised at home" is better spent.
"There are no financial resources in the United States that are
not within the borders of the forty-eight states." Grants-in-aid

are just "subsidies, doles, and paternalism," or in some writings just socialism. The dollar raised by national taxation and returned as a grant-in-aid comes back as fifty cents, reduced by "the political brokerage of the bureaucrats." The Indiana legislative resolution previously quoted in full contains a number of these phrases.

Then there are the phrases denouncing "big government" and "centralization" as inherently undesirable, and urging that government be kept "close to home" if liberty is to be protected and popular government preserved.

When one speaker solemnly asked before the General Assembly of the States in 1948, "Are we faced with an irresistible rush to centralization—then state socialism—then dictatorship?" another speaker gloomily replied: "I completely agree that a continuation in the direction of centralization toward which we are heading will eventually mean the destruction of our form of government as we have known it."

These I interpret as expressions of fear of some impending doom, and of a nostalgia for some simpler, less active system of government and society that in the minds of the speakers must have existed at some time in the past.

The rationalization of these fears into a sort of scheme of thought can be traced through an extensive literature. Although there is at least a trace of anarchist or anti-all-government feeling in this literature, in its recent forms it is directed mainly against "centralization," distant government, and "big government," meaning almost always the national government of the United States. Even though certain states have up to a quarter of a million square miles of area and up to fifteen million population, at present most of the anti-centralization argument seems to accept centralization at the state level. If a state performs a function, it is not centralization!

These speakers overlook the fact that the nineteenth-century liberal case for local self-government, upon which they unconsciously draw, centered on the small community with its face-to-face contacts and its opportunities for men to know each other intimately and to develop experience, responsibility, and the abil-

187

ity to work with others in small community affairs. Before there was much national centralization of functions there was state centralization, and it was opposed almost as strongly as national centralization is today. Now state centralization seems to be thoroughly accepted. Indeed some of those who denounce federal aid as a means of national domination over the states speak with pride of the states which are increasing state aids to local government, and must, by parallel reasoning, thereby be destroying the local self-government of the smaller units within the state. Fortunately for local financing the leaders in local government, struggling to maintain their public services, do not take so dim a view of the effects of state aid.

The whole argument against national centralization and for keeping government "close to home" is based on a confusion of physical distance to the capital with closeness to the people in the political and social senses. In small rural communities, in villages and small cities, closeness can be of both kinds, in physical distance to the city or town hall, and in personal knowledge of the local officials. But people generally have a better sense of proportion and importance than to think that such physical proximity is the determining factor in importance. The significant question is what government is most important in their lives. That will be the government that is closest to their interests and the one they follow most closely.

The physical distance to the capital is not the test; that distance to the national capital has in fact been overcome. By newspapers, radio, television, and other media of publicity, which also know something about relative importance, the national government and its important doings are brought daily into the people's homes, as no state government is. People know the President better than they do the state governor or the mayor of the city. Many know their United States senators better than their state senators or their county board or city council members, at least in the large urban places. And the national government is present in every sizable community with its post office, recruiting office, veterans' services, social security office, and agricultural and other programs.

It is the national government that takes the young men from their homes into military service, that pays out veterans' benefits and social security checks, and that tries to stabilize agricultural prices and settle major labor disputes.

Let us not deceive ourselves, therefore, about what is close to the people, or about their awareness of the relative importance of different government services. They know, as I do also, that state and local governments are important, but not more so than the national government.

Furthermore, most of them, I truly believe, are somewhat aware that government is not dangerous or against the people's interests merely because its capital is far from most of them. The national government is their government, even more than the state and local governments are, because it belongs to all of them, wherever they move in the nation or abroad. They recognize, as Hamilton, Madison, and others recognized at the beginning of the nation's history under the Constitution, that bigness is not a danger in a representative republic with federal features but a positive advantage. As it is reasoned out in *The Federalist*, no. 51 (which is probably the work of Madison though attributed generally to both him and Hamilton), small states tend to be unstable, ruled by factious majorities or even minorities, and unable adequately to provide security or liberty. "It is no less certain than it is important, notwithstanding the contrary opinions which have been entertained, that the larger the society, provided it lie within a practical sphere, the more duly capable it will be of self-government."

I think the experience of the United States supports the thesis that its big government, the national government, has been on the whole more stable, more responsive to public needs, more effective in administration, more sensitive to the needs of minorities like the Negroes, and more genuinely concerned to protect civil liberties than, on the average, the separate states have been. The fact is that the American people have popular national self-government as well as self-government by the states and local self-government in smaller places, and that each of the three is worthy to be preserved for performing the functions it is best capable of performing.

The proposition that has been put forward against grants-in-aid and against increases in national services, that the national government is breaking down because of its very size and the volume of its activities, is not supported by any body of evidence that has come to my attention. It has a plausible sound, certainly, but evidence is lacking. If national and state agencies of comparable functions are compared (the Bureau of Internal Revenue with state tax collecting agencies, the FBI with state law-enforcing departments, the U.S. Public Health Service with state health departments, and so on), I doubt that a case can be made out. That there is a difficult task of coordinating services in the President's office and in the Budget Bureau must certainly be admitted. But it has not been an impossible one.

In answering the usual arguments against grants-in-aid I have followed the course marked out by the critics and not that suggested by logic. My conclusions are, in general, that the critics have not made out a good case either that the sums going into federal aid are enticing the states into a loss of their self-government, or that the centralization and big government the critics profess to fear are inherently bad or dangerous. Centralization and decentralization or local self-government go together; each one implies the other; and under conditions of well-established popular government it is the strong and secure central governments that are most favorable to and that can most easily tolerate a considerable degree of autonomy or self-government in the parts. It is the central governments that are inherently weak and fearful that try to suppress local self-government. Such is not the case with the national government of the United States.

☆ 12

The Self-Government of the States

AT EVERY turn in the current discussion of the federal system one question arises persistently in various forms: Are not the states being deprived of their self-government? Whether the subject under consideration is grants-in-aid, the allocation of governmental functions, the distribution of tax resources, or any other question affecting national state relations, the issue of self-government for the states comes bobbing up. The discussion is subtly or abruptly turned from the question of what arrangement would be best for the national welfare, for the good of the people and the country, to the question of how it affects the powers, and the so-called sovereignty and independence, of the states.

In short the distribution of political power, the issue whether the parts or the whole, whether the states through their governors and legislatures, or the nation through Congress and the President, shall decide the question of what is for the general welfare in matters of national concern, becomes a main point of contention.

It is not an issue that noticeably divides the people, since they are represented in the governments of both the parts and the whole. Most national officials and members of Congress keep a discreet silence on the question. But since it is an issue that arises clearly in the Governors' Conference and in the publications against federal aid it is one that must be considered carefully.

The phrase "self-government" has a wide variety of uses and connotations. There is the self-government of a nation when it is free from domination by any foreign or alien nation. There is the self-government or self-control exercised by the individual over himself when he sets a standard of proper conduct for himself and abides by that standard. Between these two extremes of national and individual self-government there are intermediate levels of self-government of various political units that are smaller than and subordinate to the nation, but that each include a number of individuals and are, within the ranges of their powers and competence, superior to the individuals that compose them or that come within their boundaries.

It is only in representative or republican systems of government that genuine local self-government is known. In such places the self-government of local units consists in the right and the practice of citizens in their respective units of electing and holding responsible the officials who are to govern them in local affairs. The importance and problems of local self-government will be taken up in the next chapter.

The states in the United States stand in a somewhat anomalous position between the national government and the strictly local governments. Speaking through their governors and other leaders, they have tried for a long time to justify their positions by constitutional arguments concerning states' rights. More recently they have turned to self-government as the value to be emphasized. They set up the self-government of the states as something valuable for its own sake, necessary to "preserve our federal system," and as, indeed, a value that is superior to some of the values achieved by national action through Congress, the President, and the federal courts. State action is in this view better than national action, the smaller and more local better than the bigger and more nationwide.

This is, I believe and have tried to show in an earlier chapter, debatable, but the important point here is that the powers of the national government are now conceded to be so extensive and so deep-reaching that the question of policy is at present overriding. How much of its power shall the national government exercise, and how shall it employ that power? Shall it use its powers in any case in areas where the states may also act? If so, in what cases, when, how, and to what extent, and for what purposes?

There is always the possibility that by clumsy, excessive, and inconsiderate action the national government may be invading spheres where the states also are active or have the power to act, and that by so doing the national government may be taking away the powers of self-government that many people sincerely believe do belong to and ought to be left with the states. They may be achieving some economic or social improvement at the expense of an important political value, the autonomy of the states.

Perhaps it is best to begin by determining what self-governing powers the states have under the Constitution and then to consider whether these powers are actually declining on the basis of the evidence.

Every state has the following powers and rights:

The right to make and change its own constitution and the form of its government and to limit that government's powers, without any outside interference, by the national government or by any other state. Under the United States Constitution every state in the Union has this power, and uses it, without even reporting what it does to any other authority, much less referring it to Congress for approval. The United States Constitution requires only that the state government shall be republican in form and subordinate to the supreme law of the land; up to now Congress has never even made a serious inquiry into the forms of state government to see whether they are republican.

By its own constitution a state may not expand the powers of the state government beyond what the United States Constitution permits, but it may restrict the powers of its government to points below what the national Constitution allows, and every state has done this to some extent. It is possible that in practice some of these state constitutional restrictions on state governmental powers may serve as an excuse for a state's not performing its full constitutional duties to the nation, but I have no case in mind to cite.

The right to elect or to provide for the appointment of all its own officers and employees; to discipline and remove them; and to hold them responsible to the voters and the state's own courts.

The national government does not control or interfere with the election of state and local elective officers; and except for requiring a minimum merit system for some classes of officers who administer federal-aid funds, the nation's laws do not regulate the state's selection and control of the many state appointive officers and employers.

The right to initiate and carry out its own laws and policies without prior approval by any other authority. This right every state has and exercises to the full, as witness the tremendous and increasing volumes of laws passed in state legislatures year after year, and the increasingly large bodies of state civil servants and ever-growing state budgets to carry out such laws. In cases where states have agreements with the national government or with other states over some function, they ought to consult with those other authorities before acting, but they do not always do so, and are not required to do so—as evidenced by frequent flare-ups of interstate dissension over such matters as interstate truck taxation. Of course judicial review can usually be invoked to test the legality of state action *after* it has taken place.

The right to maintain the integrity of its body of laws for regulating the important human relations that come under state control concerning property, ordinary trade relations, domestic relations, local government within its area, and social institutions. The United States Supreme Court decision of 1938 in Erie R. R. v. Tompkins went far to ensure this right to the states and to require even the federal courts sitting in a state to conform to state court decisions as well as to state statutes in cases where they apply. The acts of Congress in the 1930s to prevent federal courts from obstructing state courts and administrative agencies in state tax cases and in cases of state utility rate regulation moved in the same direction. Federal laws fill many gaps and provide some national standards in certain fields of state regulation, but the great underlying body of law even for national purposes is state law. Witness here the great codes of state legislation and the voluminous digests of state decisions available now for every state. These are very considerably greater than they were one hundred or even fifty years ago.

Adequate constitutional powers for all state purposes. With some exceptions in the field of civil liberties, the Supreme Court has recently become increasingly generous in recognizing the right of the states under the Constitution to legislate for all their ordinary functions, for a growing body of new functions, and even for some national functions where Congress has failed to act.

Congress has supported the same policy of giving a large measure of freedom to the states not only by failing to use some of its own powers (and thus leaving the states to provide the laws) but also by positive acts to aid the states in carrying out their powers. Numerous local aspects of interstate and even foreign commerce are regulated by state laws (port and harbor facilities and regulations, tugboat service, railroad grade separations and safety at crossings, etc.), while intrastate matters are by congressional policy and Supreme Court decisions left almost entirely under state control where they do not seriously interfere with congressional regulations of interstate matters.

Since the Supreme Court gave up its "laissez-faire" ideas about inherent or natural-law restrictions upon the scope of government activities, relatively few state laws have been held unconstitutional because of a supposed lack of state power to enact them. Upheld in recent decades have been mortgage moratorium laws, fair trade acts, special chain store taxes and restrictions, laws for regulating the sale of real estate, insurance, stocks and bonds, and many other state laws that earlier might have been held to violate the contract clause or the Fourteenth Amendment due process and equal protection clauses of the Constitution. The principal areas in which the Supreme Court keeps a more watchful eye on state activity are state laws that infringe upon civil liberties, or that burden or discriminate against interstate and foreign commerce, or that cut in upon important pieces of federal legislation such as the Taft-Hartley Labor-Management Relations Act.

Broadly speaking, the states exercise today a far wider range of legislative powers than they ever did before, as will be borne out by any chronological comparison and content analysis of state legislative codes since the Civil War or even since 1900. At the same time, as we have seen, Congress has also been making wider use of its legislative powers than it formerly did, so that more points of contact, overlapping, and contradiction between federal and state laws have unavoidably developed. It is the latter fact, and not any actual decline in the total of state legislative powers, that I believe has given rise to demands for "returning" powers to the states.

A broad range of functions to perform. In utilizing their really extensive powers to legislate, the states have recently opened up wide ranges of public functions that were hardly thought of some fifty years ago. From the Civil War down to about World War I, the states made some but relatively little advance in the provision of public services. Most of them did little or nothing (other than to legislate, and that very meagerly) about highways, public health, public education, social welfare, the conservation of resources, law enforcement, the regulation of business or labor, or the promotion of agriculture. Many of them were bound by self-imposed constitutional restrictions which prevented them from spending tax revenues on internal improvements (even highways), while other self-imposed restrictions upon their own taxing powers tied them fast to archaic taxing systems that usually included a discredited general property tax as the main source of state revenue.

What most of them did was to avoid their direct service responsibilities by authorizing their local units—counties, towns, cities, villages, and school districts—to provide from local property taxes for the roads, schools, and health and welfare services that the people needed. The states in general merely supported their legislatures, courts, and executive offices, gave some support to higher education, and provided state prisons, insane asylums, and a few other such state institutions.

It was around the turn of the century (say, 1890 to 1915) that Robert La Follette of Wisconsin, Hiram Johnson and others in California, Theodore Roosevelt and Charles Evans Hughes in

New York, Joseph Folk in Missouri, and other comparable leaders carried on the Progressive struggle to awaken the states to their responsibilities and to break the rings of vested interests that were holding the states in a sort of bondage. Elihu Root of New York and other leaders threw out the warning that if the states did not begin to think about their responsibilities to the country at large, and to give the people, honestly and effectively, the services they were demanding, the people would indeed turn to Washington for help and leave the states to wither and decay.

At that time no state had a truly effective taxing system or a well-considered budget system, none had centralized purchasing, not a half-dozen had efficient personnel systems based on merit. There were practically no state highway systems, state police systems, comprehensive conservation departments, or general state departments of agriculture or of labor. There were no workmen's compensation laws until near the end of the period, only a few state departments to regulate public utilities other than railroads, in general no old age assistance laws other than those for the county poor farms, no schemes of aid for widowed mothers and dependent children—but we need not continue this listing of what the state were *not* doing.

Even when some states tried in that period to expand their services and to regulate trade and industry, they faced a Supreme Court that often invoked the contract clause and the due process clause of the Fourteenth Amendment as barriers to protect vested property interests against state regulations and taxes. They faced also the threat that if they raised their own taxes to provide new services, some of their industries might move to other states that kept their taxes lower.

But just before and after World War I the states began to pass out of the era in which their governments were primarily legislators into a new time in which they have added to their broad legislative functions a large number of important administrative services and functions, to support which they now have large budgets and extensive rosters of trained and competent personnel. If anyone will candidly lay the facts about state powers and functions today alongside the comparable facts of forty to sixty years ago, I do not see how he can reach the conclusion that the states are weaker today than they were then.

Adequate revenue-raising powers. These powers are now available to every state, at least as far as the United States Constitution is concerned. To be reasonably self-sufficient and self-governing, any state or local government has to have sufficient revenues for a decently effective support of its own functions, and should also to be able to raise much if not most of what it needs under its own taxing powers from its own people. There is no point here in speaking in absolute terms, because all governments are limited in their resources, and subordinate governments more so than central national governments.

The taxing powers of the states have already been discussed. To recapitulate briefly:

Since the adoption of the Fourteenth Amendment, the Supreme Court attitude toward state taxing powers has never been more liberal than it is today. In the legal constitutional sense the states have taxing powers that are very nearly concurrent with those of the national government. They already duplicate many national taxes.

In the practical sense, however, through two world wars, an unparalleled depression, a "cold war," and the Korean war, the national government has had to utilize certain taxes for defense and relief purposes to such an extent that the states have been reluctant to levy the additional taxes they would have needed to provide more amply for their public services. State expenditures are devoted almost entirely to nondefense purposes, and it happens in all countries that nondefense expenditures must yield to the nation's needs for defense in major wars.

Recognizing this fact, the Congress of the United States has passed a number of statutes to enable the states to increase and to hold on to their tax revenues, and has in addition provided increasingly large amounts in grants-in-aid to enable the states to undertake and carry on certain functions of real national concern.

As a result, state revenues have gone up significantly since before World War II, indeed in the entire period since World War I, despite a temporary slump or leveling off for short periods now and then. State revenues, nearly all for nondefense purposes, have gone up more than the comparable revenues devoted by the national government to its own nondefense purposes—and state revenues are still rising while federal expenditures and taxes are being reduced. Whenever defense needs can be further substantially reduced, state revenues should be able to rise even more rapidly, given a continuation of high national employment and productivity.

Among the real obstacles to further increase of state revenues are two: a natural reluctance of legislators to increase taxes, and various state constitutional restrictions that the dominant political and economic interests in the states concerned do not wish to have removed.

In short, much of the difficulty in many states is not lack of taxable resources but the lack of will to raise the money that its government needs and to remove various self-imposed tax restrictions. These self-imposed restrictions include the unwise dedication of some important revenues to certain specific purposes, and state constitutional provisions supported by state supreme court decisions that prevent some states from using, for example, the income tax as a source of revenue. Congress has been generous in allowing taxes paid to state and local governments to be deducted from a person's income before his national tax is figured, but a number of states still hold back from the imposition of state income taxes.

Relative freedom from supervision and interference. The legislation enacted by the states is not supervised by Congress, as James Madison had proposed in the Federal Convention of 1787 that it should be. The decisions of the state courts are in the great majority of cases not reviewed by any federal court, because most of them raise no "federal question." The work of most state officials and agencies goes on from day to day and year to year without any national supervision, much less any national interference. If freedom from outside supervision is any test of the possession of self-governing powers, as I think it is, then the statements so far made suggest that the states are self-governing to a very high degree.

There is, however, another side to the picture. Because the state and national governments are engaged together in a number of activities, of both national and state concern, under various contracts and other agreements including those that arise out of federal-aid programs, there are certain federal standards that the states have agreed to meet and there are various types and degrees of federal supervision to see whether the states are complying. How does this supervision affect the states?

A series of studies were carried out in Minnesota between 1946 and 1948 which suggest a number of tentative conclusions about the supervisory relations in that one state. Unfortunately the studies did not cover all federally aided functions, and the conclusions reached, even if valid, would not necessarily apply in other states. But these studies (in which I took part personally) are the best guides I have at the present, and I will summarize the conclusions here for whatever they may be worth:

The supervisory relations varied from one function to another, according to the nature of the function and the laws under which the function was administered. No two were exactly alike.

There was practically no conflict between laws, because the state laws on each function had been made by the legislature to conform to the United States law and requirements.

The relations in practice were not stiff, formal, and legalistic; instead they were *human* relations between national government personnel on the one hand and state and local personnel on the other, both groups being interested primarily in having the particular services with which they were charged performed in the best way possible.

In the initial stages of a program there were misunderstandings and disagreements, but in time these were worked out through explanations and concessions from both sides and with general satisfaction to both the national and state officials. When new personnel came in for either side, there might be another temporary period of getting acquainted.

This tendency to develop harmonious working relations was not greatly affected by the fact that during much of the time covered in the study the Republican party controlled the state administration, while the Democratic party controlled the national administration.

Relatively harmonious working relations between the national and state personnel in a field seemed to be conditioned by their common vocational and professional interest in improving the work and status of the function. They usually worked together in trying to get changes in standards, rules, budgets, and personnel requirements to advance the service. They met together in national, regional, and state conferences of officers and experts in their respective fields, to discuss and try to overcome commonly felt difficulties of administering and financing the function. There were also many telephone calls and office visits to settle various questions.

The governors and state budget officers in Minnesota were close to but somewhat outside the stream of relations between the national and state officials in particular functional fields, but they were consulted at times and they raised no sharp objections to what was being done, as happened in some states.

State legislators generally paid little attention to the interrelations between national and state officials in any field. Legislative committees dealt directly with their respective functional departments, and not through the mediation of the governor or state budget officer.

There were no "crack-down" orders from the federal to state agencies in Minnesota in the period covered by the study, nor were there any significant ones before or after. State and local officers seemed, in fact, to welcome the presence, the advice, and the help of the federal officials in their field. No doubt the latter gave the former much moral support, when questions arose in the legislature or in state budget and accounting offices, and in addition the state officials could at times justify what they did by pointing out that the federal standards (which they had had a part in making) required it.

The financial audits by federal officials were the most common type of federal supervision over state officers, and they were conducted differently for different services with very little squabbling or adverse publicity for anyone. This may be a fault, of course, because more publicity might have been desirable.

In short, the Minnesota experience for the years we studied does not reveal any excess of federal supervision over federally aided projects, or any great protest from Minnesota officials or citizens against the work of the federal agencies in the state.

The foregoing analysis of the self-governing powers of the states might seem to be conclusive evidence of the states' vitality. Nevertheless the statement is frequently made that under grants-in-aid the states are being progressively reduced to the status of "mere administrative districts" of the nation. This argument was heard long before the recent expansions of federal aid.

What is an "administrative district?" When the Post Office Department divides the national area into postal inspection districts or a state highway department divides the state area into road maintenance or highway patrol districts, then there are so-called administrative districts that can be shown upon the map. Almost every important agency of the national government uses its own scheme of administrative regions and districts. There are dozens of such schemes. For convenience, of course, the state areas are used as districts by a number of national agencies.

These administrative districts have practically no political significance. They are made and changed by central administrative agencies for their own convenience. Most people who live in the districts, including public officials, have no knowledge of their boundaries or even of their existence. The locally resident citizens within each do not elect those who are to manage the district's affairs, because such a district (a state highway patrol district, for example) is not a body politic for any purpose. It has no charter or constitution, no body of elective officers, no status in law. It is so unlike a state in these respects that it is surprising to find the term even used in this connection.

What those who use this phrase and this argument seem to have in mind is quite different. They see certain departments of the states engaged by agreement in close collaboration with national agencies, devoting much of their time and effort to the administering of functions in which the national government has some guiding hand, and they think this means the ultimate complete loss of state control. They should look a little deeper into the situation.

When a function is clearly of national concern, as already noted, there is a choice between two major alternatives: direct performance of the function by an exclusively national agency, like OASI, which by-passes the states completely, or an agreement between the national government and the several states whereby each state administers the function within its area in accordance with agreed standards, with federal aid, and under some national supervision. By the latter arrangement some of the major state departments, notably in highways and welfare, have been built up and are maintained. Are these departments mere administrative agents of the national government like the Post Office Department? The answer is obviously no. The state highway department is still the state's highway department in every important respect.

Another aspect should also be considered. Does not the federal-aid system, by giving state agencies the power to administer functions in which there is a national interest, actually give the states considerable control over national policy and effectiveness in the area, control which they otherwise would not have, in addition to giving the states the extra funds?

A politically wise Frenchman of the late eighteenth century, Comte de Mirabeau, said something that can be freely rendered into English as follows: "To administer is to govern; to govern is to reign [to be ruler]; it all comes down to that."

How often have we heard the political heads of government and legislators complain that they cannot achieve what they want and that their hands are tied because the civil servants who do the work are not responsive to their orders. When those who are doing the work "drag their feet" and continue to carry on their work in old ways, the heads of agencies may at times be practically helpless. This happens even more when a central government depends on local governments and their civil servants to do the work. State administrators have experienced this many times in trying to keep county, city, village, and township officials in line with state laws and policies when carrying out state functions in such fields as property assessment, poor relief, public health services, and education. The heads of national agencies in Washington face the same problem in trying to keep state agencies in line when carrying out federal-aid projects. The central administrator seldom dares to "crack down" on state administrators, because he knows, and he knows that the state administrator knows, how quickly he will be denounced in Congress and in the press if he tries to enforce the rules strictly.

In short, as administrators of federal programs under grants-in-aid the state governments have acquired something in the nature of an added check upon the national administration. Political power, like electricity, does not run all in one direction.

This, however, is small consolation to the state governors, who do not themselves administer the grant-in-aid programs and who often do not have much control over the officials who are in charge. It may be that the governors sometimes confuse their own powers, or lack of them, with the powers of the states, and therefore do not see the issue of state self-government as clearly as they might. But since a number of them have taken the lead in recent years in warning against what they consider the loss of the self-government of the states, it is important to try to understand their position.

From the beginning of the state governments at the time of the Revolution, state governors have struggled against great obstacles in the attempt to strengthen the powers of their office and to make the governor the undisputed head of the entire state administration. None of the very first state constitutions made any such provision, because popular distrust of a strong executive prevailed, but New York (1777) and Massachusetts (1780) adopted constitutions that looked somewhat in that direction. These two states provided also for popular election of their governors, while in other states generally the governors were elected by the legislatures and for short terms, commonly one year, and were thus under legislative control.

After the Constitution of the United States set the pattern for a chief executive who headed the entire executive branch, there was one move after another in various states to make the governor's office a replica of the presidency in this respect. The reformers wanted more freedom for the governor from legislative control, and more appointing power in his hands so that he could actually control the state administration. Progress in this direction came slowly and painfully, and has never been completed. Some governors in the present generation continue to carry on the campaign for more official powers, longer terms, better salaries, and more official help in their offices. In this effort they have considerable public support.

Substantially what is wanted by those who support this position is that all important state department heads and boards shall be appointed by and responsible to the governor. Along with this power the governor would be charged with responsibility for planning a complete state budget annually or biennially, would have control over the selection, training, and discipline of state personnel, and would supervise all state business affairs, finances, purchasing, and contracts. To assist him in handling these important duties the governor would have under his control a budget director, a state personnel board or officer, a controller of expenditures, a central purchasing officer, and other such aids.

These and other provisions represent the ideal of the state government as a completely unified business conducted according to the best standards of corporation management, with the governor as its business head as well as its political leader. The very logical and reasonable argument for this change is that state government has become a big business in every way, and that it calls for central, responsible business management. Obviously any governor in such a position would be a very powerful official.

Most states are far from having attained this supposedly ideal governmental structure. Under most state constitutions the governor is not "the executive" of the state, but only the leading member of the state executive department. Usually some important state officers are directly elected by the voters and hence are not under the governor's control. Generally also certain major departments are under ex officio boards, or under boards or commissions of appointed members, who have long and overlapping terms and are protected by law from interference by the governor.

As a result of these factors and others like them there are many frustrations in a governor's career. In the public mind he is held responsible for what goes on during his administration, yet he can do little or nothing to prevent or to cure some of the troubles. He cannot control the whole state administration, he cannot make a complete and satisfactory state budget, he cannot appoint and remove state personnel as he might desire. On top of these frustrations he finds that his term is short, his salary is generally inadequate, and his staff of help on state problems is too limited.

There is another side to the problem, however. It is this: Many if not most governors do not, in fact, have a great deal of time to spend on state business and financial problems. Some of them have little taste for it, and most of them are too busy in other ways. They are called upon so extensively to appear and to speak at public meetings and celebrations of all kinds, and must give so much time during and between election campaigns to party and campaign matters, that they have but little time or energy for anything but such "public relations" activities. Some governors do, however, by a very considerable effort manage to allocate considerable time to problems of state business management and finance.

At the same time state legislators, as a rule, are not anxious to enlarge the governor's powers over the state administration, because every increase of the governor's powers in this direction is a potential or actual diminution of the powers of the legislatures and their committees over the state administrative departments. Likewise many state department heads are happy to be able to escape strict control by the governor, the state budget officer, and any other appointees of the governor. They are content to deal directly with the appropriate legislative committees about their budgets and expenditures, instead of knuckling under to the governor and his staff.

What has all this to do with the governors' attitudes on federal grants-in-aid and on the self-government of the states? A great deal, I think. A governor finds that the state department heads (for whom the public holds him responsible) deal directly with their federal counterparts (in highways, social welfare, public health, and education, for example) on federally aided programs, and also with state legislative committees, instead of clearing everything first through officers who are under the governor's immediate control. Thus decisions can be and are made about state administrative problems with little or no consultation with the governor. This is indeed frustrating and humiliating to any governor who has to think of his office as heading the state administration, because he is the one who is held responsible.

Furthermore, federal grants-in-aid are determined for each state and for each separate program (highways, old age assistance, etc.) by Congress and the national administrators, and each program on a different basis, so that it is almost impossible for the governor's budget office to budget accurately for such aided functions. Already beset by state constitutional provisions and statutes that "dedicate" certain revenues to certain purposes (e.g., gas tax to highways, game and fish receipts to conservation services, etc.) the governor finds that he can actually budget effectively for only a small part of the state government's total revenues and expenditures.

Many a governor finds that his state administration is not an integrated unit, but more like a series of separate departments, many of which seem to report directly to national agencies. How much simpler and more businesslike it would be, reason some of the governors, if the state raised all its own revenues and could budget and control every dollar raised and spent through a state executive budget.

The position of the state governor is, indeed, a difficult one— but this is not due primarily to the federal grant-in-aid programs, although they are important factors, but to these in combination with various state-imposed obstacles in the governor's path. The latter are probably far more important. Reform often has to begin at home. If the governors could, each in his own state, bring about those changes in the state constitution and statutes that would make him truly the head of the whole state administration and relieve him of any present unreasonable restrictions upon his powers to budget for the whole state government and to control such state business activities as finances, purchasing, and contracting, the attempt to get better control over federal grants-in-aid would seem to me more realistic.

Further movement in the direction of intrastate reform to increase the governor's power and responsibility for all phases of state administration, finances, and business management is, I believe, greatly to be desired. A few states, notably New York, have already gone far in this direction. The more a state does to reform its own house, the less it will need to worry about the influence of federal grants-in-aid upon its policies and its powers of self-government, and the better prepared it will be to deal effectively with federal agencies and grants.

On the other hand the complete elimination of federal grants-in-aid would be for most states a high price to pay for the supposed advantage that some governors see in the increase of state self-government, without any assurance that the desired result would follow. Until the states generally bring about the reforms at home that will strengthen the governors' central controls over state administration, it would seem to be unwise to cut off sources of revenue like federal grants-in-aid that many states find highly important if not indispensable.

But this is not the whole story. State administrative reform will go forward slowly, piecemeal, and with occasional backslidings.

In the meantime much can be done by Congress and by the national agencies that administer federal aid to facilitate better budgeting by the states and better state supervision over federally aided programs.

There can be no good reason in national policy why the governor in any state should not be allowed to exercise such budgeting and supervisory functions over federally aided state services as he has over other state departments. To clear things with the governor should not be unduly burdensome or time consuming, although it might involve some duplication of effort. Congress should not tell any state how much power the governor of the state should have, or what sort of central budgeting it should do, but if necessary it could direct national agencies to cooperate fully with the state governor and budget agency to assist them in carrying out their responsibilities. Each state should make its own decision as to what kind of budget agency and procedure it wants —and the legislature will not always agree with the governor about this. To me the self-government of the states requires that each state be allowed to decide such questions for itself, even if it wants the office of governor to be weak and not strong; but the national government should be ready to cooperate with the state no matter what its decision, provided that no national interest is thereby injured.

But one more point remains to be made—or, rather, to be repeated with new emphasis.

Every state is a state *in the Union.* It is a part of the nation, under the Constitution, laws, and treaties of the United States. It is not a sovereign, independent state in the family of nations like Great Britain or Spain or Sweden. A state in the Union cannot escape from its obligations to the nation and avoid having to get along with a superior national government. When a state has done all that it can do to integrate its government under the state governor, his office and powers will still not be fully comparable to those of the President or of the chief executive of any other national state. To believe otherwise, as some persons seem to do, is to pursue an *ignis fatuus,* to imagine a vain thing.

As I read and appraise the evidence, the states are fully maintaining and even increasing their powers of self-government. The state governments are stronger and more active in the performance of public services than they ever have been in the past. I think they provide, generally speaking, better government and more government than they did fifty or a hundred years ago. When I say "generally speaking," I simply mean that the record shows somewhat uneven results among the states. A number have maintained high standards for many years. Others have been up and down. Changes for the worse can come very quickly in some states with changes in administration or in the party in power.

This unevenness is something that must be taken into account in any consideration of the potentialities of the states. All forty-eight have certain permanent characteristics, for better or for worse, that affect all they do, and that cannot be wished away:

Every state is different from every other in its outlook, its policy, its way of thinking, and its way of doing things.

Every state is changeable, and in some cases quickly so, when new problems, new leaders, and new aspirations arise. Progress made today can easily be lost tomorrow.

Every state tends to be local and even selfish in its point of view, ready to pursue its self-interest first of all, and not primarily interested in the nation as a whole.

Every state is competitive with every other state in trying to attract population and industries from other states.

Every state is unequal to every other state in financial capacity for getting things done as well as in other capacities.

No two states have the same balance between needs for a service and the ordinary financial capacity to supply those needs.

Within every state there are competing interests, urban-rural, or north-south, that make it difficult to maintain even a statewide program.

Taking all these factors into account, I can only say that he would be a bold and, yes, an ignorant man who would assert that there is even a good prospect that states acting individually could achieve nationwide performance of an important function according to a national plan and in the national interest. The experiences of the Greek city states in ancient times, of the thirteen United States under the Articles of Confederation, of the southern states during the Civil War, and of the present states in the Union in handling separately such problems as the incorporation of business companies, workmen's compensation, and state banking regulation, should be sufficient to destroy any hope of a uniform national policy being achieved through the action of numerous separate states.

One of the worst fallacies in political discussions is the "all-the-people" or "all-the-nations" fallacy. "If all the people" would only do so and so, or "if all the nations" would do this and not that, then we would have no more wars, no more poverty, and so on. This is mere perfectionist wish-thinking, the avoidance of real thought. "All the people" never do the same things where choice and will are involved. No two persons act exactly alike. Neither do any two nations, or any two states. Even the most powerful and brutal system of coercion does not wipe out individual differences.

Where an important national interest is involved the national government would not be justified in entrusting it to the unguided free choice of the forty-eight separate states. The laudable objective of increasing still further the self-governing powers of the states would hardly warrant any such gamble.

But, it is often asked, if the states acting separately cannot effectively develop and carry out major nationwide services in the national interest, can they not do so cooperatively? And by so acting, can they not strengthen their powers of self-government?

The means and methods of interstate cooperation are numerous and varied: formal interstate compacts approved by Congress, informal interstate agreements, conferences of state officials, reciprocal legislation, and uniform state legislation, among others. These parallel to some extent the methods of international relations. Interstate compacts are to interstate relations what treaties are to international relations. Each government maintains at least nominally a committee of its own officers entitled a Commission

211

on Interstate Cooperation to promote interstate agreements and services, and also a commission or commissioner on uniform state laws. There are numerous nationwide bodies composed of particular classes of state officials like attorneys general, secretaries of state, insurance commissioners, and so on, to deal cooperatively with what are essentially state and not national problems. The Council of State Governments, with central offices in Chicago and branch offices in New York, Washington, D.C., and San Francisco provides central secretarial services, stimulation, and guidance for numerous interstate governmental organizations and movements.

No one can seriously doubt the value of these interstate agencies or the importance of cooperative interstate action to facilitate the work of all state governments and to take on certain regional activities in watershed control and sanitation, fisheries in common coastal waters, interstate parks, bridges, and port facilities, and the like. There are persons who profess to believe that it is morally and politically more desirable to get such things done by interstate cooperation than by action of the established authorities of the national government under the Constitution.

When one looks over the entire list of achievements through interstate agreements and cooperation, however, and sees not only how comparatively small they are (with a few exceptions) and how rare it is to get the cooperation of all forty-eight states or even to get the same uniform law passed in all the states, one is forced to recognize that the possibilities are severely limited. The big jobs that need to be done cannot be accomplished by methods of voluntary interstate cooperation. Such cooperation is no substitute for national action or for joint state and national action. It is primarily supplemental and interstitial.

As I honestly believe that Congress is, in the long run, the best representative of the states and the best defender of their interests and their powers of self-government, so I believe it has not lost sight of their interests or of the national interests when using the grant-in-aid method and the tax-offset method of bringing about reasonably uniform national action. By these methods it is feasible to team up state legislative and administrative action with national standards and supervision toward the attainment of nationwide services and goals.

Congress has shown confidence in the state governments. Instead of by-passing the states and setting up its own direct services, the national government has in most cases, by proper inducements, enlisted the services of the state governments in national endeavors. If in such services the states do not decide all the major questions, they certainly do decide many of them and are consulted about the others. Thus they retain practically all their self-government even in these federally aided fields. When the alternatives are considered, I doubt that any better ones have been proposed for achieving national objectives while preserving the self-government of the states.

States that wish to free their governments for even more constructive efforts have the power within themselves to do so. Many need to modernize their constitutions in order to bring them up to the requirements of the twentieth century. They need to and they alone can strengthen and integrate their systems of state government—their legislatures, their courts, their executive and administrative agencies. They need to end the unfair apportionments of senators and representatives in their state legislatures; very few things would give urban people so much reason to increase their confidence in the states as a reapportionment based honestly on population, so that every man and woman shall count as one, and none shall count as more than one. In the process of reform, archaic restrictions on the state taxing power and unwarranted dedications of revenue to selected purposes need to be ended. The liberties of the people need to be protected by better state bills of rights, better enforced.

In almost every state there is much that needs to be done to improve popular government, and which if done would indeed give the people sound reasons for a further strengthening of their confidence in their states.

13

Self-Government at the Local Level

THERE are more than 116,000 local governments in the United States, as officially counted in 1952. They vary in numbers from 89 in Rhode Island to more than 9000 in Minnesota. Sixteen states have from 1000 to more than 9000 each. These governmental units include counties, cities, villages, towns, boroughs, school districts, and a great variety of other such entities. Each one has been established by or under authority of state law with a governing body (usually elective), various officers and employees, some public function or functions to perform, and the authority to raise, receive, and spend public funds. It is hardly necessary to add that each one is a center of political and governmental activity, and a practical example of local self-government.

Among these units and between them and the state and national governments there are so many examples and varieties of intergovernmental relations that no person could fully describe them, not even for a single state.

My purpose here is not to attempt the impossible or to bring confusion to the reader, but instead to consider briefly how *local* self-government is faring in the states. While certain state leaders have been calling attention to what they consider a decline in the self-governing powers of the states, how have the states and their governments been dealing with the local units and their powers of self-government? A short consideration of this problem will round out the general discussion and also provide some comparative standards to help in judging whether the pulse beat of self-government generally is being maintained in the nation.

The Constitution of the United States says nothing about the local units of government within the states. Following their former usage the state governments continued under the Constitution to create, regulate, and abolish local units of government, while Congress refrained from taking any action in this field. When questions have come before the Supreme Court about state control over local governments the Court has uniformly held that local governments are the mere creatures and agents of the state, authorized and organized to carry out in parts of the state's area various functions of the state itself.

As mere agents of the state the local units have no more right against the state than a state department or other state agency would have. Although a private corporation might claim that the charter granted to it by the state becomes a contract with the state, once the corporation's members have invested funds in its activities (Dartmouth College case), a municipal charter is not such a contract with the state. Consequently a state may freely change or even rescind the charter of a city or other local government. Furthermore, the due process and equal protection clauses of the Fourteenth Amendment do not protect a local government against the state that created it (City of Trenton v. State of New Jersey).

From these and other evidences it is safe to conclude that the power to create and regulate local governments within the state is one of the powers reserved to the states in the most unqualified sense. The Constitution provides no protection to local governments against their states, and the national government (except when protecting its own interests) deals with the local units only with the state's consent. In short the responsibility for the organization, powers, supervision, and general conduct of local government in every state is wholly and inescapably the responsibility of the state and its government. On the other hand the state cannot be held responsible for any failures of local government due to defects in human character and to other conditions beyond its control. It is to the legislative, administrative, and financial provisions made by the states for local governments that we need to pay attention.

Throughout the history of state control over local governments in this country the literary theory of the advantages of local self-government has had considerable vogue. That theory was mentioned in Chapter 9, above. It emphasizes the importance of self-government in numerous small units like towns, villages, and school districts, where men can know each other, meet face to face, work on common problems of the community together, and develop experience, knowledge, and a sense of public responsibility from direct participation. These values are not only good in themselves, but also are supposed to have some carry-over value for higher levels of government, because men will participate more responsibly and wisely in state and national government if they have gone through the school of experience and hard knocks in local government. This theory is still widely held, apparently, and some men go so far as to say that a system of local self-government is a prerequisite for effective national self-government. The latter proposition is hard to prove; English experience seems rather to prove the contrary, for only after Parliament had been reformed in 1832, on the basis of an approach to popular government nationally, was an effective system of local self-government set up. In any case, however, local self-government, and state and national self-government through elected representative bodies, do seem to go together.

Unfortunately for the theory of local self-government in small face-to-face communities, American society proceeded during the nineteenth and twentieth centuries to undergo great transformations that increased the mobility of the people so that many did not stay long in one place, and drew the population more and more away from the small places into larger and larger urban centers, some of metropolitan proportions, in which the people could not all know each other and only a few could get the public experience needed according to the theory. Even the experience that men had gained in the small communities from which they moved had relatively little value in deciding the questions that the big cities faced. Indeed the "small-town attitudes" of legislators and of many displaced ruralites and villagers who found themselves living in big cities were in some respects a distinct obstacle to a frank confrontation of the problems of the large urban place.

How well have the states, acting through their legislatures and governors, met the problems of local self-government in a changing society? Have they sensed at all what was coming and instituted important studies and actions looking toward better laws and organization for local governments? Have they set up effective state agencies to give aid and guidance to people in local communities who need help on local problems of organization, personnel, procedures, and finance, as well as on technical matters in such fields as public health and education?

Hindsight is clearer than foresight in most cases, and I do not wish to pass judgment on able and conscientious legislators of the past. In some states, notably New York and Massachusetts, and perhaps in others, the legislatures showed considerable prescience at various times and made valiant efforts to find better ways of governing and financing local units. In general I should say, however, that the record of the state legislatures in seeking and adopting constructive measures for improving local government has been only from fair down to poor. They are chargeable with neglect, indifference, and lack of foresight and of giving in too easily to established prejudices and vested interests rather than with actual animosity to the improvement of local governments, I believe. But the record is not a good one.

It is natural that urban places have suffered most from legislative neglect, and in this case there has also been some animosity. The traditional rural counties and townships were not pressing for important changes, as a rule; their people did not feel the need of any. It was in the growing cities that the ferment of change was felt, and the rural members and sentiments that dominated the legislatures grew positively resentful of urban claims.

New England towns, for example, even when their populations had grown well beyond any possibility of conducting the town's business in a town meeting, were only grudgingly given city charters with elective councils. It seemed easier to divide some towns into fragments in order to keep the old traditional form. Other urban places that needed better sources of revenue to meet their rising expenses for increased services, or that needed better control over their public utilities, or over land platting and city planning and housing, found it most difficult to overcome resistances and indifference in the legislatures. At times, for partisan and more sinister purposes, legislatures would enact laws to plunder a city treasury, to saddle a city with great debts, and to oust the officers whom the people had elected in order to replace them with officers more acceptable to the ruling clique in the legislature.

Are these all examples from the distant past? Some of them have happened within the past few years.

It sometimes appears to be a marvel that the spirit of local self-government in cities is not either greatly weakened or destroyed when the difficulties and obstacles that conscientious urban reformers have faced in state legislatures and even in the state courts are recounted. The legislative troubles of the cities have, of course, been increased by failures to reapportion the legislatures so as to give cities a fairer share of representation. But there is a perennial hopefulness and a resilience in the leaders in cities that make them come back time and again to renew—in local elections, in local committee and council chambers, and in state capitols—the battle for better government and for true self-government.

An important point to note here is that today about 60 per cent of the nation's people are living in urban places, and that they are steadily increasing in numbers and proportions. If urban places are not accorded real self-government, then it makes increasingly less difference if rural places fare better in this respect. In fact, however, the situation in rural places is also not what it probably should be for maximum local self-rule.

What, then, are the conditions needed for effective local self-government? Among them are these:

Areas of local government that are adequate and suitable for the functions to be performed

An appropriate organization for each type of local unit, with some flexibility and options for local variations where needed

Powers that are broad enough and flexible enough to permit local governments some freedom to experiment

A flexible array of functions, to enable the local governments to meet the changing needs of the people

Adequate revenues and sufficient borrowing powers

Suitable provisions to ensure free and honest elections

Widespread education of the people, probably at least through secondary school, including some study of basic problems of government

The last two are desirable for all levels of government and need not be separately discussed here, but the other points will be taken up in some detail.

If self-government in any meaningful sense is to be successful in achieving its assumed objectives, each unit of local government should have a sufficiently large area and population, and usually an adequate tax base. Because the legislature controls the organization or incorporation of local units, it is responsible for setting the minimum areas or populations of villages, school districts, and other units, and indeed for rationalizing the whole system of local areas in the public interest. In deference to tradition and to old theories of extreme decentralization, these minima in many states are set too low for modern requirements.

A school district that can support only a single one-room ungraded school does not meet modern educational requirements, and can be justified only in cases of extreme isolation from other settlements. To incorporate a village of a few hundred people on a small tract of platted land, with little or no potential for growth, adjacent to a city or within a metropolitan area (as can be done by the local residents under the laws of some states) is not to promote genuine self-government but primarily to invite trouble for the small place itself and also for the adjacent city or cities. Such small places cannot carry on adequately any important functions of government, but a number of them scattered around in a metropolitan area can prevent the normal expansion of adjacent cities, or the proper organization of the metropolis as a whole.

For states to permit such laws to remain in effect and to fail to provide reasonable advice and guidance to people who wish to organize such units is for the state to fail in one of its major responsibilities for local self-government. Although a few states have made some efforts to do so, I know of no state that has made a thorough study of all its local government areas with a view to establishing a more rational and workable system and more suitable areas. The fine progress that has been made recently in consolidating school districts in many states presents one noteworthy exception to these remarks. Except for these, many states appear to have far too many units and types of local governments, and new ones are being created all the time.

Furthermore, the assignment by the state to small local units of major public functions (like public health to rural townships and small villages in some states) will not strengthen the local self-government of the units concerned when they have resources and populations that are entirely too limited for the purpose. It instead prevents the performance of the function locally and finally necessitates direct state performance of some necessary services.

Because the states have complete authority over local governments within their areas, it is only through changes in state constitutions and state laws that local units can acquire the powers that they need. The state legislature sits at the center of things, presumably watching all that goes on in state and local government, and giving or denying its consent to every proposed change. Most of the proposals for significant local changes have come out of the cities, and most of them have therefore been more or less suspect. The state's confidence in its local governments has not always been high.

To think of state legislators as being always on the lookout for new and promising ways of improving local self-government is to misread their histories. Their attitudes have probably, in the long run, been far more negative than positive, more defensive of the status quo than avid for progress and reform. They have sat and acted as protectors of property taxpayers against increased local taxes, protectors of vested interests against local government competition with their businesses, protectors of public utility companies against undue local exactions, protectors of the position of the political party in power against loss of control in local governments, and protector of the state government's powers, functions, and revenue sources against the constant and insistent demands of local leaders.

All these things are probably as they should be. Local self-government is probably more valuable or at least more cherished when it has to be fought for, point by point. But the evidence is fairly convincing that state legislative attitudes help to explain why the progress toward the improvement of self-government in local communities has not been more rapid and sustained.

To carry on their routine work, to meet emergencies promptly as they arise, and to experiment from time to time with promising new functions and new ways of doing things, local governments need adequate and flexible powers, comparable in principle if not in scope with those that the states enjoy under the Constitution. In fact, however, they are everywhere bound down more or less by a rule of strict construction. They may exercise only those powers that are granted to them by the state legislatures in express words, or that are clearly implied in the powers granted, or that are absolutely necessary to the declared objects for which they have been created—not simply convenient but indispensable. In case of any doubt about a power claimed by the local government, the doubt must be resolved against the local government and the power denied. So say the state courts generally in interpreting state laws about local government. In practice the courts are not always as strict as these words imply, but the basic rule is still the one followed. Notice how this rule is practically the reverse of the rule that is applied to state powers.

The general idea behind this judicial attitude is that local governments are simply the creatures and agents of the state. If a state intended a local government to have a certain power it would have said so somewhere in the applicable laws and charters. Furthermore the legislature will soon be in session again, and at that time it can act if it wishes to authorize what the local government desires. So at least the judges reason.

Local powers are, therefore, spelled out in great detail in the state laws, and in every law there are usually numerous restrictions and directions. This, again, is quite unlike the situation that the states are in. States do not need to find in the United States Constitution or laws any specific language authorizing them to do a thing. They just go ahead and legislate on anything they believe to be within their powers, and leave it to the courts later to decide whether they acted constitutionally.

It is clear that local governments should not be granted the power to do anything whatever that they please. I believe that no reasonable person would desire to promote that kind of anarchy. State legislative supremacy over local governments needs to be maintained. What is needed is a variety of legislative devices by which broader and more flexible powers can be made available, subject perhaps to some advisory check by the state attorney general or other such officer.

Municipal home rule is one such device. Since 1875 Missouri has had in its constitution a provision authorizing cities in that state to make, adopt, and amend their own charters consistent with the constitution and laws of the state. This idea has proved to be both workable and entirely safe for all concerned when it is properly worded. It does not give cities a completely free hand, but it permits them to alter the form of their city government and to introduce new powers and functions of government from time to time without going through the legislature. It is a step toward more complete self-government. The charter making and amending procedures are carried out locally, with approval by the voters, in a manner very much like that by which states adopt and amend their constitutions. Up to now, however, just over a third of the states have authorized their cities to adopt home-rule charters.

A similar procedure for counties has been known for a generation now, but to date only six states have adopted county home-rule provisions. In many states of predominantly rural population there is perhaps little need of such a power, but in every state with metropolitan, large urban, and suburban counties some such power and procedure could prove useful in meeting the distinctive needs of such counties.

Where municipal and county home rule have not been authorized it is feasible to enact general legislation to permit cities and counties by vote of the people to adopt one or another form of government as set forth in the law. Some states have done this with a fair degree of success as shown by various local charter elections to adopt Plan A or B or C as the local form of rule. As a means of freeing local governments from old restrictive forms of government, and of giving the voters locally something to say about their governmental structure, these optional laws are a very good "second best" as compared with home rule. Here again it is surprising how little headway this idea has made among the states generally. The resistance seems to be greatest against laws permitting optional forms of government for counties. The county-manager plan is widely opposed, but in some states so is even the small commission type.

When new local government procedures, new powers, and new functions have been found to work out successfully in some places and to be in the public interest, one way to make them available to other local governments of comparable type is for the legislature to pass appropriate general laws enabling other local governments to do likewise. There is no great gain from successful local experiments if they do not become available to other local units. This method of extending local powers is being widely used today, but only some spot checks would show how widely. How many states, for example, have broad enabling acts to authorize the use of voting machines in cities, photostatic copying of public records, the appointment of a trained medical examiner to replace the elective coroner, and the many other things that have been proved by various local experiments to have a real value to the public?

Whatever the other powers granted to local governments, they

223

must also be able to raise sufficient revenue to carry out their functions. Broadly speaking, in recent decades the states have had ample powers to levy additional taxes to meet their needs, but in many instances their legislatures have lacked the will to impose what taxes were needed even to balance their budgets; whereas the local governments, especially in urban areas, have had the desire and I think the will to raise more money by taxation but have simply lacked the power to do so. At least this in general is the difference between the state and local governments with respect to revenues, as I see them.

When both the states and their local governments relied mainly upon the general property tax for their major revenues, the state legislatures developed the practice of keeping strict control over local tax rates so that the combined state-and-local rate would not too greatly outrage the taxpayers. When the states began to turn to other sources of revenue—inheritance and income taxes, both general and selective sales taxes, special corporation levies, and the like—there was some hope in local quarters that the property tax would be turned over to the local governments substantially unimpaired.

In this the local authorities were doomed to disappointment. In many instances when a state imposed a railroad gross earnings tax, or a utilities tax, or a motor vehicle tax, to put revenue into the state treasury, it at the same time exempted a part or all of the corresponding property (railroads, motor vehicles) from the property tax. Thus the property "base" on which the local governments could levy their taxes was reduced, bit by bit. Later a number of states adopted "homestead exemptions" or reductions, and provided exemptions, or lower rates at least, for veterans. Some also repealed the personal property tax—another blow to local governments. All in all the local governments fared badly, but more was yet to come.

During the 1920s and the 1930s the taxpayers organized more and more effectively to hold down and to reduce the taxes on real and personal property. Various kinds of tax limitation laws were enacted in the states. Most of these limited the rates of taxation on property. Some states also adopted constitutional amendments putting "over-all" limitations on tax rates; that is to say, they set maximum total rates for all the governments that taxed property in the county or other local unit, and arranged for dividing this total rate among the different local layers of government—such a part to the county, so much to the school districts, and so on. These measures were indeed drastic reducing remedies for the local governments. Local self-government reached a very low ebb in a number of states during this period. Public schools, police and fire departments, and other major services all suffered in consequence.

During this period also a number of states introduced state plans for approving, reducing, or vetoing local bond issues and local government budgets. State agencies made decisions on strictly local matters. "Pay-as-you-go" laws were imposed upon a number of local governments. The financial outlook for local governments and their services was never more desperate.

It was spending by the national government during the 1930s that helped to keep many local governments going. A national "municipal bankruptcy act" was also passed by Congress to help some of the more hopelessly debt-ridden local governments out of their financial troubles. There were, too, a few instances in which state legislatures began to share with local governments the proceeds of some state taxes, and in Michigan those interested in the financing of counties, townships, and school districts initiated and induced the voters to pass a measure to distribute much of the state sales tax among these local units.

In general, however, local governments throughout the nation continued to be dependent primarily upon the property tax, and remained in an unhappy financial plight, alleviated only in part by the prosperity and the new inflation that came with the wartime industrial boom. In the meantime several states, notably Pennsylvania, New York, and California, began to pay more constructive attention to local financial needs. In the 1940s Pennsylvania and New York passed broad general laws for "home-rule taxing powers" for local governments. The states have also increased substan-

225

tially their state aid to local governments, primarily for education, highways, and welfare; and there have been some additional instances of state-local tax-sharing from such sources as tobacco and liquor taxes.

Cities have also benefited to some extent here and there from state laws authorizing them to levy local sales taxes, income taxes, and admissions taxes, to name some of the more important ones, and they have also been authorized to install parking meters and to impose service charges for what they do in many places. In general, however, partly because of the inflation, the outlook for local finance is not bright—and it is the cities that in general are in the worst predicament. State aids for highways and education, for example, go largely to rural areas, to school districts, and to counties, not to cities. An important exception is the "block grant" system that has been introduced in New York, from which cities get considerable benefit.

The generally poor state of local finances in the United States in recent years is indeed surprising when one considers the general prosperity that has prevailed for the nearly ten years since the end of World War II. Certain measures of the national government, like federal aid for urban highways, for farm-to-market roads, for hospital construction, airports, and public housing, among other things, have helped considerably to enable local governments to catch up on some construction needs. But it cannot be said that the states generally have been sufficiently aware of the importance of adequate financing for maintaining the virility of their local units of government.

At several points in the preceding discussion the influence of the national government upon local government finance has been mentioned. In one way or another, time and again, the national government has taken actions that have helped the local governments very materially.

The question has arisen in connection with federal aid for airports and in other cases whether the national government should ever have direct financial relations with the local units of government. Is not this a dangerous invasion of the states' constitutional powers in the control of local government?

Various considerations have led to the creation of direct national-local arrangements. In the first place the mayors and other leaders of large cities throughout the nation have come to feel that the state legislatures, under normally rural domination, have no real interest in the problems and needs of the large cities. The United States Conference of Mayors, with headquarters in Washington, D.C., was founded partly on the thesis that the problems of the large cities are essentially national in their scope and importance, and that the state legislatures are not going to do much about them. Therefore, national action is necessary. Second, various federal-aid acts are for the support of services like public housing, airports, and urban highways in which the big city interest is very strong. Finally, the emergency relief and construction acts of the depression period in many cases called for urban cooperation with the national authorities, and at that time the legislatures generally saw no objection to such direct relations between the national and municipal authorities. It was only later that state organizations—the Governors' Conference, for instance —became sensitive about this alleged invasion of state authority over local governments by the national government.

Those who speak for the states point out, however, that aside from the dangerous constitutional precedent that may be set by direct national-municipal relations, there is the point that since all local governments exist as agents of the state, what the cities do may call for new state laws, for increased state support of the services in question, and thus the states have a great interest in all that the cities do. They urge that in general the relations between the national and municipal governments should channel through the state government. This is much the same point as is raised about direct relations between state functional departments and the corresponding national agencies. The governors who stress this point are clearly trying to maintain the unity and integrity of each state government.

This issue was fought out in the debate over the airport construction act of 1946, but the outcome was not just what the state leaders wanted. Congress in effect left it to each state to decide for itself through legislative action whether it wanted to have national-local relationships in airport construction channeled through a state office. Some states might not wish to set up a state authority for this purpose, and so it was left. It seems to me that in general Congress should respect the right of every state to control its local governments, but should not force every state to adopt the same method for handling such a matter as federal aid for airport construction.

The general conclusion of this wholly inadequate chapter is that the states have fallen short of the ideal in many respects when their actions on local self-government are considered. Many things that only the states can do to improve and strengthen local self-government they are doing poorly or even neglecting to do. Toward the larger cities in particular many a state legislature seems to have an antagonistic and competitive attitude—and yet most Americans are now living in cities, and proportionately more will do so in the future. Is this antagonism then an expression of fear of what is going to come? Or an evidence that legislators know they have not dealt entirely fairly and competently with the urban problems?

Even aside from this aspect, the states' performance in preserving and promoting local self-government generally is not all that it might have been and could yet be. Legislators have neglected general local government problems of areas, organization, and finance, have displayed a temporizing and delaying attitude, an unwillingness to try to bring the machinery and powers of local government up to date in the face of the great changes that have come over the nation. The governors, also, have in general not given enough leadership toward modernizing and strengthening local government to meet the needs created by modern conditions. There is need for much research and much fresh thinking on how to maintain the principle of local self-government in the age ahead when most of the people will be living in fairly large to very large cities. If the state governments do not do their share, they should not be surprised to find the cities appealing more and more for aid from the national government.

Is local self-government then in decline? Paradoxically, I think not. Despite what some state leaders say about the dire effects of federal grants and supervision upon the self-government of the states, I do not for a minute believe that state aid to local units and state supervision over them is in any way dangerous to local self-government.

Local self-government, I repeat, is something that has to be fought for, over and over again. Those who want to see better local governance, adequately financed, and under genuine, intelligent popular control, come back again and again from their defeats to begin the battle all over. Sometimes, of course, they win. The spirit of self-rule persists and constantly reasserts itself. I think it will continue and will win even more victories in the years ahead.

This spirit of local self-government, and the spirits of state and national self-government, need to be preserved as cooperating forces for the general strength and welfare of the nation.

☆

PART IV
Changing the System

14

A Program of Constructive Action

BEFORE outlining any suggestions for positive action to improve the federal system and intergovernmental relations, I cannot refrain from reviewing a few issues of philosophy as to what is good for America. My appeal is to every pariotic citizen to look at the situation within the United States, and at the nation's position in the world, as realistically as he can, and then to decide whether the nation's course with respect to the federal system and the relations between the national, state, and local governments needs to be changed, and if so, why and how.

We need to look at the situation not only as it is today, but also as it has developed historically, and to look ahead as prophetically as we can by projecting past trends and present conditions into the future. This will require a look at the total situation of the country, as fully as any person can survey it, and a placing of general trends and accomplishments ahead of particular present grievances, whether merely fancied or real.

Important issues cannot be wisely decided by catch words and phrases that are heavily charged with emotions, like "bureaucrat," "power hungry," and "dictator"; or by the blind acceptance of myths about the universal dangers in centralization and "big government," and the ineffable virtues and beauties of decentralization and little governments. The facts seem to reveal that there are no black and white contrasts between central and local government when genuine popular controls prevail over all levels. There are instead various shades of gray in the performance of government, and the darker grays are not by any means all at the level of central government.

Changing the System

What are, then, some of the major facts to be listed for the appraisal?

The population of the United States is only about one fifteenth of the world population, its area only about one tenth that of the habitable area of the globe. Within this area the American people have developed the greatest accumulation of material wealth and in most respects the highest standard of living ever known. They are the envy of the whole world, the object of hatred to many people.

Although they have real friends in many important lands they have also powerful enemies. They cannot maintain their place in the world or ultimately even provide for their own security by standing completely alone. The Communist nations in particular miss hardly any tricks or opportunities in their persistent and malevolent efforts to create dissension and weakness within the United States and enmity against this nation abroad. They recognize, as some Americans seem not to, that the United States is the principal bulwark of the free nations of the world against their revolutionary conspiracy to dominate all nations. If the United States weakens and goes down, what forces will be left in the world to prevent the destruction of the civilization and the free and democratic "way of life" that Americans so generally hold dear?

The population of the United States—now more than 160 million—is steadily growing in numbers and changing in age composition and other characteristics. There is complete freedom of internal migration so that constant shifts of residence are taking place—toward the great cities, toward the west, and toward the south. Agriculture is changing, modernizing, and becoming more scientific and productive, so that the problem of markets is ever present. Industry, already largely organized on a national scale and highly mechanized and productive, is finding new raw-material resources, developing new products, growing in plant and in volume of output, and also seeking new markets, at home and abroad. The up-to-date and complex system of transportation and communication is also nationwide. Advertising is largely national.

Sales organizations are local, metropolitan, regional, and national. Under these many influences the people are constantly raising their standards of living, and demanding more, newer, and better products. Their average incomes, also, are high and going higher.

To govern this great and dynamic society the nation has under one supreme Constitution a national government, forty-eight state governments, and more than 100,000 local units of government. The people have come more and more to expect national action on national problems. They have organized national associations for almost every conceivable purpose—fraternal, religious, educational, scientific, professional, financial, industrial, commercial, and agricultural—as well as in every important field of the public services and of public policy. Through these associations and by other means the people learn that their local problems are also national, or at least nationwide. Everywhere the highways are falling behind traffic needs, the public schools are already inadequate and are facing an early large influx of more children, private and public health services and facilities are not keeping up with modern possibilities of prevention and cure—and so on through all the public functions and all the genuine needs felt by the people.

In these circumstances, as given in this utterly inadequate thumbnail sketch, how shall the public services be advanced and maintained to keep up with the demands of a so-rapidly growing and changing population? How shall the work be organized, administered, and financed? What level of government or combination of levels shall handle the various tasks and under what agreements with each other as to financial aid and other conditions? How in all this organization and activity under public authority shall popular self-government and the liberties of the people be maintained? These are some of the major issues, and there are numerous others.

Faced with this great array of specific and practical problems most Americans are content to take up each one as it comes within their purview and to seek practical changes and adjustments to satisfy growing needs and to protect existing rights. This practical and piecemeal approach does not satisfy everyone, however. There are many conscientious persons who are understandably troubled

235

about a purely empirical, trial-and-error approach. They fear that when changes are made in this way, without any general plan or philosophy, important values may be lost never to be recovered.

I agree with them on the importance of theory, and of trying to see the whole probable effect before making any important change in any part of the governmental system. But a theory ought to conform to and explain the facts. From this viewpoint I find myself unable to agree with some of the particular philosophies that have been put forward in this field. I think I can distinguish in particular two such philosophies, but they overlap somewhat, and their spokesmen stand together at least in a general opposition to recent trends toward national leadership and activity in the public services. We have already considered these philosophies at some length but let me review the essentials.

One group, represented by a number of state governors and numerous other persons, espouses and sets up as a controlling value a certain view of the federal system of government under the Constitution, a view that they believe represents "the intention of the framers" of the original document. This is the view that the national government was never intended to have or to exercise some of its present powers and functions, especially in spending for the general welfare and in providing federal aid for the states; that by such actions the powers of government are becoming unduly centralized in the national government with consequent loss of self-government by the states; and that in this way the federal system as originally planned is being destroyed. Men of this persuasion agree in general that government under modern conditions must be more active and "interventionist" than it used to be in economic and social affairs, but they want more of the decisions, the financing, and the administration of services left in the hands of the states alone. In this way they believe the true federal system will be preserved.

Another and rather amorphous group puts forth a more sweeping philosophy, one that is in some respects antithetical to active and effective government. On its surface it seems to be opposed only to strength and activity in the central or national government, but on closer examination it is seen to be opposed to state and local governmental activity as well.

It is in many respects, I think, a philosophy inspired by fear and defeatism. It pictures "big government" and "centralization" as leading inexorably to "paternalism," "socialism," "the welfare state," and dictatorship, and it revives the discredited shibboleth of "states' rights." It professes loyalty to the Constitution, but seems to forget that the adoption of that Constitution by the people, with its provisions for a strong national government, was one of the greatest acts of constructive republican centralization the world has ever witnessed. The holders of this philosophy certainly think of themselves as the most loyal and patriotic of Americans, and the most strongly opposed to communism, yet they favor measures to weaken the national government and its popular support, measures that the Communists would probably be glad to see carried out in the United States.

Some of the proponents of this philosophy have taken to calling themselves "nationalists," but this is a curiously misleading term as applied to them. They are certainly "anti-internationalists," in a sense, but they are not for a strong national government. Many of them supported the so-called Bricker Amendment which would have weakened the power of the national government, acting through the President, to enter into binding national agreements. That amendment would, in my judgment, have weakened the historic freedom of the nation to conduct an effective foreign policy. It even pointed in the direction of extreme states' rights in that some treaties might have required the separate consents of every state legislature before they could have become effective. Even the Articles of Confederation did not go this far. This is indeed a curious kind of "nationalism."

In internal policy, especially, many holders of this philosophy are for weakening the national government and reviving a system of states' rights. Some of them have been leading exponents of a proposed constitutional amendment to limit the power of Congress to levy income and estate taxes (the proposed 25 per cent limitation), and a few have gone so far as to advocate taking the income tax power away from Congress entirely and vesting it wholly in the states. In this way the national government would become dependent on the states for grants-in-aid, very much as under the Articles of Confederation. Another proposal has been a drastic constitutional limitation on all nondefense *spending* by the national government, in order to exorcise the demon of "the welfare state." Under their own reasoning the holders of this view would have to oppose the welfare state at state and local levels as well.

I wish to repeat that I do not think that all proponents of changes in the fiscal and functional relations between the national and state governments accept this philosophy. Quite the contrary; many of them make only modest proposals in line with American traditions and practices. But supporting these moderates, and planning to go far beyond them, are numerous citizens who hold essentially to the views that I have outlined.

The conditions and the necessities of modern life that have led to the expansion of governmental services and controls have been largely ignored in the second philosophy thus briefly outlined— and to some extent in the first philosophy also. The great achievements of the American people, acting politically through their established system of government, in the development of the United States to what it is today have simply been taken for granted, or ignored, or held up as objects to arouse fears as to what may come next. Political activity and government as such seem to be looked upon as inherently bad and dangerous and not as essential activities and tools of a people struggling for a better life. The anti-active-government philosophy looks to the past, and those who hold it seem to yearn for something smaller, more peaceful, less hectic and demanding than what they find in the modern era— something that they think must once have existed. The escapism and the mythology about American history that underlie this philosophy are so evident that even he who runs may read them.

If their ideas were carried out to their logical conclusions, they would reverse the long-time trend toward nationhood with its unity of action as one nation. The trend toward national-state cooperation would have to give way to states' rights and the revival of rivalry, suspicion, and opposition between the national and the state governments. Grants-in-aid and other means of cooperation would largely fall by the wayside. The trend toward expansion of the public services, and toward social responsiveness on the part of government to the needs of the people, would be not merely halted but reversed. Even the development of the idea of the sharing of burdens according to ability to pay would be abandoned if the ideas of some persons in this group of believers were to prevail. The national income tax, for example, would be either drastically limited or repealed. I do not expect these ideas to prevail but I think they should be brought out into the light.

When I mention what the American people have achieved as a nation largely through politics, government, and administration, I have in mind that they have used all three levels of government, national, state, and local, as their necessary tools and instruments. They have used them not only for strictly public measures but also to foster morality, religion, home and farm ownership, industry and thrift, and the spirit of liberty and self-reliance, among other virtues, in the people. In many of the most important things in the nation's life the national government, under an able line of Presidents from George Washington to Dwight Eisenhower, has taken the lead. One of the grave questions now is how much if any of that national leadership shall be abandoned.

But what do I mean by the great achievements in politics and government that have made the United States what it is today, and in most of which the national government has had a leading part? Very few persons have ever attempted to draw up such a list as I give here, and I make no claim that this one is exhaustive or that it is the best short list that could be made. But here it is, and it represents a large part of what the United States means to me. I hope to be pardoned if I seem to wave the flag too vigorously.

★ The adoption of the Declaration of Independence

★ The successful struggle for national independence and nationhood

239

Changing the System

★ The adoption of the Constitution of the United States

★ The setting up of a complete and effective national government of three branches and a national administrative organization under the Constitution

★ The adoption of the Bill of Rights, listing the fundamental liberties of the people including freedom of speech, press, and religion

★ The practice of judicial review for protecting people's rights

★ The acquisition and development of a continental domain

★ The creation of thirty-five additional self-governing states and their admission into the Union

★ The creation of a continent-wide network of state and local governments on republican principles

★ The building up in most of the people of a tradition of representative government under popular control through free elections, and with an essentially two-party political system

★ The preservation of the Union in its gravest crisis, and the establishment of the principle that political change thereafter should be by peaceful means

★ The emancipation of the Negroes held in slavery

★ The opening of the western lands to homesteaders

★ The establishment of a unified rule of national citizenship

★ The establishment of the principles of due process of law and equal protection of the laws as binding on all the states

★ The establishment and protection of internal free trade and migration throughout the nation

★ The encouragement and promotion of the greatest and in most senses the freest system of private enterprise in the world

★ The creation of a nationwide system of free public education

★ The establishment of merit civil-service systems of a high order of honesty and effectiveness in the national government and in many state and local governments

★ The establishment of courts and of effective law enforcement throughout the nation

★ The establishment of nationwide systems of postal service, of public roads and highways, of railroads, of inland waterways, of airways and airports, and of communications by telegraph, telephone, radio, television, and other media, mostly under national laws and protection

★The adoption of nationwide port and harbor improvements and protection to ocean shipping

★ The establishment of a national system of flood control and river improvements, public drainage and irrigation, and water power developments

★ The protection of the public domain, including land, waters, game, fish, minerals, and forests, against ruthless exploitation

★ The establishment of an unexcelled system of public parks, forests, and reserves—national, state, and local

★ The provision of nationwide aid—national, state, and local— for the aged, the needy, the dependent, the blind, and other handicapped classes

★ The establishment of a national system of social security, OASI

★ The provision of public health services and hospitals everywhere

★ The provision of workmen's compensation and unemployment compensation everywhere

★ The making of elaborate and generous provisions for all veterans

★ The nationwide state and national promotion and regulation of safe banking, sound insurance, honest sales of stocks and bonds, fair trade practices in commerce, safety in industry, fair labor practices, and the settlement of industrial disputes

★ The encouragement nationally, and to some extent in states and local communities, of home ownership and family farm ownership, and the progressive elimination of tenancy

★ The national efforts to stabilize the agricultural industry, the oil industry, the coal industry, and other sectors of the economy

★ The passing of national laws to maintain high levels of employment

★ The establishment of state universities and colleges in every state, including a unique system of nationally promoted land-grant colleges for those seeking careers in agricultural and mechanical pursuits

★ The establishment of agricultural experiment stations and agricultural extension work in all states

★ The establishment of an extensive system of federal aid to assist the states in raising their standards in various public services

This is clearly only a partial list of what the nation has achieved in less than 200 years. It includes nothing about achievements in national defense, atomic energy, or foreign affairs or about numerous types of public institutions and miscellaneous national, state, and local services. But the list is already long enough to raise the question What is there so radically wrong with what the United States has achieved or the path it is pursuing that some men desire now, at this stage in the nation's development, to reduce the leadership of the national government, to "weaken" the national government?

If the services that I have listed are dangerous "socialism" or "paternalism," then I suppose that many United States citizens, myself included, must stand convicted of favoring socialism and paternalism. But I simply do not believe that these words apply to the many things I have listed—things that Americans have achieved through politics and government, largely under the leadership and direction of the national government, and with the cooperation of all levels of government and countless citizens and private groups.

As long as effective popular controls are continued over government—and they are fully as effective over the national government as they are over most state and local governments—what is the reason to fear "bigness" and "centralization" in government? I think the case against centralization and bigness has not been proved. As long as the individual is not lost sight of, it seems to me that it is just as safe and in many ways more effective and even more moral and responsible, to think in big terms and to act in big units as it is to think and act in small terms and small units. Business organizations, churches, and many other groups all seek growth and bigness. Moral virtue lies in individual choices and actions, not in the sizes of the groups through which men work.

I doubt also that anyone could show that state and local governments have, on the average, been more virtuous and high-minded in their actions or more mindful of the dignity of man or of the liberties of individuals, or have maintained higher standards of public morality, than the national government of the United States. Presidents like Washington, Jefferson, Lincoln—in fact I would say all the Presidents—have been interested primarily in establishing and maintaining honest and effective government, according to their own lights, in order to promote the national security and general welfare. They have not been interested in power for power's sake or in setting up personal dictatorships; Washington, Lincoln, and the others simply cannot be explained in such terms. Although a few have been weak and have been imposed upon by conniving friends, no President has been guilty of personal malfeasance, or of any attempt to perpetuate himself in office unconstitutionally.

What is the factual basis in American experience for the fears and the almost morbid distrust of the national government of the United States that are expressed in many current writings? On any comparative factual basis is not the record on the whole a good one? And have not the American people shown a really high capacity for self-government nationally and for keeping their national government in particular under effective control?

The evidence seems to me to indicate that, under firm and forward-looking national leadership, the state and local governments also do their work much better; and even when all-out war descends upon the nation, and the whole machinery of government, after some initial blunders and false starts, gets better organized into an effective and highly integrated working organization—all this is done without ever seriously endangering basic civil liberties, or bringing any threat of a personal dictatorship comparable to that of a Hitler or a Mussolini. The conditions of political life in the United States are not favorable to that sort of outcome.

In the whole history of government in the United States I think the evidence shows that strength and unity in government are better for the public welfare than weakness, and also that all three levels of government—national, state, and local—need to be strong and effective if the best results are to be achieved. The cooperation of all three levels is needed if goals are to be attained. The better organized the governments are, the better staffed they are, the better financed they are, the more cooperative and effective they are.

For these reasons, I favor strong and efficient governments at all levels, and I truly believe that much progress has been made in this direction in recent decades. My view, in short, is that no fundamental change is needed in the relations between the national and state governments: no weakening of the national government, no great shifting of functions, no important reallocation of revenues or of taxing power, no basic change in federal-aid programs or policies, no diminution of the autonomy of either the national or state governments.

Looking at the conclusions I have reached after long study of the subject of intergovernmental relations, I am indeed surprised to find what a conservative I have become or have always been. I have the temerity to suggest that if others who write on this subject would do more fundamental studying and thinking about the subject in all its complexities and fullness of details, and would candidly consider the alternatives and not expect perfection, they would probably come out not very far from where I do.

My personal suggestions for improving intergovernmental relations are, in general, for going forward steadily along the lines of recent developments, for testing, adjusting, and improving relations progressively, and not for any sweeping changes or for any attempt to "return" to some supposedly better arrangement that is presumed to have existed in the past. In any case, unless all the nation's social and economic developments of many decades can also be reversed, I see no chance of changing greatly the major governmental developments that they have evoked. The social, the economic, the political, and the governmental practices of any society are unavoidably and necessarily interwoven and interdependent, as integrated aspects of the entire social life.

But improvements are always possible and desirable. No system of government can stand still. I therefore present the following modest list of suggestions for policies and actions to be carried out at the several levels where the power to do so rests.

Put national security and defense ahead of other considerations as long as the present world tensions prevail. Do nothing to weaken the national government in its ability to perform any part of its allotted work—in foreign affairs, in military affairs, or in domestic affairs. A national government that is indifferent to the people's needs at home cannot count upon their complete loyalty and enthusiasm in the struggle against subversion at home or against attacks from abroad.

Remember that the reasons for doing the utmost for national security are to protect the way of life that the people have found to be good, including freedom of speech, press, and religion, popular elections and control of government, equal protection of the laws, free public education, protection to the consumer against fraud and profiteering, and various public health and welfare services. These things need to be continued and also improved as far as they can be, even while defense is a first consideration, yes, even during war.

Endeavor to strengthen and improve government at all levels, national, state, and local.

Try to turn the emphasis of the states' leaders from the issue of states' rights to the problem of *states' duties* under the Constitution to work for the general welfare.

Remember that all levels of government are parts of a highly effective and complex system of organization. All are needed for producing the services now rendered and for continuing the American system of popular control of government.

Keep the present autonomy of the national and state governments, and try to increase that of the larger local units.

Call upon the leaders and citizens in all units of government, national, state, and local, to do what they can in their several governments to improve popular government. Don't leave it all up to the national authorities.

Extend and improve the political and economic education of the people.

Don't make a scapegoat of the national government and blame it and its policies for all local and state difficulties. Many if not most of those difficulties are produced at home and are remediable only at home, through changes in state constitutions, state laws, and state and local practices.

Leave or put powers and functions where they can be *effectively* exercised and performed. If that means a sharing of responsibilities among various units and several levels, well and good. The problems of intergovernmental cooperation can always be worked out if *service and not power* is set as the goal.

Put a large question mark opposite the statement that weakening the national government will strengthen the state governments, and ask for the evidence. The city-states of ancient Greece, the United States under the Articles of Confederation, and the states'-rights-worshipping states in the Confederacy of 1861–65 had the satisfaction of claiming to be sovereign and independent states, but they obstructed each other, even fought with each other in some cases, and stood in the way of central united action to such an extent that in the end they suffered the loss of all their pretensions. "In Union there is strength." This implies having a central government to do things for common purposes, which thus saves the strength of the members that might otherwise be wasted in strife, in duplication of effort, and in attempts to do things beyond their natural powers.

Remember that local self-government implies the necessary existence of strong central government. The stronger the central government, the more easily it can tolerate strength and activity in the member states of a union, but the central authority must always have the supreme and guiding hand.

Look with much skepticism on any statement about "transferring" a whole function or activity from the national government to the states, or from the states to the local governments. The

246

transfer will be no transfer at all, but rather a weakening and possible ultimate destruction of the function, if the units to which it is to be transferred are incapable of handling it, or are subject to pressure groups that will not permit it to be performed.

If public ratemaking is involved, watch out that the unit to which the power is to be transferred is not practically in league with the private interests that want to profiteer at public expense, or at the expense of consumers elsewhere.

If the ownership and management of public lands and other property are involved in the transfer of control, watch out that the governmental unit to which the control is to go is not already committed to private exploitation of the resources even to the point of destruction. "Don't set the wolves to watch the sheep!" is an old and useful warning. Leave the control where it can be *effectively* exercised in the general public interest.

Remember that for most regulatory and management purposes, the area and jurisdiction of the regulating or managing authority ought to be such as to include all that is to be regulated and managed. For greater equality of treatment, greater efficiency, and as a practical matter, the state governments should consider whether the control of subversion in all its forms is not strictly a national responsibility, and whether the provision of veterans' benefits of all kinds should not be a charge primarily if not wholly on the national budget.

Remember in fiscal matters that the defense needs of the nation are completely incalculable. Do not let the nation get into a position where it does not have adequate taxing, borrowing, and spending power for every national need, both nondefense and defense. This applies at all times, before a war comes and after a war, as well as during hostilities.

Leave the states also with their present broad taxing powers under the Constitution of the United States, and if the tax system in your own state is inadequate or unfair examine first your *state* constitution and laws and policy to see whether the fault is not there.

Continue and expand the efforts of the national government to

247

protect the taxing powers of the states against destructive inter-state competition and against methods of evasion of state taxes through interstate commerce and the postal system.

While defense expenses have to be high, continue efforts to keep other expenses (national, state, and local) within reasonable limits, even postponing some desirable improvements if necessary. *Indeed, this should be done at all times.*

Restrict all new national spending on domestic functions to sit-uations in which there is a clearly demonstrated national need and national interest.

Keep in mind in all revenue adjustments that within the states it is the large cities that have the greatest need for financial aid today.

Remember that local governments are very dependent upon the general property tax. Both state and national governments should provide appropriate payments in lieu of taxes for property they take off the tax rolls, especially when such property produces a revenue.

Do not be misled into trying to itemize in long lists of details all the powers or all the specific functions and activities of na-tional, state, and local governments. A constitution is better for being brief and allowing for a great deal of flexibility, change, and growth. A rigid code listing the exclusive powers and func-tions of the national, state, and local governments, if it could be worked out at all, would be a Pandora's box of ill-will, strife, and litigation. Keep the present flexibility between national and state functions under the Constitution.

Keep the internal compulsive powers (eminent domain, taxa-tion, police power, civil draft, and penal power) intact under present rules as to priorities. All units of government have to use all of them in varying amounts, degrees, and forms, and in many different situations.

Remember that functions such as roads, health, education, wel-fare, and law enforcement overlap and affect each other in so many ways that they cannot be separated out from each other and put in separate non-communicating compartments. Education includes health education; sick children are likely to be poor students in school; roads carry school buses and sanitary vehicles; and law enforcement is needed to make all other functions effective. The same interrelationships exist to some extent among all other functions of government.

As between the levels of government, continue to work out divisions of labor and support so that in any broad function like public health each level of government will do that part of the work which it can do best, and each level will support the function according to its *interest* as modified by its *ability*.

As for the national government, let Congress consider giving up as soon as possible the "government towns" at atomic energy plants and elsewhere. Let them go under the ordinary state laws on urban government, and let the people living in them vote in them and be responsible for their government and, as far as reasonable, for their finances.

Continue the basic federal-aid policy and program of the nation toward the states, and expand and improve state aids to local units, because grants-in-aid seem to offer the best available compromise plan for the financial health of state and local units, for the strengthening of the states, for equalizing common burdens, and for promoting intergovernmental cooperation. State and local governments like individuals need various incentives to do their best work.

When told that grants-in-aid are destroying the self-government of American state and local governments, ask to see the historical evidence, and analyze it independently. I don't think a good case has been made out against the federal-aid system.

Where the service is one that ought to be provided as nearly as possible on an equal basis throughout the nation, for reasons of national welfare, make the federal grants to the states serve as equalizers of the cost burden; that is, give proportionately larger grants to the states of lower average income—in proportion to their service needs and in inverse proportion to the incomes of the people.

249

Follow the same principle of equalization in state aids to local units for functions of statewide concern.

Avoid "open-end" grants-in-aid as much as possible; that is, make it possible to budget and appropriate definite amounts each year where this can be done. But some welfare grants may work better if left as "open-end" grants.

Encourage state budgeting of federal aids as fully as possible. Many governors and state budget officers are trying to do a good job of integrating their state administrations, and effective central budgeting of all major funds is important to effective control and integration.

Consolidate some of the minor federal-aid programs in public health, and in education, into larger ones, and give increased flexibility and freedom to the state governments in the spending of them, but require at least some notice to be given to the appropriate federal agency of each important change to be made by any state.

Continue to require minimum standards of performance, with adequate reporting and accounting, from all units of government that receive grants-in-aid, and reasonable matching of funds where feasible and justifiable.

Reduce the amount of supervision and paper work that is required of state and local governments to a more reasonable minimum.

Continue in every feasible way to reduce the human frictions and irritations that unavoidably arise when agents from one level of government supervise the work of officers and employers at another level. Supervision is most effective when it takes the forms of assistance, cooperation, and friendly encouragement among equals.

Consider whether in the light of the current and increasing crisis in the support of public education, in view of rapidly rising school populations and the shifts in population from place to place, some program of federal aid or loans for school construction may not be necessary in the national interest for the next ten years or more. This may be especially needed in the states directly affected by the Supreme Court decision against segregation in the public schools.

Wherever a state legislature wishes it, let federal grants designed for local governments be cleared through the state treasury or other appropriate agency, but do not force this by national law upon any state.

Taxes that are collected by one level of government, but whose proceeds are shared by law between several levels of governmental units, are suitable in state-local relations, because local governments are dependent upon the state government for their powers to tax, to spend, and to perform functions.

Remember that although it is the urban places that particularly need financial aid at the present time, school districts almost everywhere are also in great need. Tax-sharing would be appropriate in both cases.

Remember that the dedication by constitution or law of particular tax revenues to specific expenditure purposes is generally conceded to be harmful to sound budgeting at every level of government.

Continue the present almost complete freedom from such dedications in the national government.

Eliminate dedications in the states by state action as soon as this can reasonably be done.

Have Congress repeal the present laws designed to require state dedication of gasoline taxes to highway purposes and game and fish license revenues to the corresponding conservation purposes.

Keep Congress, which is the best representative of the interests of all the states, as the agency to settle questions of the adjustment of national to state interests.

Encourage the formation for study and report purposes of a commission or at least an interdepartmental committee in Washington with a small research staff, and a cooperative advisory group from the states representing the legislatures, the governors, the state budget officers, and the principal state functional departments (highways, health, education, welfare, airports, and agriculture). Have this committee or commission conduct the investigations needed to iron out any difficulties that crop up in the administration of federal aid. A separate but similar study arrangement for frequent review of overlapping tax and revenue problems and for promoting intergovernmental cooperation in tax administration might also be desirable. The principal classes of local governments (cities and counties at least) should regularly be represented on any such study groups.

Remember that the whole field of intergovernmental relations is an intensely practical one, because it is so full of the problems of human relations. In every field a somewhat different pattern develops because of the nature of the function, the laws, the personalities of the officials, and many other factors. This being so, work with and from what has already been devised to what is practically attainable. Do not reason out a theory unrelated to the facts and then prescribe it and force it upon those who must administer the program. Remember the words of Robert Browning:

> The common problem, yours, mine, everyone's
> Is not to fancy what were fair in life
> Provided it *could* be; but finding first
> What *may* be, then find how to make it fair
> Up to our means—a very different thing.

☆

SUGGESTIONS FOR FURTHER
READING AND INDEX

Suggestions for Further Reading

THAT the interest in the problems of federal government and intergovernmental relations is widespread is attested to by the already voluminous and rapidly growing body of publications that are devoted to these problems.

The Library of Congress issued on November 6, 1953, a 73-page selected bibliography *Intergovernmental Relations in the United States*. This mimeographed list was prepared at the request of the Commission on Intergovernmental Relations by W. Brooke Graves, chief of the Government Division of the Legislative Reference Service of the Library.

In May 1954 the Joint Reference Library (located at 1313 East 60th Street, Chicago) issued its own selected bibliography in 39 pages entitled *Federal-State-Local Relations*, which it had prepared for the American Municipal Association and the Council of State Governments.

These basic lists are indispensable for the research-minded.

Also useful for research is *Federalism and Intergovernmental Relations: A Budget of Suggestions for Research*, prepared by William Anderson on behalf of the Committee on Public Administration and the Committee on Government of the Social Science Research Council, and published by the Public Administration Service, Chicago, in 1946. This research handbook contains a highly selective bibliography (pages 181–92) for the United States and several other countries with comparable federal systems.

For the reader not especially intent upon research there are a few accessible books and reports that would add considerably to the discussion in the foregoing chapters.

The oldest and in some ways still the best of these is *The Federalist*. This collection of 85 essays written in 1787 and 1788 by Alexander Hamilton, James Madison, and John Jay, strong proponents of the adoption of the Constitution, deals in a vigorous,

255

lucid, and fundamental manner with the need for a national government strong enough to provide for national security and the general welfare, yet so constructed and organized as to protect personal liberties and to preserve popular control over the government.

Two fairly small books on the American federal system in general are a 15-year-old one, by George C. S. Benson, *The New Centralization, A Study of Intergovernmental Relationships in the United States* (New York: Farrar and Rinehart, 1941; 181 pages); and a recent one, by Leonard D. White, *The States and the Nation* (Baton Rouge, La.: Louisiana State University Press, 1953; 103 pages). Both these books present some views that are not the same as the views on the same subjects that I have presented herein.

The Council of State Governments has recently prepared three important monographs: *State-Local Relations* (1946; 228 pages); *Federal Grants-in-Aid* (1949; 322 pages); and *Federal-State Relations* (1949; 297 pages). The first two of these were published by the Council in Chicago. The third one is a report prepared by the Council for the Commission on the Organization of the Executive Branch of the Government (the first so-called Hoover Commission). This report and the report of the Committee on Federal-State Relations that served under the first Hoover Commission were published together with other materials in one volume under the title *Federal-State Relations* as United States Senate Document No. 81, 81st Cong., 1st Sess.

A study of *The Administration of Federal Grants to the States* prepared by V. O. Key, Jr., for the Committee on Public Administration of the Social Science Research Council was published in 1937 by the Public Administration Service, Chicago (388 pages). There is no later work that covers this subject comprehensively. However, a series entitled Intergovernmental Relations in the United States as Observed in the State of Minnesota, of which six numbers have already been published by the University of Minnesota Press with more in prospect, covers a part of the ground intensively and also shows some of the impact of such grants on the state. Similar but shorter studies have begun to appear in various other states. One of the best and most recent is *The Impact of Federal Grants-in-Aid on California*, by Earl C. Segrest and Arthur J. Misner (Berkeley, Calif.: Bureau of Public Administration, University of California, 1954; 347 pages).

The report of the Commission on Intergovernmental Relations and the various committee reports and other documents prepared for it should be especially useful for a more complete understanding of the national grants-in-aid to the states.

On the subject of overlapping taxes and tax sources a study now twelve years old but still a mine of useful information is *Federal, State, and Local Government Fiscal Relations*, Senate Document No. 69, 78th Cong., 1st Sess. (Washington, D.C.: Government Printing Office, 1943; 595 pages). This publication embodies a report of a Committee on Intergovernmental Fiscal Relations to the secretary of the treasury.

More recent studies are James A. Maxwell, *The Fiscal Impact of Federalism in the United States* (Cambridge, Mass.: Harvard University Press, 1946; 427 pages); United States Treasury Department, *Overlapping Taxes in the United States* (mimeographed; Washington, D.C.: Treasury Department, January 1, 1954; 144 pages); and Kenneth W. Gemmil and others, *Federal-State-Local Tax Correlation*, a symposium arranged and published by the Tax Institute, Princeton, N.J. (1954; 248 pages).

As a reference work on constitutional questions the following is unexcelled and indispensable: Edward S. Corwin, editor, *The Constitution of the United States: Analysis and Interpretation*, Senate Document No. 170, 82d Cong., 2d Sess. (Washington, D.C.: Government Printing Office, 1953; 1361 pages).

In January 1954 Columbia University, as a part of its bicentennial program, conducted an important conference on federalism at Arden House with both foreign and American scholars participating. The papers read at those sessions and parts of the panel discussions are included in *Federalism Mature and Emergent*, edited by Arthur W. Macmahon (Garden City, N.Y.: Doubleday, 1955; 558 pages).

Finally, *State Government* (a monthly magazine) and *The Book of the States* (biennial; latest issue Volume X for 1954–55, 676 pages), put out by the Council of State Governments, Chicago, are indispensable for anyone trying to keep abreast of current developments. For state-local relations the *National Municipal Review*, published by the National Municipal League, New York City, is also very useful.

Index